Research Alert
Yearbook
2015

Anne C. Whitaker
Editor, Research Alert

WHITAKER & COMPANY, PUBLISHERS, INC.

WHITAKER & COMPANY, PUBLISHERS, INC.

14305 Shoreham Drive, Silver Spring, Maryland 20905-4481
301-384-1573
www.Research-alert.net

Joel Whitaker, Publisher
Donna Whitaker, Director of Operations

ISBN-13:978-0-940195-06-6

CONTENTS

Advertising & Marketing

Advertisers pay big bucks to celebrities to endorse their products. But do those endorsements make a difference? That's one of the questions answered by researchers, and the results were surprising.

When it comes to advertising, ads shown on TV (especially alcohol) are most influential to teens/young adults, while celebrity endorsed brands are only memorable when closely related to the celebrities fame.

Hispanics were more likely to be influenced by family/online ads, while Millennials were more likely to remember ads about fast food and quick-service restaurants.

Underage Youth More Likely to Drink Alcohol Brands Shown on TV

Alcohol brands shown on popular youth television programs are three times more likely to be consumed by underage drinkers compared to other alcohol brands, providing new and compelling evidence of a strong association between alcohol advertising and youth drinking behavior.

A new study from the Center on Alcohol Marketing and Youth (CAMY) at the John Hopkins Bloomberg School of Public Health and Boston University came to this conclusion after examining whether exposure to brand-specific alcohol advertising on 20 popular youth television shows was associated with brand-specific consumption among underage drinkers.

The find was published in *Alcoholism: Clinical and Experimental Research* and comes on the heels of a study from the same researchers earlier in July which discovered underage drinkers are heavily exposed to magazine ads for the alcohol brands they consume.

"Taken together, these studies strengthen the case for a relationship between brand-specific alcohol advertising among underage youth and brand specific consumption," said lead author Craig Ross, PhD, MBA, president of Virtual Media Resources in Natick, Massachusetts.

Among youth, alcohol is the number one drug and responsible for 4,300 deaths per year.

Differences In How, Why Consumers Remember Celebrity Endorsed Brands

Consumers who are shown two ads featuring the same celebrity are more likely to forget when the celebrity is endorsing a product only moderately associated with the celebrity's fame, according to a new study from the University of Arkansas.

Katie Kelting, a marketing researcher at the U of A, found consumers are more likely to remember the product if it is either a really good or really bad fit with the reason for the celebrity's fame.

The study cites as an example of a moderate fit a State Farm commercial featuring Cleveland Cavalier LeBron James.

The study continues saying that as an industry or product, insurance does not fit James' celebrity; it is a product that neither enhances his celebrity nor detracts from it.

Conversely, the study showed that consumers experience a relatively high level of recall when a product is endorsed that is highly matched with the celebrity's expertise or image, such as James selling a sports drink or basketball shoes.

As for a low fit or match, that would be LeBron James starring in a fast food commercial. James is one of the world's premiere athletes, not to mention arguably one of the best basketball players ever. This would be a low match because general perception is that someone does not reach peak physical condition by frequently eating McDonald's.

Kelting, an assistant professor of marketing in the Sam M. Walton College of Business, said "The same thing happens with low and high matches, a low match is just weird enough for people to remember. It may not make sense to them, and they may not feel particularly good about it, but they will remember it, more so than LeBron James endorsing an insurance company."

2014's Most Memorable Ads
Among Millennials

Fast food and quick-service restaurant (QSR) ads performed well with Millennials (18-33) last year, says Nielsen in a review of the most memorable English- language ads among this demographic, according to Nielsen.

Wendy's spot, "Pretzel Bacon Cheeseburger be with You Song" emerged as the leader with a brand memorability index of 338, meaning that it was 3.38 times more likely to be remembered and associated with the right brand among Millennials than the typical ad.

The study also notes that food ads comprised of either of the top 10 ads among African-American Millennials and nine of the top 10 among Hispanic Millennials, though they didn't have quite the same appeal among Asian-Americans of this age, who only placed three in their top 10.

Overall, humorous ads and those that "touted an own able campaign concept" appeared to be the most memorable.

Among advertising categories, QSRs were second in ad spend through the first three quarters of the year with $3.4 billion ad buys, though that trailed the automotive category ($8.4 billion) by a significant amount.

Hispanics More Likely to be Influenced
By Family, Online Ads

Hispanics are more receptive to online advertising than non-Hispanics, but also rely more on their family when making purchase decisions, according to a recent Specific Media study produced with SMG Multicultural and conducted by Millward Brown Digital.

Hispanic survey respondents were more likely than non-Hispanics to report being persuaded to make purchases after viewing several types of digital ads, and were significantly more likely to view Smartphone ads as useful, relevant, influential and informative.

Separately, the study found Hispanics to be heavy TV multi-taskers, noting also that they're more likely to engage with brands online if a TV ad directs them to the brand's online presence.

Finally, Hispanics reported being influenced by family when making purchase decisions to a greater degree than non-Hispanics, with the difference particularly acute when it came to the reported influence of children (50% of Hispanics vs. 28% of non-Hispanics).

Where You'll Place Ad Dollars, 2015-2019

TV and out-of-home advertising have the healthiest future, while the outlook for print (at least in print format) is dim.

That's the conclusion PwC reaches in its just-released annual Entertainment & Media Outlook report. As consumer behavior migrates online, so will advertiser spending, PwC says, with two notable shifts expected to take place in 2019.

The following is a look at some of the highlights for major media markets covered by PwC, ordered by projected size in 2019 and specific to the U.S.

Online Advertising

Online advertising is expected to overtake TV advertising in size in 2019, with online reaching $83.9 billion (compared to TV's projected $81 billion) on the back of a 2014-2019 compound annual growth rate (CAGR) of 11.15%.

As expected, mobile's share of online ad spending is expected to grow throughout the forecast period, increasing from a forecast 30% share this year to a predicted 46% share in 2019, buoyed by a 2014-2019 CAGR of 25.6%.

Of the "wired" internet advertising types, paid search is expected to retain its dominance, growing from $19.7 billion this year (51% share of wired internet advertising) to $22.1 billion in 2019 (49% share). Paid search's CAGR of 3.2% will be eclipsed, however, by video ads' forecast CAGR of 15%, which will take desktop video from an estimated $3.8 billion in revenues this year to $6.6 billion in 2019.

Meanwhile, among the other "wired" internet advertising categories, display ads are predicted to have the slowest growth, with a CAGR of 1.8%. Display ad revenues are forecast to grow from $12.2 billion this year to $13.2 billion in 2019.

TV Advertising

TV advertising spending is projected to grow from $69.2 billion last year to $71.1 billion this year and $81 billion in 2019 (2014-2019 CAGR of 3.2%), at which point it will cede its status as the top media advertising market.

The researchers note that: "While the growth of Internet advertising has taken some revenue away from traditional TV, it has not, so far, had a particularly damaging impact. Advertising campaigns tend to use digital advertising as a complement to TV advertising, both are often used

rather than one replacing the other. Online TV/video Internet advertising is not solely controlled by specialist online TV services. The traditional networks have also entered this space (through services such as ABC Online, CBS.com, Fox.com, NBC.com) so – as Internet advertising grows more popular – these services will also benefit from additional revenues."

Even so, online is predicted to comprise just a small portion of overall TV advertising revenues. Indeed, just $6.8 billion of the $81 billion in TV advertising revenues forecast for 2019 (or about 8.4%) are expected to be from online TV, despite online TV advertising revenues' CAGR of 14.4%.

Broadcast networks are forecast to see a higher advertising CAGR (3.7%) than cable networks (3%).

Radio Advertising

The radio advertising market in the US is expected to remain relatively flat over the duration of the forecast period, increasing marginally from $17.4 billion this year to $18.1 billion in 2019, and with a 2014-2019 CAGR of 1.1%.

Not surprisingly, terrestrial radio online advertising will be the fastest-growing segment, with a CAGR of 8.6%. However, as with TV (and unlike print and out-of-home), digital ad revenues will represent just a fraction of overall radio revenues. Forecast to comprise 6.8% share of total radio ad revenues this year, online radio is projected to grow to 9.1% share of radio revenues by 2019.

The dominant form will continue to be terrestrial radio broadcast advertising, although terrestrial radio ad revenues are predicted to remain stagnant between this year ($16.1 billion) and 2019 ($16.3 billion).

Magazine Advertising

The magazine advertising market is composed of two main segments: consumer magazines and trade magazines.

The consumer magazine advertising market in the U.S. is projected to be valued at $16.8 billion this year, and will remain essentially flat through 2019, when its value is predicted to be $17 billion. Growth in digital advertising (2014-2019 CAGR of 17.6%) will be just enough to offset declining print revenues (CAGR of -8.2%). In fact, digital advertising is projected to overtake print advertising as the dominant source of consumer magazine advertising revenues in 2019 ($8.7 billion and $8.4 billion, respectively).

Meanwhile, the trade magazine market is smaller, but following similar trends. With an overall CAGR of just 0.8% between 2014 ($4.5 billion) and 2019 ($4.7 billion), digital will close in on print advertising, with the former boasting a CAGR of 11.9% as opposed to the latter's -5.3% projected CAGR. As such, digital ad revenues are projected to increase from 31.6% of trade magazine ad revenues this year ($1.4 of $4.5 billion) to 47.4% share in 2019 ($2.2 of $4.7 billion).

Newspaper Advertising

The hardest hit of the media types examined, newspaper advertising is the only market expected to decline between this year and 2019, falling from $20.2 billion to $16 billion. Unlike magazine advertising, digital advertising in the newspaper market is simply not growing quickly enough (2014-2019 CAGR of 3.4%) to offset print advertising losses (CAGR of -8.7%). Forecast to account for 23.6% of newspaper ad revenues this year, digital is expected to grow to 33.9% share of revenues in 2019.

Meanwhile, each of the three major segments of print advertising (classified, national and retail) is forecast to drop by an annual rate of at least 8%, with classified having the worst outlook (-9.1%).

Out-of-Home Advertising

Out-of-home (OOH) advertising has the strongest prognosis of the traditional media types, though its healthy outlook is mostly the result of strong projected growth in digital out-of-home advertising. Overall, OOH ad revenues are predicted to grow from $8.4 billion last year to $8.9 billion this year and $10.7 billion in 2019, for a 2014-2019 CAGR of 4.8%.

During the forecast period, digital is expected to grow at a compound annual rate of 9.8%, bringing it from 34.7% share of total OOH ad revenues this year to 43.5% share in 2019.

Cinema Advertising

The smallest medium of those listed, cinema advertising is predicted to grow from $814 million last year to $839 million this year and $898 million in 2019, for a 2014-2019 CAGR of 2%. Cinema advertising revenues will continue to be dwarfed by box office revenues, which are expected to grow at a 4% annual clip from 2014 ($10.4 billion) through 2019 ($12.5 billion).

How Do Consumers Find Out About New Products?

Consumers' top purchase influencers are also their top sources of new product awareness, according to results from a recent Nielsen report. The study, based on a survey of 30,000 consumers across 60 countries, found that friends and family (56%) and TV ads (52%) are the leading sources of information about new products for consumers.

Still, the Nielsen survey results indicate that fewer consumers rely on these sources than did 3 years ago, with this particularly the case for TV ads.

(It's worth noting that a 2013 survey from Ipsos found TV ads and word-of-mouth to be the leading sources of new product and brand discovery for U.S. consumers, while the global average placed the internet at the top of the heap, followed by TV ads.)

Nielsen's latest survey segments the results into earned, paid, and owned media, noting that for the purposes of the study, a new product is defined as any item that the consumer has never purchased in the past. The results indicate that for product awareness:

- Among earned media, "active internet searching" (44%, up from 39% in 2012) and social media postings (26%, up from 15%) are rising forces;

- There has been very little positive movement over the years in paid media, with TV ads and print declining as sources of product discovery, while other paid media remain generally flat; and
- Almost half of the respondents find new products by seeing them in-store, steady from 2012, although fewer than one-third (31%) attribute product discovery to receiving a free sample (down from 56% in 2012).

The report notes that traditional media still are effective sources for introducing youth to new products, demonstrating that TV in particular still reach Generation Z (15-20) and Millennials (21-34).

Indeed, the Nielsen results find youth far more likely to have learned of new products from internet ads and video-sharing websites, while being less likely to have done so through outdoor ads, or direct mail.

Meanwhile, radio is another medium that continues to reach Millennials, according to results from both studies.

In other interesting results from the Nielsen survey:

- Affordability and convenience are the top drivers behind new product purchases, followed by brand recognition and novelty, with affordability playing a stronger role among older than younger generations;
- 4 in 10 respondents in Latin America said they wish more products fitting a healthy lifestyle were on the market, though that figure drops to 19% in North America;
- One-quarter of respondents in North America said that they had bought a new product because it was from a brand they like, and 18% said they had done so because it was from a well-known or popular brand, with brand-name recognition again more important to older consumers;
- Some 26% of respondents globally said they wish more ecologically friendly products were available on the market and 16% wish more products were committed to positive social impact, though only 10% said they have purchased a new product because it was from a brand that cares about the environment and just 7% due to the brand's corporate social responsibility; and
- Although youth – Gen Z (62%) and Millennials (66%) – were the most likely to say they had purchased a new product on their most recent grocery shopping trip, almost half of Baby Boomers (ages 50-64) and one-quarter of respondents from the Silent Generation (65+) said the same.

Overall, while Gen Z (62%) and Millennial (66%) respondents were the most likely to say they had purchased a new product during their last grocery-shopping trip, more than 4 in 10 Baby Boomers (50-64) and one-quarter of respondents from the Silent Generation (65+) agreed.

Why You Should Keep Advertising In Magazines: Audience Grows 7.6%

Don't fail to keep promoting your brands in magazines.

That's the clear message from the latest Magazine Media 360° Brand Audience Report from the **MPA – The Association of Magazine Media**, which covers both print and online readership.

U.S. magazines' total print and digital audience rose 7.6% to 1.68 billion in July from 1.57 billion in July 2014, the report said. But note that "magazines" now includes not only the familiar print versions, but mobile.

And that's where most of the growth came from. The total mobile Web audience jumped 58.3% to 445.5 million from 281.4 million, and the size of the audience accessing magazine content via desktops or laptops edged up 3.2% to 256.9 million.

Digital growth more than offset a smaller decrease in magazines' total print audience. But some *print* categories were doing well.

For example, some food and epicurean titles enjoying big increases. *All recipes* — Meredith Corp.'s new food title based on the Web site of the same name — saw the audience for its combined print and digital editions soar 38.9% to 7.5 million, with most of this in print. EatingWell was up 9.9% to 5.74 million, *Vegetarian Times* jumped 35.7% to 2.45 million, and *Every Day with Rachael Ray* edged up 1.9% to 5.21 million.

Smaller increases were seen at *Food Network Magazine,* up 0.5% to 12.4 million, and *Bon Appetit/Epicurious,* up 0.4% to 6.64 million.

A number of automotive enthusiast titles also saw their combined print and digital editions grow, with *Car Craft* up 3.4% to 1.93 million, *Motor Trend* also up 3.4% to 7.34 million, *Popular Mechanics* up 3.3% to 7.6 million, and *Street Rodder* up 4.3% to 2.11 million.

Last but not least, some highbrow journals experienced growth in this category, with *New York Magazine* up soaring 34.5% to 2.38 million, *The New Yorker* up 7.2% to 4.49 million, and *Vanity Fair* up 2% to 6.93 million.

Truth in Advertising: Who's Got It, and For What Formats?

Nielsen has released its latest "Global Trust in Advertising" report, a biennial examination of the different forms of advertising that consumers around the world trust and act upon.

Trust by Format

As Nielsen notes, "the proliferation of online ad formats has not eroded trust in traditional paid advertising channels."

In fact, among paid media channels, traditional media outperform online and mobile ads in trust; TV ads lead all paid media with 63% of global respondents reporting complete or somewhat trust, followed by newspaper (60%) and magazine (58%) ads.

And the digital format that earns trust from the most respondents – online video ads (48%) – remains below radio and pre-movie ads (each at 54%); the least-trusted traditional media formats.

Surprisingly, the report finds little change in the results from the last edition released in 2013.

Since then, ads on TV (+1% point) have seen a negligible increase in trust, while other traditional media formats such as print, billboards, radio and movies have seen declines of just 1-3% points. None of the digital formats analyzed – including online video, paid search, social ads, and mobile ads – saw an increase in trust from the last report, a fairly intriguing result given the proliferation of such advertising over the past couple of years.

Meanwhile, earned and owned media continue to largely engender more trust from respondents than paid media. Among all the available options, global respondents were by far the most likely to trust recommendations from people they know (83%), proving yet again the power of word—of-mouth.

Results from the study likewise show that respondents are more trusting of consumer opinions posted online and editorial content such as newspaper articles (each at 66%) than of paid media in general, though TV ads are almost on par.

As for owned media, 7 in 10 respondents reported completely or somewhat trusting branded websites, the top result, followed by brand sponsorships (61%) and opt-in emails (56%), with these latter two ranking in the midst of the variety of traditional media formats.

Trust by Generation

Of note, the survey – conducted online earlier this year among more than 30,000 consumers in 60 countries – indicates that Millennials (aged 21-34) report the highest levels of trust in almost all of the 19 formats listed (which include recommendations and consumer opinions online).

In fact, the only format for which Millennials did not indicate the most trust was radio ads, where they were slightly edged by Gen Xers (35-49).

For the most part, though, there were only minor differences in the levels of trust shown by Millennials, Gen Z (ages 15-20) and Gen X (35-49) respondents. Several channels earn considerably less trust from older generations, with the Silent Generation generally the least trusting across formats.

The biggest gaps in trust between Millennials and Silents were seen in formats including: branded websites; consumer opinions posted online; TV ads; brand sponsorships; ads before movies; billboard ads; and each of the digital formats identified.

By comparison, the levels of trust placed in recommendations, editorial content, newspaper ads, opt-in emails, and radio ads were more consistent across generations.

Singling out Millennials, the report shows that while they have more trust in digital ad formats than older generations, the same general order of trust applies to them as with consumers overall: earned media first, followed by a mix of traditional and owned media; with digital formats trailing.

Which Forms of Advertising Do Consumers Act Upon?

The Nielsen study also looked at self-reported response to advertising, measured as the percentage of respondents who always or sometimes take action on the ads in question.

The results show that the majority of formats found a greater share of respondents reporting action than trust. It was in this area that digital ad formats found some footing, with action generally outpacing trust by a larger degree than for traditional and earned media.

Even so, the top formats in terms of action are broadly consistent with the trust rankings:

- Recommendations from people (83% always or sometimes taking action);
- Branded websites (70%);
- TV ads (69%);
- Consumer opinions posted online (69%); and
- Newspaper ads, opt-in emails, and editorial content (each at 63%).

The greater levels of reported action for digital formats means that they don't all occupy the bottom rung. For example, ads served in search engine results (58% reporting frequent action) and ads on social networks (56%) exceed levels for radio (54%) and ads before movies (54%).

Which Themes and Emotions Drive Impact?

As Nielsen's study reminds, successful campaigns depend not only on reach, but also on delivery of the right message. As such, the report looks at the types of themes that resonate with consumers, finding that ads depicting real-life situations resonate the most with global respondents, cited by 44%.with consumers, finding that ads depicting real-life situations resonate the most with global respondents, cited by 44%.

There's considerable variance in the responses when sorting by region, though. In North America, for example, humorous ads (50%) were cited significantly more often than ads depicting real-life situations (24%). This supports other pieces of research that find humor to have particular appeal among North Americans.

Europeans, like Americans, were most apt to point to humorous ads as resonating with them. Those in Africa and Asia were most likely to point to real-life situations, while in Latin America the highest response came for health-themed ads.

In sorting the results by generation, the survey noted some interesting results:

- Real-life situations, sports-themed and competitive ads tended to have consistent appeal across generations; but
- Humorous, health-themed, value-oriented, and pets/animal-centered ads showed the highest appeal among older generations; while
- High-energy and aspirational ads, as well as celebrity endorsements, tended to resonate more strongly with youth.

There was one theme that emerged from the findings: kids and family find meaning with Gen Xers. Indeed, family-oriented and kids-centered ads each demonstrated the strongest levels of resonance with this generation (presumably due to their being most likely to have kids in the home).

How Long Before An Internet Radio Listener Hears an Ad?

Internet radio listeners spent roughly 14 minutes on average listening to music before hearing their first ad during Q3 2015, per XAPPmedia's latest Internet Radio Ad Load Report.

That includes 41% hearing an ad within the first 10 minutes of listening, up from 32% the prior quarter.

By comparison, the newly-launched (as of Q3) Apple Music served an ad within 10 minutes for about three-quarters of sessions, for an average of slightly less than 9 minutes of listening before the first ad.

The overall ad load for the 5 publishers tracked in Q3 was 2 minutes and 21 seconds per hour, down 21 seconds per hour from Q2. This average masked an increase of 10 seconds/hour for 3 of the publishers, which was more than offset by a 56 second/hour cut for the other two.

Super Bowl Advertisers Mercedes-Benz and BMW See Biggest Increases in Car Shopper Interest on edmunds.com

Mercedes-Benz and BMW saw the most compelling spikes in traffic on edmunds.com after their ads ran during Super Bowl XLIX, according to a real-time analysis by the car shopping website.

By the end of the game, the Mercedes-Benz AMG GT had the biggest cumulative spike in traffic, with a 2189% jump over previous Sunday averages on edmunds.com. The BMW i3 captured the second most buzz on edmunds.com; its cumulative traffic climbed 583%.

"Even though these two advertised vehicles are likely to be sold in small volume to niche audiences, the BMW and Mercedes brands will enjoy the overall buzz they have generated, especially as both continue their efforts to grow their overall reach into new car shopper segments," said edmunds.com Sr. Analyst Jessica Caldwell. "Both brands will be quite happy that the millions of dollars they invested had the desired effect."

Edmunds.com also tracked the immediate traffic lifts enjoyed by Super Bowl advertisers during and after their commercials ran:

- Chevrolet sponsored the pre-game show and showed four Colorado ads; site traffic to Colorado pages increased 25% during the pregame and 1104% during the first quarter of the game;
- During the third quarter of the game, Dodge Challenger ads lifted its traffic on Edmunds 232%;
- Fiat 500x increased 3981% in the moments following its second quarter ads; interest remained high in the third quarter, delivering a 986% life for the vehicle;
- Jeep Renegade was advertised in the third quarter of the game and traffic to its pages immediately increased 1031%; during fourth quarter the increase was 5720%;
- Kia Sorrento traffic increased 213% immediately following its third quarter ad;
- Lexus NX's second quarter ad generated an increase of 341%. The brand did even better immediately after its RC 350 ad ran in the third quarter, increasing vehicle's page traffic

on Edmunds 5702%. The RC continued to enjoy success in the fourth quarter with a 690% lift in traffic to its pages on edmunds.com;

- MINI sponsored an early part of the pre-game show and showed five ads; site traffic to MINI Cooper increased 48% during that period;
- Nissan brand consideration increased 90% immediately following its second quarter ad; and
- In the moments following its halftime ad, Toyota Camry site traffic increased 364%

Super Bowl Ad Rankings Go to the Dogs

Anheuser-Busch's 'Lost Dog' spot was ranked the top commercial in the 27th annual USA TODAY Ad Meter, the most widely recognized barometer and industry-leading tool used to measure public opinion surrounding Super Bowl advertising.

AB won for the third straight year, taking home its 13th Ad Meter title in three years.

The top five ads, as voted upon by this year's Ad Meter panel, including final ratings are:

1. Anheuser-Busch — Lost Dog (8.10)
2. Always — Like a Girl (7.10)
3. Fiat — Blue Pill (6.87)
4. Microsoft — Braylon (6.74)
5. Doritos — Middle Seat (6.71)

Some services are more popular in some markets than others: San Francisco (48%) edges Washington DC (47%) in Netflix penetration, while Washington, DC (24%) takes the lead over Seattle (23%) in Amazon Instant prime penetration, with San Francisco further back (18).

Seattle, meanwhile, has the largest share (9%) of homes with access to Hulu Plus.

The Super Bowl Ad Meter was created by USA TODAY in 1989 to gauge consumers' attitudes about television's most expensive commercials.

Alcohol

Alcohol is the number one drug among youth, responsible for 4,300 deaths per year. And the majority of alcohol consumed by youth are brands advertised on television programs aimed towards them.

Alcoholic preferences may be determined by education and income level, and the U.S. widened their lead over France in wine consumption.

Underage Youth More Likely to Drink Alcohol Brands Shown on TV

Alcohol brands shown on popular youth television programs are three times more likely to be consumed by underage drinkers compared to other alcohol brands, providing new and compelling evidence of a strong association between alcohol advertising and youth drinking behavior.

A new study from the Center on Alcohol Marketing & Youth (CAMY) at the John Hopkins Bloomberg School of Public Health and Boston University came to this conclusion after examining whether exposure to brand-specific alcohol advertising on 20 popular youth television shows was associated with brand-specific consumption among underage drinkers.

The find was published in *Alcoholism: Clinical and Experimental Research* and comes on the heels of a study from the same researchers earlier in July which discovered underage drinkers are heavily exposed to magazine ads for the alcohol brands they consume.

"Taken together, these studies strengthen the case for a relationship between brand-specific alcohol advertising among underage youth and brand specific consumption," said lead author Craig Ross, PhD, MBA, president of Virtual Media Resources in Natick, Massachusetts.

Among youth, alcohol is the number one drug and responsible for 4,300 deaths per year.

Distillers Shipped More Spirits, Saw Revenue Rise 4% in 2014

U.S. consumers drank about 2.2% more distilled spirits — whiskey, bourbon, vodka, gin, etc. — last year than a year earlier, according to the Distilled Spirits Council of the U.S., which represents American distillers. That translates to a total of 210 million cases of product Frank Coleman, a DISCUS senior vp, attributed the growth picture to a continued fascination with American Whiskies in the U.S. and abroad, continued innovation in flavors, especially flavored whiskeys, premiumization, continued "restraint" on hospitality taxes by legislatures, and the growth in small distillers, which expands grassroots and consumer interest in the category.

Also helping: improved market access, including the repeal of the country's last ban on election-day alcohol sales in South Carolina, spirits tastings expansions in five states, local alcohol elections, especially in Texas where 64 out of 81 wet-dry alcohol elections passed last year, and the continued spread of Sunday sales.

David Ozgo, DISCUS senior vp-chief economist who compiles the figures, noted that 35.7% of all spirits sales, a total of 75 million cases, are in the value category; 36.3% (76.3 million cases) are in the premium category; 19.6% (41.1 million) are in high-end spirits, and 8.4%, or 17.8 million cases, are in the super-premium category.

Value products volume slipped 1.3% last year. That wasn't surprising, Ozgo said, given that the economy has been improving. When the economy improves, people start trading up. Indeed, last year premium spirits volume grew 3.1%, high-end products grew 5.8% and super- premium rose 5.1%.

Looked at in terms of price segments, value products sales slipped $31 million. Premium products sales grew $145 million, high-end jumped $433 million and super-premium grew $351 million.

Drunk Driving Declines as Drug Use Behind the Wheel Rises

The U.S. spent decades successfully campaigning against drunk driving to make roads safer, but use of marijuana and prescription drugs is increasingly prominent on the highways, raising new questions about safety, according to studies released by the Department of Transportation's National Highway Traffic Safety Administration.

The latest version of NHTSA's Roadside Survey of Alcohol and Drug Use by Drivers, supported that the number of drivers who had alcohol in their system has declined by almost one-third since 2007, and by more than three-quarters since the first Roadside Survey in 1973.

Yet that same survey found a sizable increase in the number of drivers using marijuana or other illegal drugs.

The 2014 survey found that almost one in four drivers tested positive for at least one drug that could affect safety.

"America made drunk driving a national issue and while there is no victory as long as a single American dies in an alcohol-related crash, a one-third reduction in alcohol use over just seven years shows how a focused effort and cooperation among the federal government, states and communities, law enforcement, safety advocates and industry can make an enormous difference," said NHTSA Administrator Mark Rosekind. "At the same time, the latest Roadside Survey raises significant questions about drug use and highway safety. The rising prevalence of marijuana and other drugs is a challenge to everyone who is dedicated to saving lives and reducing crashes."

Nearly 8% of drivers during nighttime weekend hours were found to have alcohol in their system, and just over 1% were found with 0.08% or higher breath alcohol content. This number is down by around 30% from the previous survey in 2007 and down 80% from the first survey in 1973.

However, even as drinking and driving continues to decrease, use of illegal drugs or medicines which can affect road safety is mounting. The amount of weekend nighttime drivers with evidence of drugs in their system rose from 16.3% in 2007 to 20% in 2014 and the number of drivers with marijuana in their system grew by roughly 50%.

"Drivers should never get behind the wheel impaired, and we know that marijuana impairs judgment, reaction times and awareness," said Jeff Michael, NHTSA's associate administrator for research and program development. "These findings highlight the importance of research to better understand how marijuana use affects drivers so states and communities can craft the best safety policies."

Americans' Alcohol Preferences, By Education and Income Level

Self-reported alcoholic consumption is far higher among Americans from high-income ($75k+) than lower-income households (<$30k), with 78% of the former and 45% of the latter occasionally drinking, according to a Gallup survey.

Similar discrepancies were also found by education level, and among drinkers, those with higher annual household incomes and education levels reported being more frequent drinkers.

Interestingly, middle- and lower-income drinkers favor beer over wine and liquor, though wine edges beer as the most common alcoholic beverage among higher-income Americans.

Wine is a clear winner among college graduates, while beer takes precedence among those with some college education and those with a high school education or less.

U.S. Widens Lead Over France in Wine Consumption

Larger discretionary income levels for consumers contributed to Americans purchasing more wine, marking a 1% growth rate to 328.6 million 9-liter cases, according to the Beverage Information & Insights Group's 2015 Wine Handbook.

The U.S. continued to lead the wine market in 2014 after surpassing France in 2013. U.S. wineries grew to 8,287 in 2014, an increase of 525. This may explain why domestic wine growth increased 1.3%, while imported wine growth decreased by 0.7%.

Wine consumers matured in 2014, demonstrated by the increase in sales of wines in the $10 to $20 price range. Sales of wines priced below $10 slowed. Box wine brands saw double-digit increases and consumers began purchasing smaller 187-ml wine bottles, primarily for consumption at outdoor events.

With California facing its fourth year of major drought, which has caused production struggles, Oregon and Washington experienced record-size wine crops in 2014. Some wine suppliers raised prices, finding that consumers are more likely to purchase a new brand at a higher price point, than to remain with a familiar brand that raises its price.

Table wine grew to 300.8 million 9-liter cases, a 0.9% increase over 2013. The champagne and sparkling wine category grew for its 13th consecutive year to 18.2 million 9-liter cases, up 4.0%.

Designated Drivers Supported by 98% of Americans

Ninety-eight percent of Americans think that having a designated driver who agrees to do the driving is important when planning to go out with friends when there will be drinking, according to a new Road Safety Monitor (RSM) poll conducted by the **Traffic Injury Research Foundation USA**, Inc. (TIRF USA) and sponsored **by Anheuser-Busch**.

The public opinion poll conducted in October and November 2015 investigated Americans' opinions and behaviors in relation to this issue and is based on a sample of 5,009 drivers, aged 21 years or older.

"Fatalities involving alcohol-impaired driving have declined to approximately 10,000 in comparison to previous years, which recorded averages of 13,000 to 14,000 according to official statistics. When using a longer look back period, drunk-driving fatalities have actually decreased 53% since 1982", explains Ms. **Tara Casanova Powell**, Director of Research at TIRF USA.

"Although this drop reveals progress in reducing the problem, data from recent years suggest that these declines may have plateaued since 2010, which means that alcohol-impaired driving requires continued attention and action if further improvements are to be realized."

The good news is that progress has been made and that Americans clearly consider this to be a top priority compared to other road safety and societal issues. Such levels of concern suggest there is support among the public to further reduce the problem.

To illustrate, a majority of Americans (78%) are concerned about the issue of alcohol-impaired driving. However, the poll also found that 8% of respondents self-reported alcohol-impaired driving when they thought they were over the legal limit.

When asked about reasons for engaging in this type of behavior, more than half of those respondents who indicated they had driven in these circumstances answered that they thought they were capable of driving at the time. In particular, 44% of these respondents thought they were okay to drive and 12% thought that they could drive very carefully when they thought they were over the legal limit.

According to Dr. **Ward Vanlaar**, Vice President Research of TIRF in Canada and a co-author of the study, research has clearly demonstrated that today the majority of Americans realize driving while impaired is dangerous; however, some people simply do not understand the risks they pose to themselves and others.

"It is clear that while many people have gotten the message through education and enforcement, there are some drivers who believe they are less impaired, or better able to manage the effects of impairment, and do not realize they are unsafe to drive," says Vanlaar. "Also, our results are consistent with other research and indicate that young male drivers are at a heightened risk for driving drunk. This speaks to the importance of tailored approaches toward groups at risk."

One simple solution that can help is to educate the public about alternatives to driving such as using a designated driver who agrees to do the driving on a night out with family or friends, a taxi or public transportation where it is available.

The poll asked respondents about their behaviors in this regard and revealed that 70% of Americans reported that they had been a designated driver, 45% have used a designated driver and 28% have used some other form of transportation such as a taxi or bus.

Casanova Powell explains that in absolute numbers, this corresponds to an estimated 140 million drivers aged 21 years or older who have been a designated driver, 90 million who have used a designated driver, and 56 million who have used some other form of transportation.

To provide a more general picture, 51% of Americans reported either using a designated driver or alternative transportation (an estimated 103 million drivers aged 21 years or older) and 78% reported using a designated driver, being a designated driver, or using alternative transportation (an estimated 156 million drivers aged 21 years or older).

"Although designated driver programs alone will not solve the problem," Casanova Powell says, "they can be a part of the solution, and the fact that so many drivers have already relied upon such alternatives shows that providing alternative solutions to drivers can help to encourage better decisions after a night out."

Brands

Brand communication methods, social media interactions, honesty and authenticity are the top influences for customer loyalty when brand shopping.

Many top brands are gravitating to Instagram to expand their client base (unsurprisingly, Instagram is extremely popular with teens). Netflix and Amazon top most lists, along with Apple and Google.

How Consumers Want to Communicate With Brands

Some brand communication methods — such as sending useful information or tailored emails based on past purchases — resonate well with consumers, but other proactive outreach methods are disliked by many, according to results from an SAP SE poll conducted by Ipsos.

Thirty-seven percent of respondents said they like it when companies they have bought something from adjust offers to them based on where they live, with 18% disliking this and 31% saying it depends on the company.

While research has found personalization to influence consumers' purchase decisions — with emailed product recommendations one of the favored forms, the SAP study finds a little more indecision on the part of its respondents.

Roughly one-third say they like it when companies have bought from tailor their mailings or emails based on what they know about past purchases.

But 22% dislike this practice and 36% believe it depends on the brand.

The tide is more adverse when it comes to consumers being asked if they want alerts or information sent to their phone, with more disliking (34%) than liking (29%) this.

Similarly, more dislike (34%) than like (27%) offers to help via chat or phone before the consumer has asked for assistance.

It is worth noting that in each case more than one-quarter find this dependent on the brand, suggesting more could be willing recipients of this type of communication.

Asked about the channels they prefer to use when they want information about a company's products and services, consumers pointed to email (28% share of respondents) first, followed by telephone (23%) and in-person (16%).

Just 4% said that social media is their preferred channel.

However, social media is a preferred channel for sharing positive reviews.

Among the 48% of respondents who make an effort to tell people online when they really like a product or service, 19% most often communicate the positive feedback on their own social media sites.

That rivals the 20% who most often post on review websites such as Consumer Reports of Yelp or Amazon.

Top Brands Ranked by Customer Loyalty

Mobile, digital, and social brands continue to exhibit loyalty supremacy, with new brands and categories making up more than a third of this year's Top-100 leaders list, according to Brand Keys Loyalty Leader 2014 report.

Topping this year's list is Apple, Amazon, What's app, Google, YouTube, and Kindle.

Thirty six of the top-100 Loyalty Leaders are new brands or categories.

Most new arrivals facilitate communication and social outreach: tablets, smartphones, and social networks, with What's App (instant messaging), Netflix, and Amazon (video streaming), Instagram, and PayPal (online payments) now representing that trend.

Other, new, non-digital/social categories include Fast-Casual Restaurants (Chipotle, Panera, Chick-fil-A), Insurance (USAA), Credit Cards (Discover, American Express), and Beer (Sam Adams).

Dunkin' Donuts was the only non-digital/social brand in the top-10, up 7 spots from last year, but not astonishing when you realize their customers have rated them #1 in the out-of-home coffee category for years.

The 2014 Brand Keys Loyalty Leaders top-10 rank as follows:

1. Amazon: tablets
2. Apple: tablets
3. Apple: smartphone
4. YouTube: social networking
5. What's App: instant messaging
6. Amazon: online retail
7. Google: search engines
8. Kindle: e-readers
9. Samsung: smartphones
10. Dunkin' Donuts: coffee (out-of-home)

Forty-five percent of the top-100 brands account for consumer outreach and engagement via cellular and social networks, and the phones, smartphones, computers, and tablets needed to meet ever-increasing expectations related to outreach and personal connectivity the consumer uses as a yardstick to measure brands.

Last year beauty and personal care brands accounted for approximately a fifth of the top-100 but this year represent only 13%.

Traditional retail brands were down 50%. The ineptitude for many retailers to provide meaningful differentiation — beyond low-lower-lowest pricing strategies — has seriously eroded loyalty levels in the retail category. That and a shift to buying online and via mobile devices

Retail brands that remain among this year's Loyalty Leaders include J. Crew (#50), The Gap (#80), Macy's (#88), Victoria's Secret (#75) and T.J. Maxx (#92).

Six automotive brands made the top-100, including: Hyundai (#23), Ford (#26), Toyota (#48), Jeep (#70), Nissan (#94), and KIA (#99).

Nissan appears on the list for the first time while Ford and Toyota moved up the list +12 spots each, Jeep moved up +11.

The brands that showed the greatest loyalty gains this year were:

- Netflix (+79)
- Estee Lauder (+31)
- MAC Cosmetics (+28)
- HTC smartphones (+26)
- Cover Girl (+25)

With a few exceptions, it turns out that the biggest Loyalty Leader losers were primarily categories, with certain categories just disappearing.

Those categories included Breakfast Cereal, which should not come as a shock to anyone.

Perennial Loyalty Leaders absent from this year's list include Pepsi and Coke, ABC News, NBC News, CBS News, the Today Show, Bing, and Yahoo.

When it comes to the search category, only Google (#7) appears.

Not surprisingly General Motors did not make this year's list.

McDonald's, which had appeared since the List's 1996 inception, dropped off the top-100 list too.

In a study conducted earlier this year by Brand Keys, Millennials, a key audience for fast food chains, reports a 20% decrease in visits to them, with 42% reporting increased visits to fast-casual restaurants, a category whose brands *have* shown up for the first time on this year's list.

Other brands *not* appearing on the loyalty Leaders List this year included Ben & Jerry's, Canon (point-and-shoot cameras), H&M, Haagen-Daz, Skechers, Skype, Southwest Airlines, Walgreens, and Walmart.

Brands with the greatest loyalty and engagement erosion:

- Max Factor (-20)
- Clinique (-16)
- Grey Goose (-13)
- Revlon (-13)
- Apple Computers (-11)
- Costco (-11)
- Sam's Club (-11)
- Sam's Club (-11)

While it is true that some of the shifts are due to the creation and adoption of new categories and brands that better meet — even exceed — customer expectations, brands that understand that real emotional connections can serve as a surrogate for added-value.

The brand which have made loyalty and emotional engagement one of their real strategic priorities and KPIs will always show up at the top of a consumer's list.

Top Brands Are Gravitating to Instagram And Attracting More Engaged Audiences

Instagram continues to build its user base — and it's becoming a favorite of top brands too.

A new study from Simply Measured notes that 86 of the Interbrand 100 had an account on the mobile network during Q3 2014, up from 54 a couple of years earlier.

Moreover, the number of brands posting at least once a week has almost doubled during that time frame, jumping from 38 to 73.

The study details brands' growing efforts on the platform (20 now post at least daily, more than triple the amount doing so last year) are paying off in the form of larger audiences, as 34 more brands this year have at least 10,000 followers and 15 more have at least 100,000 followers.

More importantly, the data reveals that growth in post engagement is outpacing brand adoption of Instagram.

In other words, Instagram users are proving receptive to brand content, and engagement rates have not dampened as a result of increased brand activity.

In fact, the average engagement per post for top brands using the platform is now five times higher (18,822 likes and comments per post) than it was two years ago (3,648).

In an interesting analysis, the study notes that comments on posts tend to occur quickly, as half are made in the first 6 hours after posting and three-quarters in the first 48 hours after posting.

Not too surprisingly, the time distribution of comments for high-performing posts (those with double the average engagement) is quite different to low-performing posts (those with half the average engagement).

The most engaging posts take more than 13 hours to get to half of their comments, while the least engaging takes less than three hours to get to that mark.

For the Simply Measured analysts, this represents another reason to focus on quality.

Brands should remember that Instagram doesn't filter its feed — so users scroll through a single stream, and only top quality images and video with catch their attention long after posting.

The single stream also means that brands have to be careful about how they time their posts.

As Instagram doesn't resurface content (as does Facebook, for example), marketers must be cognizant of brand activity on the platform so as to avoid being lost in the clutter.

The data indicates that automotive brands are the most heavily represented from the Interbrand 1000, though its media brands that are the most active, also drawing the most engagement.

Those sectors — along with luxury and apparel — are said to have found the most success thus far.

Other actionable data offered in the report:

The average caption is 138 characters long including hashtags, but there is no statistically significant correlation between caption length and engagement;

Posts that include at least one @mention (which represent 36% of posts tracked) have engagement levels 56% higher than those that don't include a mention;

Almost nine in 10 posts from top brands include a hashtag, and these posts average 12.6% more engagement than those lacking a hashtag (note that hashtags are important for content discovery on Instagram); and

While only about one in 20 posts were tagged with a location, these averaged 29% higher engagement than those without a location tagged.

Taking Stock With Teens – Fall 2014

Piper Jaffray has completed its 28th semi-annual Taking Stock With Teens market research project, which indicates increased spending across categories despite decreased optimism about the economy.

Key findings from the survey in fashion, beauty and personal care, digital media, food, gaming and entertainment include the following:

Spending rebounds as teen employment figures improved modestly and parent contribution returned to historical levels in the 70% range. Yet, teen perception of the economic climate worsened with roughly 73% seeing the economy as saying the same or getting worse, up from just 57% a year ago.

Male spending increased in the spring while females turned this fall and contributed to gains year over year and sequentially in total spending. This is the first period of improved spending, specifically on fashion-related goods, in nearly two years.

Fashion spending improves with a mid/high single digit increase in apparel spending. Beauty spending increased, mainly on color cosmetics, while spending declined in accessories.

Shopping frequency stabilized after several years of declines but remains below historical averages, suggesting capacity rationalization is needed as teens continue to shop "on demand." While teens still prefer to shop in-store for their fashion needs, they are increasingly shopping online and via mobile, preferring sites associated with stores versus pure play e-commerce sites.

Teen closets are diverse. A key fashion trend among teens is the spirit of choice – demand for action sports, fast fashion, refined classics and fashion athletic brands stabilized or increased. Demand for legacy brands stabilizes – AE, A&F, Hollister and Aero – but is still significantly below peak mindshare and current capacity.

These generations of teens are creating their own "stories" through purchases, experiences and activities in order to cultivate their personal brands, primarily in domains like social media and friend networks.

Friends and the Internet dominate teen influences and combine in social media environments. Instagram and Twitter are the two most used social media sites, implying teens are increasingly visual and sound bite communicators.

The percentage of teens asking for a GoPro as a gift more than doubled sequentially and more than quadrupled year-over-year.

Apple remains the top consumer electronics brand for teens. 67% own iPhones, up 6% from spring 2014. Seventy-three percent

of teens expect their next phone to be an iPhone.

A key food trend amongst teens is the increasing consumption of organic food, especially among upper-income teens.

Mobile gaming interest declines to 80%, but of those that play 22% spend money on virtual goods or extra levels, up 4% from spring 2014.

World's Most Valuable Brands

Apple and Google retain the top positions on Interbrand's Best Global Brands ranking for the second year in a row, with both exceeding $100 billion in brand value — the first time in the history of Best Global Brands that two brands have each exceeded $100 billion.

Apple (#1), valued at $118.9 billion, increased its brand value by 21%, while Google (#2), valued at $107.43 billion, increased its brand value by 15%.

"Apple and Google's meteoric rise to more than $100 billion is truly a testament to the power of brand building. These leading brands have reached new pinnacles — in terms of both their growth and in the history of Best Global Brands — by creating experiences that are seamless contextually relevant, and increasingly based around an overarching ecosystem of integrated products and services, both physical and digital." said Jez Frampton, Interbrand's Global Chief Executive Officer.

When determining the top 100 most valuable brands each year, Interbrand examines three key aspects that contribute to a brand's value:

The financial performance of the branded product and service;

The role the brand pays in influencing customer choice; and

The strength the brand has to command a premium price or secure earnings for the company.

Top risers in 2014 include Facebook (#29, +86%), Audi (#45, +27%), Amazon (#15, +25%), Volkswagen (#31, +23%), and Nissan (#56, +23%).

There were also five new entrants to the list in 2014: DHL (#81), Land Rover (#91), FedEx (#92), Huawei (#94), and Hugo Boss (#97).

In 2014, the cumulative brand value of the automotive brands popping up on the Best Global Brands ranking increased 14.6%, with all 14 brands collectively making up a combined brand value of $211.9 billion.

This past year proved to be a record one, with three out of the five Top Risers coming from the automotive sector.

Included in this year's top 14 automotive brands: Toyota (#8, +20%), Mercedes-Benz (#10, +8%), BMW (#11, +7%), Honda (#20, +17%), Volkswagen (#31, +23%), Ford (#39, +18%), Hyundai (#40, +16%), Audi (#45, +27%), Nissan (#56, +23%), Porsche (#60, +11%), Kia (#74, +15%), Chevrolet (#82, +10%), Harley-Davidson (#87, +13%), and Land Rover (#91, NEW).

Since 2004, Toyota has been the most valuable automotive brand on the Best Global Brands ranking and remains a commander in green technology development.

Overall, the technology sector leads as the most valuable category, with 13 of the top 100 brands this year hailing from this sector.

The category grew 11.3% year-over-year, and collectively is worth $493.2 billion in brand value.

Unsurprisingly, Facebook (#29, +86%), Apple (#1, +21%), and Google (#2, +15%) represent this year's fastest growing brands, yet a number of one-time leaders experienced an abrupt decline in brand value.

Nokia, a Finnish communications and information technology developer, (#98, -44%) experienced the largest decline in value among the top 100 brands, falling from #57 in 2013 to #98 this year.

Nintendo (#100, -33%) had another difficult year, falling 33 places to take the #100 position this year with a brand value of $4.1 billion.

Possibly somewhat surprising, financial services brands experience growth in brand value, with all 11 financial services brands on this year's list ranking increased in brand value: American Express (#23, +11%), HSBC (#33, +8%), J.P. Morgan (#35, +9%), Goldman Sachs (#47, +3%), Citi (#48, +10%), AXA (#53, +14%), Allianz (#55, +15%), Morgan Stanley (#63, +11%), Visa (#69, +10%), Santander (#75, +16%), and MasterCard (#88, +13%).

Both the biggest jump and biggest fall came from the technology sector, Facebook had the biggest jump while Nokia had the biggest fall.

While the composition of the top 10 remained largely the same as last year (with the rankings remaining intact among the top 6), McDonald's dropped 2 spots to #9, while Intel dropped 3 spots and out of the top 10 (#12).

The Importance of Honesty and Authenticity for Brands

Consumers believe that honesty and authenticity are the top attributes for brands to display, particularly to Millennials, according to new studies by Mindshare North America and Cohn & Wolfe.

The desire for openness and authenticity from brands can be juxtaposed against other research finding that the public's trust in major corporations is declining, and that advertising practitioners suffer from lower honesty ratings than auto mechanics.

Against this backdrop of skepticism and shortage of trust, it is no wonder that consumers are looking for authenticity from brands.

A recent study from Cohn & Wolfe confirms this. It found that 63% of consumers surveyed across 12 global markets would buy from a company they recognize as authentic over and above its competitors.

Moreover, 6 in 10 would recommend an authentic organization to family and friends.

A leading 91% of respondents agreed that it is important for companies to communicate honestly about their products and services, and 87% agreed that companies should act with integrity all the time.

By comparison, only 6 in 10 felt that it is important that companies have products or services they cannot live without.

A new study from Mindshare North America finds that it is vital that brands communicate their good intentions to Millennials, for whom "friendship values" are a building block of identity.

Among the 1,000 Millennials aged 18-34 who participated in the study, a majority believe that the following show that brands have good intentions:

Supports employees (62%);
Follows through (57%);
Puts people over profits (57%);
Works for a better world (54%); and
Helps people (52%).

Communication

Communication is key. Whether it's what American adults use to communicate or how consumers want brands to communicate with them, communication is the most important. That being said, face-to-face tops social as the favorite word of mouth vehicle.

How Consumers Want to Communicate With Brands

Some brand communication methods — such as sending useful information or tailored emails based on past purchases — resonate well with consumers, but other proactive outreach methods are disliked by many, according to results from an SAP SE poll conducted by Ipsos.

Thirty-seven percent of respondents said they like it when companies they have bought something from adjust offers to them based on where they live, with 18% disliking this and 31% saying it depends on the company.

While research has found personalization influences consumers' purchase decisions — with emailed product recommendations one of the favored forms -- the SAP study finds a little more indecision on the part of its respondents.

Roughly one-third say they like it when companies tailor their mailings or emails based on what they know about past purchases.

But 22% dislike this practice and 36% believe it depends on the brand.

The tide is more adverse when it comes to consumers being asked if they want alerts or information sent to their phone, with more disliking (34%) than liking (29%) this.

Similarly, more dislike (34%) than like (27%) offers to help via chat or phone before the consumer has asked for assistance.

It is worth noting that in each case more than one-quarter find this dependent on the brand, suggesting that more could be willing recipients of this type of communication.

Asked about the channels they prefer to use when they want information about a company's products and services, consumers pointed to email (28% share of respondents) first, followed by telephone (23%) and in-person (16%).

Just 4% said that social media is their preferred channel.

However, social media is a preferred channel for sharing positive reviews.

Among the 48% of respondents who make an effort to tell people online when they really like a product or service, 19% most often communicate the positive feedback on their own social media sites.

That rivals the 20% who most often post on review websites such as Consumer Reports of Yelp or Amazon.

American Adults' Use of Communication Devices, by Age

Asked how frequently they used each seven modes of communication, adult respondents under the age of 50 reported that texting was the form of communication they more frequently used, followed by emails for those aged 30-49 and phone calls using a cell phone for those aged 18-29.

Some 38% of 18-29-year-olds said they had posted or read messages on a social media site "a lot," while 14% had frequently used Twitter recently.

Both figures were far higher for the 18-29 bracket than for older age groups.

Face-to-Face Tops Social As W-O-M Vehicle

Both Millennials and Gen Xers say they're more likely to spread the word about their favorite brands and products face-to-face than via social media, according to results from a CrowdTwist study. Beyond those two leading word-of-mouth vehicles, though, email proves more popular among Gen Xers while texting is more apt to be used by Millennials.

The results are from a survey of 1,208 North American consumers ages 18-69, from which subsets of 403 Gen X consumers (born between 1965 and 1980) and 402 Millennials (born between 1981 and 1997) were examined in separately-released reports. (The report examining Boomers has yet to be released; presumably, face-to-face will also be a more popular W-O-M vehicle than social media among this group of respondents.)

Millennials (50.5%) and Gen Xers (49.6%) were equally as likely to say they are extremely loyal or quite loyal to their favorite brands. Of these two sets of respondents, though, Millennials appear to be the group more likely to switch brands.

With consumers increasingly modifying their shopping habits due to loyalty programs, preventing churn is paramount for those marketers using a loyalty or reward program. For both cohorts, the top reasons given for abandoning a loyalty program were:

- The rewards not being compelling or relevant;
- Being tired of waiting for points to accumulate; and
- Not having enough ways to earn points.

When it comes to earning those points through non-purchase activities, answering a survey is easily the favorite method for Gen Xers (78.2%) and Millennials (74.4%). Of note, among the various activities listed, checking-in at a location ranked higher for Gen Xers than Millennials, while the opposite was true for watching videos.

Consumer Experience

Consumer experience can affect how frequently a shopper may buy products from someone, or if they ever will again. Consumers are most likely to attribute a positive experience with a company by how quickly their request is dealt with. The biggest customer experience failures seem to be with long waits/poor response times, poorly empowered and trained customer service. Ideally, customers prefer experiences with companies that have fast responses and a simple purchasing process.

How Do Consumers Say They'd Respond
To Positive Customer Experiences?

Some 82% of consumers have had a positive experience with a company recently, finds Verint in a survey of 18,038 respondents across 9 countries. Consumers were most likely to attribute a positive experience to the company dealing with their request quickly, while a sizable proportion also said that the company understood their issue and history.

That implies a level of desire for personalization in the customer interaction, though there appears to be some tension on this front.

Indeed, when presented with pairs of statements and asked to choose the one they agree (presumably more) with, consumers responded as follows:

- 52% chose the statement "I like it when service is personalized to me and my interests" versus 48% who chose the statement "I am suspicious about how my data is used"; and
- 51% chose the statement "Customer service is an experience that should reflect me as a person" against 49% who chose the statement "Customer service is a transaction – it shouldn't matter who I am".

While the results imply that there's some appetite for personalization, they also show that there's a demand for simple, fast and effective service.

The research shows that consumers will reward companies that provide an excellent customer experience.

In fact, roughly 6 in 10 said that they would tell friends and family about a customer experience that went the extra mile, and almost 4 in 10 would write a positive review.

Interestingly, respondents were more than three times as likely to tell friends and family about a positive experience (61%) as they were to talk about it on social media (17%).

This fairly low figure comes despite other research suggesting that consumers are more likely to praise than complain about a company's customer service on social media.

Nevertheless, the Verint study indicates that customer service can affect perceptions and even loyalty. When asked what frustrates them enough to make them switch providers to a competitor, survey respondents pointed first to finding a cheaper alternative (31% share) but second to impolite, rude or uninterested staff (16%).

As for customer loyalty? Globally, Verint finds that the highest portion of customers have stayed with their bank for more than 3 years (80%), with sizable proportions also staying loyal for that long to mobile phone companies (65%) and utility companies (62%), among others.

On average, though, just 41% of customers have stayed loyal to an online retailer for more than 3 years, presumably as price is a more important factor in that sector.

Consumers Wary of Sharing Personal Data With Retailers

Only four in 10 consumers surveyed in 12 countries say they're comfortable receiving personalized text message offers from retailers, and even fewer are comfortable sharing personal information while making purchases, finds Zebra Technologies in a recently-released study.

The results are interesting in light of separate research from Aimia finding that most consumers will share at least some information with companies.

According to the Aimia survey, of more than 20,000 consumers across the globe, more than eight in 10 respondents will share name, email address and nationality with companies, and at least seven in 10 will share their date of birth, hobbies and occupation.

Within the U.S., 51% of 18-34-year-olds reported being willing to share their mobile phone number with companies, though that figure dropped to 30% among Boomers.

The report stresses that trust, rather than desire for rewards, is at the heart of willingness to share information. And more than two-thirds of respondents reportedly said they "understand why they have to share personal information with companies to receive better offers."

That type of rationale recently came under fire in a University of Pennsylvania survey entitled "The Trade off Fallacy". According to that study, "a majority of Americans are resigned to giving up their data – and that is why many appear to be engaged in tradeoffs."

Of the 1,506 U.S. adults surveyed, 91% disagreed (71% strongly) that "if companies give me a discount, it is a fair exchange for them to collect information about me without my knowing." (Perhaps it's the knowing part that they were hung up on?) Further, 55% disagreed (38% strongly) that "it's okay if a store where I shop uses information it has about me to create a picture of me that improves the services they provide for me."

The results from the Zebra Technologies survey align closer with that sentiment than do the results from the Aimia survey. In looking at privacy concerns with regards to retailers, the Zebra study found that just 27% of respondents are comfortable sharing personal information while making a purchase online, and only 25% are comfortable sharing their data when making a purchase in-store.

Comfort with websites' tracking behavior and with sharing social media profile information with retailers turned out to be even lower (each at 20%).

Concerns with protection of the data may be behind those low levels of comfort. When respondents were asked their level of trust in various companies and institutions to protect their personal data and use it to provide something of value, just 38% of respondents indicated some level of trust with retailers. (By comparison, the highest level of trust – 62% – was for hospitals and healthcare companies.)

Nevertheless, 70% of respondents seem to feel that they would be encouraged to share personal information with retailers for some type of reward or perk.

That suggests that rewards may prompt data sharing even if trust isn't necessarily there. While that appears to be in conflict with the Aimia report, the difference may be due to the verticals involved.

In other words, consumers may want rewards when shopping, but be more driven by trust when dealing with other types of companies (the Aimia report was not limited to retailers).

What Wins Customers Back
After a Customer Experience Failure?

Roughly three in four consumers surveyed across nine countries have experienced their "worst customer experience (CX) failure" within the past 2 years, according to a report from SDL.

Customers most often ascribed failures to the post-sale support of the customer journey stage, with long waits/poor response times (35%), poorly empowered (31%) and trained (30%) customer service the most commonly-cited reasons for CX failures. So can customers be re-engaged?

Apparently, the desire is there, as 82% of customers experiencing a "worst CX" said they are interested in fixing the problem.

But while the desire to fix a problem might be there, the survey also finds that only about 1 in 5 customers experiencing a "worst CX" event will consider doing business with the company again.

That's in line with other research from Accenture, in which 73% of US customers who had switched providers in the previous year due to poor service said they would not consider switching back to their original provider or doing business with them again.

The study finds that customers who had returned to a company post-failure were most likely to attribute that to:

- The company owning the failure and admitting its mistakes (29% share);
- Receiving a genuine, personalized apology (22%); and
- The company giving discounts, credits, rebates on products/services where the failure was experienced (21%).

Far fewer (8%) said they had returned to the company in question because it showed them how they had improved their business as a result of the experience. This appears to be a minor influence on consumers, despite the sample overall indicating that this *would* win them back.

In other interesting results from the survey:

- Communications service providers emerged as the "worst offenders" for CX failures, a result in keeping with prior research;
- Pleasant and helpful customer service (35%) and well-trained and knowledgeable customer service (27%) were the leading reasons given for CX success;
- Some 64% of customers experiencing a CX failure stopped recommending the brand (22%), looked for alternatives (30%), or disparaged the company (12%);

- By contrast, 98% of customers will engage in a positive activity after experiencing a CX success, most often by recommending them to others offline (72%); and
- CX success is most commonly attributed to the combination of humans and technology, while humans are most commonly blamed for failures.

Fast Responses Top Ideal Customer Experience

Customers (aged 18-65) around the world are most likely to identify an "ideal" customer experience with companies' fast responses to inquiries or complaints (47% citing as a top-3 element) and a simple purchasing process (also 47%), according to a new study released by the Economist Intelligence Unit (EIU).

Interestingly, those factors far outweigh others such as personalization of the experience (12%) and customized offers based on preferences (7%). That doesn't necessarily mean those aren't important — personalization appears to be influential in the retail space — but rather that consumers want the basics covered first.

Failure to provide those basics can lead to lost business, per the report.

A majority of respondents said they had stopped doing business with at least one company during the previous year due to a negative experience, with this subset of respondents pointing to slow responses to inquiries and complaints, inaccurate or misleading product information, and delays in delivering the product or service as the aspects of the experience that "annoyed" them the most.

Overall, 71% of respondents said their typical response to a bad experience is to stop doing business with the company. A slight majority (55%) typically tell friends and family about it in person or by email, while 42% said they complain to the company and 26% post a comment on social media.

Meanwhile, consumers typically respond to an "outstanding" experience by making a mental note to buy from the company again (69%), telling friends and family (51%) and posting a comment on a social media site (23%).

In consumers' eyes, the obstacle that most prevents companies from providing an "ideal" experience is a lack of interest in customer satisfaction, cited by 45% of respondents.

That's an interesting result, as an accompanying survey of global executives found them most likely to describe their customer experience focus as being on building relationships with customers to increase satisfaction.

That survey also found the largest proportion of executives pointing to silos within the organization (36% selecting as a top-2 choice) as the obstacle standing in the way of improving the organization's customer experience.

For executives, organizational silos count as a bigger hindrance than a lack of integrated information systems (27%) or inflexible technology and application infrastructure (17%).

Consumers also see the need for companies to improve their coordination.

Asked about companies they already buy from regularly, consumers said that the most important improvements that could be made to the overall quality experience were to provide better links between in-store and online services (32%) and provide better coordination across different parts of the business, such as marketing and customer service (30%).

Other findings:

- Disparities in the channels executives are using to interact with customers and those consumers are using to learn about and compare products. For example, just 25% of executives reported using search engine tools to interact with customers, and even fewer (19%) said they use independent websites. But these were among consumers' preferred channels for learning about and comparing products, cited by 69% and 46%, respectively; and
- Respondents were most likely to think that the retail and consumer goods industries provide the best overall customer experience, with the telecommunications industry lagging in the list of five identified industries. Executive respondents also tabbed retail as the industry with the best customer experience, but placed telecommunications ahead of consumer goods manufacturing.

U.S. Companies with the Best and Worst Customer Experience Ratings

Consumers gave Publix the best customer experience rating of 293 companies measured by the Temkin Group, narrowly supplanting last year's leader, H- E-B.

Indeed, supermarkets occupied five of the Top 12 positions this year, with retailers and fast food chains also well-represented. Those industries – plus parcel delivery services and banks – comprised the only five of 20 measured to average a "good" rating.

Meanwhile, on the other end of the spectrum, Coventry Health Care had the worst customer experience rating, as it did last year.

Internet service providers, TV service providers and health plans each received "poor" ratings on average.

Overall, 37% of companies rated this year (excluding utilities, which were a new addition) had an excellent (5%) or good (32%) rating. That's virtually unchanged from the past 2 years.

Industries with the Worst Customer Service, According to U.S. Adults

Government offices and the telecommunications industry (telecom, TV, internet) have by far the worst customer service, according to an Ipsos survey of U.S. adults.

The results of the survey, which asked respondents to identify up to 3 industries from 7 identified, are somewhat surprising in that insurance (13%) and airlines (12%) are among the least-cited in terms of bad customer service.

The study asked "If you had a bad experience with customer service, how likely are you to post a review or comment online, or on social media"?

Word of advice; don't get Millennials upset, 63% of 18-34 year olds described themselves as very/somewhat likely to post a bad experience, with only 37% of the 55+ year old segment.

However, good or positive service can help your bottom line just as dramatically as the "torpedo effect" associated with a negative experience:

• More than two-thirds of American consumers say they're willing to spend 14% more on average with a company that they believe delivers excellent service;

• Nearly half of the survey's respondents say they always tell others about good service interactions (46%), telling an average of eight people; and

• Two in five Americans (42%) say that a recommendation from a friend or family member is most likely to get them to try doing business with a new company, even more than a sale or promotion (34%) or a company's reputation (15%).

Consumer Satisfaction

Loyalty programs are becoming more popular with consumers than transactional desires such as rewards, points and discounts to more personal and emotional benefits such as ease of understanding and relevance of offers.

A majority of consumers want to hear from a retailer via email or advertising when it is offering a sale or promotion and almost half would want to hear from one when an item they've been looking at becomes cheaper.

Women are more likely than men to want to be made aware of sales, promotions, or discounts.

Top Reasons Consumers Continue
To Participate in Loyalty Programs

Once consumers sign up for a loyalty program, their attention shifts from transactional desires such as rewards points and discounts to more personal and emotional benefits such as ease of understanding (81%) and relevance of offers (75%), according to a COLLOQUY survey of more than 2,000 U.S. and Canadian loyalty program members.

A majority (54%) also continue to participate because it supports their lifestyle and personal preferences, per the survey, which found some differences among Millennials from other generations.

For example, lifestyle considerations are more important to Millennials (born 1981-1997; 63%) than to Gen Xers (born 1965-1980; 53%) and Baby Boomers (born 1946-1964; 46%).

The program having a smartphone app is likewise more important to Millennials (59%) than Boomers (31%), as is a mobile payment option (42% vs. 15%) and the inclusion of a competitive game or social aspect (27% vs. 7%).

When Do Consumers Want to Hear From Retailers?

A majority (57%) of U.S. adults would want to hear from a retailer via email or advertising when it is offering a sale or promotion, and almost half would want to hear from one when an item they've been looking at becomes cheaper, according to survey results from Emarsys. In each case, women are significantly more likely than men to want to hear from a retailer or e-commerce company.

Indeed, women were 40% more likely to want to be notified in the event of a promotion (66% vs. 49%) and 38% more likely to want that in the event of an item becoming cheaper (54% vs. 39%).

Beyond those top two reasons, though, there was less enthusiasm for emails and ads from retailers and e-commerce companies.

Only about one-quarter want to hear from one when something they've been looking at is close to selling out (26%) or when a holiday is coming up (25%). Even fewer (23%) want to be emailed or otherwise advertised to after visiting a company's website, store or social media page, with this desire highest among men aged 18-34 (39%).

Of note, desire to hear from retailers and e-commerce companies is generally higher among consumers with children in the household.

The survey looks further at retailers' emailing practices and advertising channels.

Specific to email, the survey hones in on consumers' responses to constant spamming with unwanted emails, finding that more than 9 in 10 would have some form of negative response, most commonly unsubscribing immediately from all email communications with the company (65%). This response was more likely among older consumers and women.

Among the other potential responses, around 1 in 7 (14%) said they would shop at a competitor instead, with this inclination highest among men aged 35-44 (28%). Only 6% said they would "rant on social media to my followers."

Interestingly, while 1 in 10 men (including 19% of those aged 18-34) reported that they would complain on social media, this response was almost non-existent among women (3%).

Turning to the most persuasive advertising channels, the results confirm several other recently-released studies in showing TV ads to be the most influential. Indeed, almost half (48%) of the respondents cited TV ads as effective in persuading them to buy companies' products, putting TV well ahead of print (38%) and email (35%).

Notably, 18-34-year-olds emerged as the age group *most* likely to cite TV as being effective, at a significantly higher rate than those aged 65 and older (56% and 37%, respectively).

Although only 22% of the survey respondents cited social ads as being persuasive, that figure was almost double among 18-34-year-olds (43%).

Finally, just one in eight (12%) adults (and 24% of those aged 18-34) surveyed said that mobile ads – whether served via browser, in-app, or by geotargeting – are effective in persuading them to buy products from companies. That doesn't seem to be the result of lesser reach, though: fully 83% of respondents reported owning a smartphone and/or tablet.

Consumers: Reviews Important
In Determining E-Commerce Site Legitimacy

More than three-quarters of U.S. consumers use customer reviews to determine the legitimacy of a site that sells brand name products, finds BrandShop in a recent survey of 1,055 U.S. adults aged 18-65.

The amount and quality of information is also used by a majority (59.5%) of respondents, though fewer determine legitimacy based on the quality of the site design and experience.

Other results from the survey confirm Amazon's power in the e-commerce space, with almost eight in 10 respondents saying they usually purchase products online from the e-commerce platform.

Still, a majority of those surveyed said they would prefer to buy clothing and apparel (56.7%) and electronics (55.9%) directly from a brand instead of a 3rd party retailer like Amazon. And given a bad experience with a product, respondents are more likely to hold the brand accountable than the retailer that sold it.

What Causes Consumers to Lose Trust in Digital Brands?

A majority of consumers don't trust websites that suffer from security and usability issues, says Neustar in recently-released research, although inaccurate content is the most common complaint of those identified. Indeed, 91% of the more than 750 adults surveyed for the report said that they don't trust websites that contain errors or mistakes.

Close behind, almost nine in 10 (88%) reported not trusting websites that frequently go down (i.e. off-line and unavailable). Another usability issue relates to slow load times, with two-thirds saying they don't trust websites that take too long to load.

A range of security concerns also affect trust, per the report:

- Three-quarters don't trust websites when identity and authentication procedures appear too easy;
- More than 6 in 10 don't trust the websites of companies that have had breaches; and
- Some 55% don't trust websites that do not have security safeguards to protect their personal information.

By comparison, fewer (31%) lack trust in websites that only rely on passwords to identify and authenticate.

(The focus on security may be a reflection of the survey being conducted by the Ponemon Institute, which researches privacy, data protection and information security policy.)

Interestingly, the report notes that "respectful advertising (less aggressive banner ads)" placed last out of 11 factors deemed important to the website experience, trailing security, performance and content factors.

Still, respondents don't like interruptive ads. Among 10 reasons for disliking a website, ads that interfere with content (55%) and ads that redirect users to sites they don't want to see (52%) were the most commonly cited. (Cue hand-wringing about the rise of ad blocking.)

Yet, despite all the research about the importance of relevant ads, just 15% of respondents said that ads of no interest to them are a reason for disliking a website. Those results suggest that consumers are fine with ads, as long as they stay in the background.

Meanwhile slow page loads were one of the more commonly-cited reasons to dislike websites, cited by half of the respondents. Respondents appear to be most impatient with social media, entertainment, e-commerce and travel/hospitality websites, as fewer than 1 in 8 would be willing to wait an additional (to what is not specified) 5 seconds for them to load.

In other intriguing results from the survey:

- Almost 8 in 10 respondents worry about security when site performance is sluggish;
- Speedy checkout (41%) is important to almost twice as many consumers as quick navigation to another page (23%), and important to almost three times as many consumers as accessing the home page (16%);
- Roughly 7 in 10 consumers report having left a website due to security concerns;
- Only about 1 in 4 have high expectations for e-commerce site security, while 95% do so for the security of banking and financial services sites;
- Almost one-quarter of respondents don't have a positive perception of a company's brand a year after a data breach;

- Some 55% say that security is important (top-3 box score on a 10-point scale) to their perception of a brand, and half say that data privacy is important to their perception.

Customer Satisfaction with Automobiles Drops To Lowest Point Since 2004

Customer satisfaction with automobiles has dropped three points this year to an index of 79 on the American Customer Satisfaction Index (ACSI)'s 100-point scale, marking its third consecutive year of declines and the lowest rating since 2004 (also 79).

In fact, just two of the 27 nameplates tracked (Honda Acura and BMW) improved their satisfaction rating from last year. The report traces the drop to higher recalls, with car owners reporting a 40% increase in recalls compared to Q2 2014.

The study finds higher satisfaction among car buyers with foreign-made cars over domestic ones, as 77% of the above-average nameplates are imports.

Toyota's Lexus (84) scored highest among all vehicles, while Fiat Chrysler had the lowest score (73).

What Are Consumers' Top Customer Service Irritants?

Roughly 9 in 10 consumers have contacted customer service at some point in the past year, according to a recent survey from the Consumer Reports National Research Center.

The study found that poor experiences abound, with half of respondents reporting having left a store without making an intended purchase because of poor service, and 57% hanging up the phone without resolving their issue. So what are their top irritants?

The survey identified numerous pain points and asked respondents to rate them on a 10-point scale, from "not annoying at all" to "tremendously irritating."

The top irritants in terms of the percentage "highly annoyed" by the practice, were:

- Not getting a live person on the phone (75%);
- Customer service being rude or condescending (75%);
- Getting disconnected (74%);
- Getting disconnected and being unable to reach the same rep again (71%); and
- Being transferred to a representative who can't help or is wrong (70%).

By comparison, while a majority find sales pitches and overly pushy salespeople to be irritating, these aren't quite as frustrating.

Good customer service is particularly important given that a majority (53%) of U.S. customers say respectful and knowledgeable representatives can calm angry callers.

That's notable in light of a study from Mattersight released earlier this year that found nearly two-thirds of U.S. consumers who contact customer service centers are frustrated before they even start talking to a representative.

Other results from that survey indicated that a majority of respondents want call center agents to acknowledge the importance of their problem.

That and an apology seemingly can go a long way: in a global survey conducted by SDL, customers who had returned to a company after a bad service experience were most likely to attribute their return to the company owning the failure and admitting its mistakes (29% share) and receiving a genuine, personalized apology (22% share).

Customer Service Satisfaction, by Channel

American adults are most likely to rate companies' customer service via phone (90%) and online chat (85%) as meeting or exceeding expectations, according to a Northridge Group survey.

That result is likely related to these being the only channels through which a majority of respondents expect their issue to be resolved the first time they contact the company.

The phone is still the preferred method of customer service contact for half of respondents, ahead of email (27%) and online chat (14%).

Indeed, 77% reach first for the phone when they have an urgent customer service issue or inquiry, though email (47%) is a more common first touchpoint than the phone (24%) when it comes to a non-urgent issue.

Just 2% of respondents reported that social media is their preferred method to contact a company with a customer service issue or inquiry. Fully one-third said they usually get no response when contacting a company via social media.

Customers Loathe Pay TV and ISPs, Love Their Smartphones

Customer satisfaction with information services – including subscription TV, Internet, wireless and fixed line telephone, and computer software – drops 3.4% to an ACSI score of 68.8 on a 0 to 100 scale, the lowest level in seven years.

According to the American Customer Satisfaction Index (ACSI), customer satisfaction with subscription TV service deteriorates further, tying Internet service providers (ISPs) at 63 – the worst score among 43 industries covered by the Index. ACSI data, which is based on 14,176 customer surveys collected in the first quarter 2015, show the decline results from poor customer service combined with higher prices.

"There was a time when pay TV could get away with discontented users without being penalized by revenue losses from defecting customers, but those days are over," says Claes Fornell, ACSI Chairman and founder. "Today people have more alternatives than ever before. Consumer abandonment of pay TV is shaking up the industry and lower satisfaction could mean even more cord cutting by subscribers ahead."

The ACSI report includes ISPs, subscription television service, fixed-line and wireless telephone, and computer software. The report also covers cell phones, part of the durables sector, as well as detailed data for the top-selling smartphone brands available to U.S. consumers.

Subscription TV: Cable Companies Crash —The ACSI reports huge drops in customer satisfaction for Comcast and Time Warner Cable, following their failed merger. Already one of the lowest-scoring companies in the ACSI, Comcast sheds 10% to a customer satisfaction score of 54. Meanwhile, Time Warner Cable earns the distinction as least-satisfying company in the Index after falling 9% to 51. Joining Time Warner Cable in the basement is ACSI newcomer Mediacom Communications (51), which serves smaller markets in the Midwest and South.

With a 4% gain to an ACSI score of 71, Verizon's FiOS service takes the lead from DIRECTV (-1% to 68) and AT&T's U-verse (unchanged at 69). Cablevision Systems enters the ACSI as the highest-scoring large cable company; however, it only ties the lowest-scoring satellite provider, DISH Network (67).

Charter Communications (+5% to 63) is going on a merger binge of its own with plans to acquire Time Warner Cable and Bright House Networks (65), which would make it the second-largest cable TV company in the country. Although Charter shows the most improvement in the industry, it may be difficult to maintain customer satisfaction momentum as the company combines operations with other providers. ACSI data suggest that mergers usually result in lower customer satisfaction, at least in the short term.

"Cable companies are trying to strengthen their positions through consolidation, but the benefits to consumers of one coaxial cable company absorbing another are questionable," says David VanAmburg, ACSI Director. "The AT&T-DIRECTV merger may be different, however, because it would allow AT&T to deliver TV service via multiple technologies."

Lack of Choice Leaves Customers Dissatisfied With ISPs – Sixty-one percent of U.S. households have just one or no high-speed Internet provider servicing their region and the lack of customer choice contributes to weak customer satisfaction. Even as Internet usage grows, customer satisfaction with ISPs remains unchanged at an ACSI score of 63 and tied with subscription TV for last place among 43 industries. Customers are frustrated with unreliable service, slow broadband Internet speeds and rising subscription prices – and they resent being locked into service contracts.

Two large ISPs do improve and their gains are sizeable. AT&T (U-verse) picks up 6% to an ACSI score of 69, taking the lead from Verizon (-4% to 68). Time Warner Cable gains 7% to 58. Bright House Networks matches the industry average at 63; Cablevision Systems and Frontier Communications debut at 61.

Several ISPs suffer large drops in customer satisfaction, including CenturyLink (-8% to 60), Cox Communications (-9% to 58) and Charter Communications (-7% to 57). Comcast stays at the bottom of the category, slipping 2% to 56.

Apple Challenges Samsung for Cell Phone Lead; Customers Happiest with No-Contract Wireless Carriers

Customer satisfaction with cell phones is unchanged at 78, the highest score yet for the industry. The majority of new cell phones sold today are smartphones, which generally have higher satisfaction than feature phones. With some of the strongest scores in the entire ACSI, the two largest smartphone manufacturers lead the way: Apple and Samsung Electronics. Apple advances 1% to 80, going head-to-head with Samsung (-1%).

"Despite its high-scoring phones, Samsung may find it difficult to chip into Apple's market share because of the need to overcome the brand appeal that is Apple's mainstay," says VanAmburg. "Samsung gained an initial advantage as the first manufacturer to introduce large screens for smartphones, but with the launch of large-screen phones by Apple, its loyal customers have little reason to look elsewhere."

Nokia, whose devices and services business has been assumed by Microsoft Mobile, is down 3% to 75, falling behind Motorola Mobility (+3% to 79). For BlackBerry, only the most satisfied customers remain, which pushes its score up 5% to 78.

Apple may share the lead with Samsung in overall scores, but in terms of smartphone devices, Samsung's Galaxy Note 4 takes the lead (86). Apple does not appear to have gained any advantage from the major redesign of its iconic iPhone in terms of user satisfaction. Several smartphones score 82: iPhone 6 Plus, iPhone 6, Galaxy S5 and Galaxy Note 3. Motorola's Moto X is next at 81, followed by the LG G3, iPhone 5 and Galaxy S4 (all 80).

Meanwhile, customer satisfaction with wireless telephone service is down 2.8% to 70. The aggregate of smaller wireless companies has the highest customer satisfaction and even shows slight improvement (+1% to 79). Smaller companies tend to be no-contract carriers with lower fees, which many customers see as better value.

In its first year as an ACSI-covered company, the prepaid phone provider TracFone Wireless takes the lead at 77. Verizon Wireless drops 5% to 71. Both T-Mobile and AT&T improve to tie at 70, while Sprint falls 4% to 65.

Fixed-Line Phone: No Longer Much of a Focal Point – Customer satisfaction with fixed-line telephone service falls 5.5% to 69 as landline usage continues to shrink; more than 44% of homes now forgo fixed-line service in favor of wireless.

Despite slipping 3% to 76, the average ACSI score of smaller local and long distance providers is much better than that of large providers. Vonage and Bright House Networks are near the top of the category (both 73). CenturyLink dips 1% to 70, while Verizon declines 7% to 68. Cox Communications drops 3% to tie Verizon and, just a notch below, Cablevision Systems enters the Index at 67.

AT&T's landline service suffers the most, down 10% to 65. Nevertheless, AT&T stays ahead of both Comcast (-4% to 64) and Time Warner Cable (-3% to 63).

Customers Less Satisfied with Energy Utilities, Shipping and Healthcare

Following yet another harsh winter, customer satisfaction with gas and electric service providers is down 2.7% to an ACSI score of 74.3 on a 0-100 scale, according to the American Customer Satisfaction Index (ACSI).

"Higher cost tends to weaken customer satisfaction, particularly when spending is not discretionary, as is the case with commodities such as energy," says Claes Fornell, ACSI chairman and founder. "It is not as much the cost of energy per se, but that usage was high and took a bigger bite out of household income."

The ACSI report covers customer satisfaction with three utility categories (cooperative, investor-owned and municipal) and two health care service industries (hospitals and ambulatory care), along with consumer shipping and the mail services of the U.S. Postal Service (USPS).

Investor-Owned Utilities: Rising Cost of Electricity and Natural Gas Dampens Satisfaction

Household satisfaction with investor-owned utilities falls 1.3% to an ACSI score of 74.

Among the largest investor-owned utilities, the highest-scoring companies are both natural gas suppliers – Atmos Energy (ACSI score of 82) and CenterPoint Energy (81).

FirstEnergy is next at 79 and posts the largest gain (+8%); it now ties Sempra Energy. Dominion Resources, PPL and NiSource all come in at 78, followed by Southern Company, Entergy (+1%) and NextEra Energy (+1%) at 77. The only other providers to improve are Xcel Energy (+1% to 76), Public Service Enterprise Group (+3% to 72), and PG&E (+1% to 71).

Most utilities have moved in the opposite direction, with DTE Energy and Exelon deteriorating the most (-8%). Duke Energy (-6%) also declines, while Eversource Energy (formerly Northeast Utilities), hurt particularly hard by winter storms, falls 7% to the industry low of 66.

Municipal Utilities: Smaller Companies Hit Hardest; Salt River Project Maintains Lead

Most large municipal utilities improved from a year ago, but smaller providers, which make up a majority of the market, drop to a combined ACSI score of 73.

The Salt River Project (SRP) leads in customer satisfaction for a fifth straight year, edging up 1% to 80, and CPS Energy advances 3% to 77.

Meanwhile, the Los Angeles Department of Water & Power (LADWP) slips 1% and scores far below for customer satisfaction at 68.

Cooperative Utilities: Best in Category Smaller rural cooperative utilities hold a strong lead over the other utility categories, but slip 1.2% to an ACSI score of 80. Despite a 1% downturn, Touchstone Energy Cooperatives remains one of the Index's top-scoring energy utilities at 80, followed by the aggregate of smaller co-ops (-3% to 78).

Health Care & Social Assistance: Patient Satisfaction Continues to Fall

Patient satisfaction is down 3.2% to an ACSI score of 75.1, the lowest level in nearly a decade.

According to patients, ambulatory care such as office visits to doctors, dentists and optometrists (76) is better than hospital services (74) by a significant margin, but quality of care is less satisfactory and both categories weaken from a year ago.

Demand for health care services is rising, with preliminary figures on household health care spending up nearly 6% in 2014 – the largest increase since before the recession.

This is probably in part a result of growth in the number of Americans with health insurance. During the same period, the rate of growth in the health care workforce slowed, which likely contributed to less efficient access to care.

However, since the middle of 2014, the health care sector has been adding workers at a significantly faster pace, which may lead to higher levels of patient satisfaction in the near future.

"Health care is a non-discretionary expense that consumers delay at their own risk," says ACSI Managing Director David VanAmburg. "While consumers might postpone a vacation or the purchase of a new pair of shoes, they rarely have the flexibility to put off healthcare regardless of cost or quality of care.

The influx of the newly insured is putting pressure on a system that is still playing catch up. Rising demand that is outpacing supply, coupled with increasing healthcare costs, is a formula for lower satisfaction."

Outpatient hospital care shows improvement (+5% to 80), but considerably lower satisfaction with inpatient services and poor emergency room service (-10% to 64) has caused overall patient satisfaction with hospitals to worsen.

Consumer Shipping: Steady from a Year Ago

Customer satisfaction with shipping is stable at an ACSI score 81.

Both FedEx and UPS are steady with identical ACSI scores of 82, while the USPS gains for its Express and Priority Mail delivery business (+3% to 75).

However, regular mail service falls for a second straight year. With a tightening budget, higher postage rates and shrinking mail volumes, satisfaction with USPS regular mail service sinks to 69, its lowest level in nearly 20 years.

Digital Devices/ Computers

Digital devices have become a part of everyday life.
Some 21% of U.S. adults report going online almost constantly, while another 42% go online several times a day. A little more than two-thirds of American adults (68%) now own a smartphone, representing a rapid rise from about half that proportion (35%) in mid-2011.

Mobile devices represent the two fastest-growing consumer electronics products this year when measured by absolute percentage point growth (rather than relative increase), with tablet penetration up 9% points to 54% and smartphones up 8% points to 72%.

More Than 1 in 3 Young Adults Online "Almost Constantly"

Some 21% of U.S. adults report going online "almost constantly," while another 42% go online "several times a day," according to the Pew Research Center.

The data shows that the percentage that are online "almost constantly" is highest among 18-29-year-olds (36%), college graduates (29%) and those with incomes of at least $75,000 (28%). These groups also over-index in their smartphone ownership, according to earlier Pew data.

Indeed, mobile connectivity is linked to the frequency of going online in the latest data from Pew.

In revealing that about three in four Americans use a smartphone, tablet or other mobile device to access the internet at least occasionally, Pew notes that 27% of these adults go online "almost constantly," compared to 21% on average.

Brands Boost Email 25%;
54% of Opens on Mobiles, Tablets

Brands continue to increase their email volume, registering a 24.8% year-over-year rise in Q3, according to Experian Marketing Services data. That represents the 12th consecutive quarter of increases and the 11th of double-digit increases.

The report indicates that 54% of email opens took place on mobiles (42%) and tablets (12%), though these devices accounted for a smaller share (40%) of email clicks (32% mobile; 8% tablet).

Of the six industries analyzed, multi-channel retailers saw the largest share of opens (61%) and clicks (54%) from mobile devices, while business products and services companies saw the smallest share (30% and 18%, respectively).

Increasing Amount of Gen Xers Own The Tech Trio: Smartphone, Computer and Tablet

Roughly 37% of adult in the United States own a smartphone, computer *and* tablet, according to survey results from the Pew Internet & American Life Project.

In looking at how the ownership of all three devices breaks out among demographic groups, the study indicates that it is highest among 30-49-year-olds (51%), college graduates (53%), and those coming from households with at least $75k in annual income (60%).

Last year, a survey from Deloitte found that 37% of Americans aged 14 and older owned the trio of devices, with that figure up to 51% among Millennials (14-30).

Email Click-to-Open Rates, by Device, Q2 2013-Q3 2015

While mobile click-to-open (CTO) rates dipped slightly on a quarter-over-quarter basis in Q3 (to 13.7%), they remained up from the year-earlier period (12.1%) and continue to close the gap with desktop CTO rates, per Yesmail's latest quarterly report.

Email-driven mobile revenue also grew in Q3, by 9.9% year-over-year, with smartphones accounting for 56.6% of mobile revenue, up from 41.6% a year earlier.

Apple devices continue to dominate revenues derived from mobile email, accounting for 77% share this past quarter.

The iPhone comprised 34% share of orders (up from 23% during Q3 2014), taking share from the iPad, which accounted for 43% of orders (down from 58% during the year-earlier period).

Average order sizes on mobile ($103.80) continued to lag desktop ($136.70), though.

The Demographics of U.S. Smartphone and Tablet Users

A little more than two-thirds of American adults (68%) now own a smartphone, representing a rapid rise from about half that proportion (35%) in mid-2011, details the Pew Internet & American Life Project in a recent study.

Tablet ownership has also been on a rapid upward trajectory, increasing from 3% of American adults in 2010 to 45% this year. So who owns these devices?

Not surprisingly, smartphone ownership is highest among youth, with 86% of 18-29-year-olds reporting ownership of a smartphone, although 30-49-year-olds (83%) are close behind. A majority (58%) of 50-64-year-olds also own a smartphone, though adoption falls to 30% among those aged 65 and up.

It's a slightly different pattern for tablet adoption, with ownership highest among the 30-49 group (57%), followed by the 18-29 bracket (50%). While ownership is again lower among older generations, the gap isn't as large as with smartphones, as 37% of those aged 50-64 and 32% of adults aged 65 and older report owning a tablet.

Smartphone and tablet ownership also have different patterns when sorting by gender and race/ethnicity. While smartphone ownership is slightly higher among men (70%) than women (66%), the opposite is true for tablets, owned by 47% of women and 43% of men.

And while tablet ownership is considerably higher among non-Hispanic whites (47%) than Blacks (38%) and Hispanics (35%), smartphone ownership rates are generally consistent, highest among Blacks (65%) and lowest among Hispanics (64%).

Smartphone and tablet ownership patterns are more similar when looking at income and education, with penetration rising alongside educational attainment and household income.

For example, adults with at least a college degree are almost twice as likely as those without a high school degree to own a smartphone (81% vs. 41%). And while a bare majority (52%) of lower-income (<$30k) adults own a smartphone, that figure rises to 87% among those in higher-income ($75k+) households.

The gaps in ownership are wider, however, among tablet owners. For example, adults in higher-income households are more than three times as likely as those in lower-income households to own a tablet (62% vs. 19%). And those with at least a college degree are more than twice as likely as those without a high school degree to own the device (67% vs. 28%).

The Pew study also looks at ownership of several other devices, including computers, game consoles, e-readers, MP3 players, and gaming devices.

Unlike with mobile devices, penetration rates of these other gadgets have either stalled or gradually declined in recent years, with e-reader ownership down substantially this year (19%) from early last year (32%). Some notable demographic results from these analyses include:

- Computer ownership being far higher among non-Hispanic whites (79%) than Blacks (45%);
- A majority of adults in the 18-29 (56%) and 30-49 (55%) brackets owning a game console, with this figure down to 8% among those aged 65 and older;
- Gaming console ownership being higher among women (42%) than men (37%);
- About half (51%) of adults aged 18-49 owning an MP3 player;
- E-reader ownership being consistent at 18-19% across age groups; and
- Ownership of portable gaming devices being broadest among 18-29-year-olds (21%) and higher-income households (21%).

North American Email Engagement Trends: Click Rates Continue Slow Decline

North American email open rates are down slightly year-over-year so far in 2015, details Epsilon in its latest quarterly email trends analysis.

But while open rates have been generally steady or increasing over the past couple of years, the same can't be said for click rates, which continue to gradually decline, down to an average of 3.6% in Q2.

Click rates have decreased on a year-over-year basis each Q2 going back at least as far as 2010, when they stood at 5.3%.

The "Business Publishing/Media General" sector recorded the highest click rate (6.8%) and click-to-open rate (24.4%) of all those measured, while the "Business Products and Services General" industry registered the lowest click rate (2.1%) and click-to-open rate (7.6%) of the industries tracked.

Separately, the report demonstrates that triggered emails continue to see significantly higher open and click rates than BAU (business as usual) emails. Indeed, the 12.1% click rate for triggered emails is the highest rate registered in at least 2 years.

Tablets, Smartphones Fastest Growing Consumer Electronics

Mobile devices represent the two fastest-growing consumer electronics (CE) products this year when measured by absolute percentage point growth (rather than relative increase), with tablet penetration up 9% points to 54% and smartphones up 8% points to 72%, according to the CEA.

In fact, smartphones are now the third-most commonly owned CE product, behind TVs (98%) and DVD/Blu-ray players (78%), while tablets have cracked the top 10 (#9) for the first time, replacing basic cell phones, which fell out of the top 10.

Other fast-growing CE products (by year-over-year percentage point gain in household penetration) include:

- Wearable fitness trackers (+6% points to 11%);
- Digital media streaming devices such as Apple TV or Roku (+5% points to 29%); and
- In-vehicle communication devices such as navigation, back-up cameras and hands-free calling (+4% points to 34%).

Digital Estimated to Influence Half of In-Store Retail Sales

Digital technologies influenced an estimated 49% of in-store sales last year ($1.7T), in line with previously-released projections and up from 36% the year prior, says Deloitte.

Mobile's influence, as expected, has been growing quickly, directly impacting 28% of in-store sales last year, accounting for about 57% of digital's total impact.

Digital's influence continues to be greatest in the electronic and home furnishings categories, according to the study, which forecasts 64% of in-store sales to be impacted by digital technologies this year.

In related news, a recent study from 4INFO and Nielsen Catalina Solutions found that mobile display ads can drive in-store CPG sales, with the analysis of 83 mobile campaigns finding that the return on ad served (ROAS) was 257%, indicating a $2.57 incremental sales lift for each dollar spent on mobile ads.

In other interesting results, mobile was found to drive twice the sales lift of desktop when measured by total sales per thousand impressions ($30 and $13, respectively), while an examination of ad clicks versus sales lift found no correlation at all between those who click and those who buy.

U.S. Now Sees More Mobile-Only
Than Desktop-Only Adult Internet Users

There are now more mobile-only than desktop-only adult internet users in the U.S., says comScore, as the former accounted for 11.3% share of connected adults in March, versus 10.6% share for the latter.

Interestingly, the milestone was reached as a result of an uptick in multi-platform users rather than a hike in mobile-only users, which had been in the 11-12% range for the six months prior.

Instead, the share of adult internet users who access the internet using only desktops almost halved over the space of year, from 19.1% in March 2014 to 10.6% in March of 2015.

Tablets Now Reportedly in a Majority of U.S. Households

Tablet penetration has reached 51% of US households as of February, up 13% points year-over-year, according to Nielsen in a recent study.

Tablet penetration stood at 50% or higher in 20 local markets, led by Atlanta (62%) and San Francisco (61%), with Phoenix (+23% points) and Miami (+19% points) registering as the markets with the largest year-over-year gains.

Beyond Atlanta and San Francisco, other markets with high tablet penetration include:

- Washington, DC (59%);
- Baltimore (58%); and
- Boston (56%).

The study also reports that smartphone penetration reached 78% of American mobile subscribers aged 13 and older in February, a figure slightly higher than comScore's recent tally of 76.6%, although that covered the 3-month period ending in February, rather than just February.

The 5 markets with the highest rates of smartphone penetration in February, per Nielsen, were:

- Dallas (88%);
- Houston (85%);
- Baltimore (84%);
- Charlotte (84%); and
- Denver (84%).

Smartphone penetration climbed by 8% points year-over-year, led by Seattle (+15% points), Baltimore (+14% points) and Charlotte (+12% points). Consistent with previous research from Pew, the Nielsen data indicates that smartphone penetration is higher among Hispanics (82%) and African-Americans (83%).

Turning to smart TVs, which are now owned by 16% of households, the report notes that Houston, Seattle, San Francisco and New York lead the way, each with a penetration rate of 21% of households.

Finally, some 42% of US households in February had access to Netflix, Amazon Prime, or Hulu Plus, per the report, a figure unchanged from November 2014. Subscription video-on- demand penetration is now in at least half of households in Washington, DC (52%), San Francisco (52%), Seattle (50%) and Portland (50%), though the only change from November is a single-point gain in Portland.

Netflix (38%, up 2 points from November) remains the SVOD market leader by household penetration and continues to add subscribers.

It's followed by Amazon (14%, up a point from November) and Hulu Plus (7%, also up a point).

Drugs/Pharmaceuticals

The use of alcohol and cigarettes by American teens reached their lowest points since 1975, and the use of some especially dangerous illicit drugs such as MDMA (ecstasy, Molly), heroin, amphetamines and synthetic marijuana also showed a drop this year. Use of Marijuana, however, remained the same.

Use of Marijuana and prescription drugs on United States highways is increasingly prominent, raising new questions about safety.

Ecstasy, Heroin, Synthetic Marijuana, Alcohol, Cigarette Use Declined Among U.S. Teens in 2015

The use of licit and illicit drugs by American teens show that some important improvements are taking place, according to the results from the latest national survey in the Monitoring the Future series.

The use of alcohol and cigarettes reached their lowest points since 1975 when the study began. Use of some especially dangerous illicit drugs — such as MDMA (ecstasy, Molly), heroin, amphetamines and synthetic marijuana — also showed a drop in use this year. However, use of Marijuana remained the same.

The study tracks the trends in substance use by polling over 40,000 8th, 10th, and 12th-graders each year in about 400 public and private secondary schools across the contiguous 48 states.

Alcohol

Use of alcohol by U.S. teens continued its long-term decline. Those in grades 8, 10, and 12 displayed a further decline in the proportion of students reporting any alcohol use in the year preceding the survey.

"The recent peak rate in annual prevalence of alcohol use was in 1997, at 61% for the three grades combined. Since then, there has been a fairly steady downward march in alcohol use among adolescents," said Professor Lloyd Johnston, the study's principal investigator. "The rate has fallen by about a third, to 40%. More importantly, the percentage who report binge drinking has fallen by half, from 22% to 11%."

Some 12th-graders drink even more heavily than five or more drinks in a row, reporting 10 or more, or 15 or more, drinks in a row on at least one occasion in the prior two weeks— dangerously high levels of consumption that the investigators have labeled "extreme binge drinking."

Peer disapproval of binge drinking had been rising since 2000 among teens, though it did not rise further in 2015. Declines in availability may be another contributing factor to the declines in teen drinking.

"In recent years, there has been a fair decline in all three grades in the proportion saying that alcohol is easy for them to get, with the steepest decline among the youngest teens," Johnston said. "This suggests that state, community and parental efforts have been successful in reducing underage access to alcohol."

Illicit Drugs

Multiple illicit drugs dropped in use this year.

There were declines in use of MDMA (ecstasy, Molly), heroin, synthetic marijuana ("K2," "Spice") and amphetamines.

Investigators say there were no statistically significant increases for any of the more than 50 classes and subclasses of drugs that MTF tracks among 8th, 10th and 12th-grade students.

The use of MDMA, known as ecstasy and more recently Molly, has been tumbling in use since around 2010. Inclusion of Molly in the question about perceived risk to the user produced a considerable jump in the proportions of 8th and 10th-graders saying MDMA use is dangerous to the user.

Reported availability of ecstasy (MDMA), specifically, has been declining since the peak year of use in 2001, but there was little further decline in 2015.

Heroin, which is one of the most dangerous illicit drugs, is of particular importance. The amount of secondary school students using heroin has been declining steadily in the past few years, and it continued to fall a little in some grades in 2015.

Among 8th-graders, the proportion reporting any heroin use in the prior 12 months fell significantly from 0.5% to 0.3%; and their annual prevalence is down by two-thirds since 2008, when it was 0.9%.

In both 10th and 12th grades, annual prevalence fell in 2015 by one-tenth of 1% to 0.5% (not a statistically significant change, but the decline for the three grades combined was significant). Both of these upper grades did have an annual prevalence above 1.0% at the beginning of the 2000s, so their rates of heroin use have now fallen by more than half.

This year's improvements were almost entirely in taking heroin using a needle, which is the most dangerous form of use. There was little change in the taking of heroin without a needle.

Synthetic marijuana has been sold over the counter in multiple states — notably in gas stations, convenience stores and head shops. It is often imported from overseas and can be very potent and unpredictable both in its chemical content and in its effects, resulting in a number of emergency room admissions.

Use fell by a statistically significant amount in 2015 for the three grades combined. The proportions saying they used any synthetic marijuana in the past 12 months now stand at 3%, 4% and 5% in grades 8, 10 and 12, respectively—down substantially from the 4%, 9% and 11% observed in those same grades in 2012.

"While there has been some increase in the proportion of students seeing use of this drug as dangerous, it hardly seems enough to account for the considerable declines in use, which leads us to conclude that efforts to reduce availability have been successful to some degree," Johnston said.

"Efforts at the federal and state levels to close down the sale of these substances appear to be having an effect," Johnston said.

The use of amphetamines also showed some decline in 2015.

While the fall in annual prevalence for the three grades combined from 6.6% to 6.2% did not reach statistical significance, the decline in past 30-day prevalence from 3.2% to 2.7% did, suggesting that the decline is fairly recent. Reported availability of amphetamines has been in decline in all three grades for some years.

Among the many other drugs covered in the study, none showed significant increases or decreases in use this year. A number already have shown appreciable declines in use in the past, such as "bath salts," LSD, other hallucinogens, salvia, crack, methamphetamine and inhalants.

The most widely used of all the illicit drugs, marijuana, showed no significant changes in annual prevalence this year in any of the three grades, separately or combined.

While the use of pot rose for several years, the annual prevalence of marijuana has essentially leveled out since around 2010.

This year, 12% of 8th-graders, 25% of 10th-graders and 35% of 12th-graders reported using marijuana at least once in the past year.

However, their daily or near-daily marijuana use (defined as smoking marijuana on 20 or more occasions in the past 30 days) is of more importance. These rates stand at 1.1%, 3% and 6% in 8th, 10th and 12th grades, respectively.

In other words, one in every 16 or 17 high school seniors is smoking marijuana daily or near daily. While these rates have changed rather little since 2010, they are from three-to-six times higher than they were at their low point in 1991.

Teens using cigarettes also reached an all-time low in 2015.

Drunk Driving Declines as Drug Use Behind the Wheel Rises

The U.S. spent decades successfully campaigning against drunk driving to make roads safer, but use of marijuana and prescription drugs is increasingly prominent on the highways, raising new questions about safety, according to studies released by the Department of Transportation's National Highway Traffic Safety Administration.

The latest version of NHTSA's Roadside Survey of Alcohol and Drug Use by Drivers supported that the number of drivers who had alcohol in their system has declined by almost one-third since 2007 and by more than three-quarters since the first Roadside Survey in 1973.

Yet that same survey found a sizable increase in the number of drivers using marijuana or other illegal drugs.

The 2014 survey found that almost one in four drivers tested positive for at least one drug that could affect safety.

"America made drunk driving a national issue and while there is no victory as long as a single American dies in an alcohol-related crash, a one-third reduction in alcohol use over just seven years shows how a focused effort and cooperation among the federal government, states and communities, law enforcement, safety advocates and industry can make an enormous difference," said NHTSA Administrator Mark Rosekind. "At the same time, the latest Roadside Survey raises significant questions about drug use and highway safety. The rising prevalence of marijuana and other drugs is a challenge to everyone who is dedicated to saving lives and reducing crashes."

Nearly 8% of drivers during nighttime weekend hours were found to have alcohol in their system, and just over 1% were found with 0.08% or higher breath alcohol content. This number is down by around 30% from the previous survey in 2007 and down 80% from the first survey in 1973.

However, even as drinking and driving continues to decrease, use of illegal drugs or medicines which can affect road safety is mounting. The amount of weekend nighttime drivers with evidence of drugs in their system rose from 16.3% in 2007 to 20% in 2014 and the number of drivers with marijuana in their system grew by roughly 50%.

"Drivers should never get behind the wheel impaired, and we know that marijuana impairs judgment, reaction times and awareness," said Jeff Michael, NHTSA's associate administrator for research and program development. "These findings highlight the importance of research to better understand how marijuana use affects drivers so states and communities can craft the best safety policies."

E-commerce

E-commerce and mobile-commerce spending on digital content and subscriptions increased 27% year-over-year in 2014, almost doubling the overall retail digital commerce growth rate of 14% and ranking as the fastest-growing spending category.

Fastest Growing Retail Digital Commerce Categories in 2014

E-commerce and mobile-commerce spending on digital content and subscriptions increased 27% year-over-year in 2014, almost doubling the overall retail digital commerce growth rate of 14% and ranking as the fastest-growing spending category, according to a comScore report.

Digital spending in the consumer packaged goods (21%), apparel & accessories (20%) and sport & fitness (17%) categories also saw high rates of growth, while the jewelry & watches (-1%) and computer software (-4%) categories were the only to see declines in spending.

Separate results from the report indicate that e-commerce (desktop) spending grew by 12.5% year-over-year (to $236.9 billion), with mobile commerce spending up by 27.5% (to $31.5 billion).

Education

The saying if you love what you do, you'll never work a day in your life might be true for some majors, but business majors are a completely different story. Those who majored in business are the least likely of those who majored in the four large major categories (social sciences/education, sciences/engineering, arts and humanities, and business) to express strong enthusiasm in the work they do now, regardless of their post-graduation career path. The year someone graduates won't hamper their income.

Those who earn their degree at 25 or older have personal income later in life that are comparable to those of traditional graduates (those who earn their degree before turning 25). The only debt that college loans don't top? Mortgages. Students think debt is a necessary part of life.

In U.S., Business Grads Lag Other Majors in Work Interest

College graduates in the United States who majored in business are the least likely of those who majored in the four large major categories — social sciences/education, sciences/engineering, arts and humanities, and business — to express strong enthusiasm in the work they do now, regardless of what career path they may have gone into after graduation.

Less than two in five college graduates with a business-related degree (37%) firmly agree that they are genuinely passionate about the work they do, notably lower than majors in the social sciences/education (47%), sciences/engineering (43%), and arts and humanities (43%).

These discoveries come from a large sample of college graduates of all ages, but even among recent graduates — those graduating between 2000 and 2014 — the patterns hold, with business majors slightly trailing all of the majors, though they are statistically tied with arts and humanities.

More commonly, business majors also trail by a substantial margin behind their academic peers in the critical area of purpose well-being.

In contrast to clear majorities of social sciences/education (56%), sciences/engineering (54%), and arts and humanities (53%) majors who are "thriving" in their purpose express well-being, fewer than half of those who majored in business (48%) are thriving.

Business is the most common field of study among undergraduates, with roughly a fifth of all college graduates saying they majored in this subject.

However, business majors with postgraduate education are far more likely to be thriving in their purpose well-being (56%) than business majors without such education (46%).

Yet business majors still display a lower level of thriving in their purpose well-being compared to those who studied other subjects after college, counting the social sciences/education (63%), sciences/engineering (63%), and arts and humanities (62%).

Additionally, postgraduate education is predictive of solid interest in a person's work, everything else being equal — 52% of those in this group strongly agree that they are deeply interested in their work, compared with 38% of people who only possess and undergraduate degree.

However, those with postgraduate education, business majors continue to be less likely than other college majors to strongly agree that they are seriously interested in their work.

Furthermore, there is little difference between business majors with postgraduate studies and those without in terms of conveying a strong interest in their work — 43% vs. 36%, respectively.

By comparison, those with post graduate degrees in other majors are far more likely than their undergraduate-only peers to say they are strongly interested in their work.

College Graduation Year Doesn't Hamper Income

Despite delaying their college education, nontraditional college graduates — those who earn their degree at age 25 or older — have personal income later in life that is comparable to those of traditional graduates, or those who earn their degree before turning 25, according to Gallup.

Gallup's study is based on surveys with almost 4,000 traditional college graduates and roughly 7,500 nontraditional college graduates who obtained their degree between 1990 and 2014.

Presently, the average age of a traditional graduate who earned their degree between 1990-2014 is 33 years old, compared to 45 years for nontraditional graduates.

This may indicate that nontraditional graduates are "paying" for delaying their education because, all things being equal, older individuals would expect to out-earn their younger counterparts, not tie with them.

But, of course, all things are not equal — and it is likely that many of these nontraditional graduates, had they not gone back to college, would be earning much less than traditional college graduates.

The percentage of nontraditional college graduates has nearly doubled in recent decades, from 16% in the 1970's to 32% for 2000-2014 graduates, according to the Gallup-Purdue index.

Colleges are noticing a rising number of older students on campus, as adults look to develop new skills, change careers or simply finish their education.

College Loans Top All Debt Except Mortgages, And Students Think Debt Necessary Part of Life

College enrollment is projected to increase almost 9% in the United States from 2014-2022, according to a new report from **Mintel**.

The growing student population is more diverse than ever before with attendees no longer solidly 18-24 years old, and women projected to comprise the largest percentage in history. As attendance rises, so too does educational debt.

Student debt has climbed steadily, growing from 8% to 10% of the total consumer debt in the U.S. since the fiscal third quarter of 2011, making it greater than any type of U.S. consumer debt with the exception of mortgages.

According to Mintel data, some 30% of those who have educational loans have monthly loan payments greater than $300, while 5% have monthly payments $1,000+. College students have altered their attitudes toward financial services adjusting to residual effects of the Great Recession with over half considering debt as necessary in today's world.

Family/Parenting

Family can have an impact on a child's future. Children living in the South get more playtime with their parents than kids living in any other region of the country.

Millennial Moms spent over $750 billion in the United States in 2015. With the number of Millennial Moms expected to at least double over the next decade, their economic impacts will only increase. Moms are slightly more likely than the overall internet browsing population to visit YouTube on a monthly basis.

Parents In The South Play More With Their Kids

Children living in the South get more playtime with their parents than kids living in any other region of the country, according to new research commissioned by the Toy Industry Association's (TIA) Genius of Play initiative, which aims to raise awareness about the developmental benefits of play.

In a national online survey conducted by PlayScience, an innovation and development company focused on play and learning, parents of children between the ages of 2 and 10 years old were asked how often they play together as a family. The following findings were revealed:

- **76%** of parents in the **South** said they play with their kids at least once a day
- **46%** of parents in the **West** said they play with their kids at least once a day
- **40%** of parents in the **Midwest** said they play with their kids at least once a day
- **38%** of parents in the **Northeast** said they play with their kids at least once a day

Parents admit that the biggest barrier they face when it comes to making time to play with their children is lack of time – in other words, they are "busy taking care of other things."

And while many parents agree that play has positive benefits, those who devote less time to playing with their kids define play as "fun" and prioritize teaching their children values and helping with schoolwork.

"It's no surprise that lack of time and parental perceptions of play impact how often parents play with their children," said Steve Pasierb, Toy Industry Association President & CEO. "However, child development experts agree that play teaches children many important values, such as empathy, in addition to cognitive, social and creative skills that simply can't be learned in a classroom setting. Playing together as a family has additional benefits, allowing parents and children to learn from one another, grow together, and build lasting memories."

"We're thrilled to see that Southern families recognize the benefits of play and we encourage the rest of the country to get on board and make play an important part of their kids' day!" added Pasierb.

Millennial Moms Expected to Add $750 Billion to U.S. Economy

With a tap, swipe or click, 13 million Millennial Moms will spend over $750 billion in the U.S. this year. And their economic impacts will only increase as the number of Millennial Moms is expected to at least double over the next decade, according to just-released research by BSM Media.

With the top of the curve still to be reached, knowing the demands and expectations of Millennial Moms will drive even more business growth, likely to historic levels.

Technology use, purchasing behaviors, social trends, voting power and much more are detailed in a new book by marketing to moms expert Maria Bailey, *Millennial Moms, 202 Facts To Help*

Drive Brands and Sales. Debuting last week as an Amazon #1 PR and Marketing "Hottest New Release", the book features an in-depth look at the background and influence of these moms, plus tactics to empower companies that want to tap in to this lucrative consumer group.

What makes Millennial Moms tick?

Social shopping is standard for Millennial Moms. 90% say they take a picture from a store's fitting rooms to garner friends' opinions on a potential clothing purchase.

Millennial Moms carry at least two wireless devices. In fact, the majority totes between three and four devices and over 10% say they always carry five or more tech gadgets.

Millennial Moms are pragmatic. 90% will not purchase a product without reading a review first.

Transparency is a must. More than half of these young mothers rate transparency as "extremely important", trusting brands that are open about their products.

Education and healthcare are the most important political issues for Millennial Moms. Politicians will do well to tap in to the Millennial Mom vote, with an estimated 85% saying they will cast their ballots in the election.

In an easy-to-read format with charts, quick insights and interviews with Millennial Moms, Bailey's new book is a must-read for anyone interested in this unique generation that is the largest cohort in history.

"They are uber-spending, hyper-connected moms who exert massive influence on everything they touch, from push presents to half birthdays and customized everything," explains Bailey, the author of this latest book based on five years of research on Millennial Moms.

"Everyone needs to understand these high tech, value-seeking mothers who are constantly raising the bar and changing the rules.

Top-Indexing YouTube Video Categories Among Mothers

Mothers are avid viewers of YouTube videos, being slightly more likely than the overall internet browsing population to visit YouTube on a monthly basis, according to data from Compete.

While music (26%) videos capture the greatest share of mothers' viewing, this demographic under-indexes the average viewer when it comes to watching music videos.

Instead, the top-indexing categories for mothers are family (+63%), how-to (+37%) and animals (+34%), per the report.

Tooth Fairy Pays Record $255 Million For Lost Teeth in 2014

The recovering U.S. economy is benefitting kids, with the average gift from the Tooth Fairy reaching a new high of $4.36 last year, up from $3.50 in 2013, according to Delta Dental's The Original Tooth Fairy Poll.

The Tooth Fairy left a staggering $255 million for lost teeth based on Delta Dental estimates in 2014.

The Original Tooth Fairy Poll has generally been a good indicator of the economy's overall direction. In fact, the trend in Tooth Fairy giving has tracked with the movement of the Standard & Poor's 500 index (S&P 500) in 11 of the past 12 years.

In 2014, both the average Tooth Fairy gift and the S&P 500 posted double-digit gains for the third year in a row, with 24.6% and 11.4% increases respectively.

"As leaders in the dental benefits industry, we keep our eye on all kinds of economic indicators, and the Tooth Fairy's record giving tracks with big gains in the major stock indexes in 2014," said Jennifer Elliott, vice president of marketing at Delta Dental Plans Association.

The Tooth Fairy Leaves More than Money

Delta Dental's survey found that in 88% of the homes she visited, the Tooth Fairy left cash for kids, either by itself or in combination with other gifts.

Kids who got a gift in addition to or instead of cash most often received a toy, game, toothbrush, toothpaste, book, doll, stuffed animal or dental floss.

Other findings from The Original Tooth Fairy Poll, which surveyed more than 1,000 parents nationwide, include:

- The Tooth Fairy visited 81% of U.S. homes with children who lost a tooth;
- The amount of spare cash on hand (44%) or the child's age (39%) are the most mentioned reasons for how much is left by the Tooth Fairy;
- The Tooth Fairy was more generous with first-time tooth losers, leaving more money for the first tooth in 40% of homes. On average, the amount given for the first tooth was $5.74, a 27% increase from 2013;
- The Tooth Fairy was stingiest with kids in the Midwest, leaving just $2.83 per tooth. Kids in the South raked in the dough, receiving $5.16 per tooth. And kids in the West and Northeast didn't fare so bad either, receiving $4.68 and $4.16 respectively.
- Kids with younger parents also received more money from the Tooth Fairy. Kids with parents under age 35 received the most ($5.40 per tooth), followed by kids with parents ages 35 to 44 ($4.24 per tooth) and parents ages 45 and older ($2.45 per tooth); and

Most kids seem satisfied with their gift. Only 17% of parents can recall their child asking the Tooth Fairy for more money. And fewer (11%) say their kids have asked the Tooth Fairy for a gift instead of or in addition to money

Finance/Income

Among affluent, Gen Xers (34-50) now outnumber Baby Boomers (51-69) for the first tie, with the former accounting for 37% of all affluent and the latter 32%.

Affluent Millennials are open to non-financial brands. At the same time, once they become customers with a financial institution, they're considerably more likely than their Gen X counterparts to claim loyalty to it. Student debt has climbed steadily, growing from 8% to 10% of the total consumer debt in the U.S. since the fiscal third quarter of 2011, making it greater than any type of U.S. consumer debt with the exception of mortgages, and students think debt is a necessary part of life.

Perhaps surprisingly, Millennials are leading among Americans who save their money with 56% reporting they are good savers, compared with 43% of Gen Xers and 48% of Baby Boomers.

Gen X Now Reportedly The Largest Generation of Affluents

Among affluent, Gen Xers (34-50) now outnumber Baby Boomers (51-69) for the first time, with the former accounting for 37% of all affluent and the latter 32%, according to Ipsos' latest annual survey of affluents in the U.S. The results are essentially switched from last year, leading Ipsos to declare this "a changing of the generational guard." Even so, Boomers continue to lead on one important front.

Indeed, Boomer respondents reported a median household net worth of $913K, almost twice the figure reported by Gen Xers ($552K). Millennials (18-33), who comprise one-quarter of affluents, reported a median net worth of $516K, not far behind Gen Xers; Seniors (70+), the smallest group (5% share) of affluents, reported the highest median net worth, of $1.42 million.

The Ipsos survey notes that affluent Gen Xers are far from being a monolithic group, a point that is often mentioned about Millennials, but less so with respect to Gen Xers. Younger Gen Xers (under 40), for example, tend to have similar tastes to Millennials in various areas (such as social media, entertainment trends and organic food), while older Gen Xers share more psychographic traits with Boomers.

That's interesting in light of other research on Gen Xers. Recently, the Pew Research Center revealed that 58% of Gen Xers identify with their generational label, compared to 78% of Boomers. An earlier study from MetLife, meanwhile, found that just 41% of Gen Xers related most to their own generation, while 28% related most to Baby Boomers.

When it comes to the various traits they ascribe to their generation, the Pew survey discovered that Gen Xers are roughly in the middle of Millennials and Baby Boomers (perhaps a function of using averages). The Ipsos survey, for its part, shows that while 54% of Gen Xers aged 34-41 agree that they "like to stand out from others," only 41% of those aged 42-50 agree.

Overall, the Ipsos study reveals that 23% of American households (and 28% of American adults) qualify as being affluent, on par with last year's results.

Among the $2.7 trillion in annual consumer spending by affluents (which represents an uptick from last year), the largest expenditure categories are:

- Automotive;
- Home and garden;
- Personal insurance;
- Travel;
- Education;

Those results signify a greater spending role for travel and electronics than in last year's survey.

Not surprisingly, affluents tend to live in urban areas, with 44% living in 10 major cities. The top 5 cities by share of affluents are:

- New York City (10% of affluents);
- Los Angeles (7%);
- Chicago (5%);

- San Francisco (4%); and
- Washington, DC (4%).

Affluents living in these cities tend to exhibit different characteristics, with those in New York City showing an above-average inclination to value their cultural or ethnic heritage and to have an interest in fashion and luxury. Affluents in San Francisco skew heavily Asian-American (29% of San Francisco affluents versus 8% nationally) and tend to be more liberal, with interests in hybrid vehicles and organic food.

By comparison, affluents in Los Angeles have stronger interests in automobiles, luxury, fashion and entertainment. (One wonders if these differences in interests are restricted to affluents, or are city-wide…)

In other highlights from the report, affluent Millennials spend 10.4 hours a week with social media, almost twice the affluent average of 5.5 hours per week.

Although Facebook and YouTube are the top social platforms for affluents overall and Millennials in particular, the youngest group is more heavily drawn to Instagram (54% using) and Snapchat (35%) than the affluent population as a whole (29% and 13%, respectively), with this likely a reflection of the traditionally younger audience of these platforms.

Affluent Millennials Say They're Loyal To Their Financial Institutions

Affluent Millennials are open to non-financial brands, finds a report from LinkedIn conducted by Ipsos that looks specifically at affluents in the U.S. At the same time, once they become customers with a financial institution, they're considerably more likely than their Gen X counterparts to claim loyalty to it.

The subset of affluents examined was defined as those living in households with investable assets in excess of $100,000.

(A separate definition of affluents – those living in households with annual income of at least $100,000 – finds that 28% of the U.S. adult population qualifies, with 22% of these being Millennials aged 18-32. Two-thirds of those qualified on the basis of their parents' income rather than their own.)

Affluent Millennials in particular provide both opportunities and challenges for traditional financial brands, according to the LinkedIn study results.

For example, 69% of affluent Millennials reported being open to financial offerings from non-financial brands, compared to 47% of affluent Gen Xers.

At the same time, 47% of affluent Millennials said they are "very" loyal and plan to do more business with the financial institutions they work with (compared to 27% of affluent Gen Xers), and another 48% claim to be "somewhat" loyal to them (versus 59% of affluent Gen Xers).

It's worth noting that as a subset of the 1,500+ survey population, affluents may be a relatively small sample, so while the results are thought-provoking, the comparisons may not be statistically significant.

Nevertheless, affluent Millennials are also more likely than their older counterparts to consider their financial institutions a one-stop shop, per the study's results.

Among those with multiple checking accounts, 54% hold them all with the same institution, versus 33% of affluent Gen Xers. Similarly, among multiple account holders, affluent Millennials are more likely than affluent Gen Xers to keep their retirement accounts (42% vs. 24%), brokerage accounts (37% vs. 23%) and savings (39% vs. 23%) accounts with the same brand.

While that may present opportunities for traditional brands, the report also suggests that there is a "very high risk" of traditional brands losing out to outsider brands.

Trust can be a differentiator, as the report's authors link affluent Millennials' higher degree of loyalty to their higher level of trust in their current financial institutions.

LinkedIn has some other suggestions for the factors that matter to affluent Millennials: a strong and positive social presence; a relationship with the company; influence of family and friends' relationship with the company; and the company's purpose (such as a social mission).

In other interesting study results:

- Affluent Millennials appear to want to perform their own research, make investment decisions and execute trades (in comparison with Gen Xers), but at the same time are more likely to consider a financial advisor a must-have.
- Affluent Millennials (27%) are more likely than Millennials or Gen Xers (18-19%) to believe that in the future banks will no longer be primary financial institutions. They're also more likely to predict a cashless society and a sharing-based economy.
- Affluent Millennials have loftier goals than affluent Gen Xers, being 3 times more likely to want to start a charitable foundation (19% vs. 6%) and start a business (30% vs. 11%). They're also 50% more likely to want to buy a second home (27% vs. 18%).

American Adults' Feelings of Financial Responsibility, by Age

Three-quarters of American Millennials (18-34) feel that they are financially responsible and generally do not spend beyond their means, according to results from an Ipsos and Wells Fargo survey.

However, Millennials are less likely than adults ages 55 and older (87%) to feel financially responsible, and are about twice as likely to say they tend to spend their money and not think twice about it (36% vs. 19%).

The survey also finds that Millennials (69%) are significantly less likely than adults aged 55 and up (87%) to know and understand the financial process involved in the purchase of a home, presumably as they're less likely to have been through that process.

College Loans Top All Debt Except Mortgages, And Students Think Debt Necessary Part of Life

College enrollment is projected to increase almost 9% in the United States from 2014-2022, according to a new report from **Mintel**.

The growing student population is more diverse than ever before with attendees no longer solidly 18-24 years old, and women projected to comprise the largest percentage in history. As attendance rises, so too does educational debt.

Student debt has climbed steadily, growing from 8% to 10% of the total consumer debt in the U.S. since the fiscal third quarter of 2011, making it greater than any type of U.S. consumer debt with the exception of mortgages.

According to Mintel data, some 30% of those who have educational loans have monthly loan payments greater than $300, while 5% have monthly payments $1,000+. College students have altered their attitudes toward financial services adjusting to residual effects of the Great Recession with over half considering debt as necessary in today's world.

Recession Alters Attitudes

Many college students saw their parents and families hurt by the recession and as a result are much more conservative than people of older generations when it comes to their attitude about investing. In fact, 73% believe that the recent recession demonstrated how important it is to save for retirement.

Similarly, 74% of college students feel that the primary purpose of money is to purchase security. One thing that provides financial security is good credit – 71% of U.S. college students agree that having good credit is the most important factor in achieving financial success.

While 71% of college students are confident in their ability to manage their day-to-day finances, including 68% of females and 75% of males, a full 58% think credit cards can be difficult to manage.

"Unfortunately, debt is considered necessary by today's standards, and 52% of college students agree. Many (38%) find it acceptable if it is used to buy something that is really desired. However, the negative effects the recession had on their parents and families have left college students much more conservative with their finances. To most, money means security and college is a time for students to learn how to manage it so they can begin to exert their financial independence," said **Robyn Kaiserman**, Financial Services Analyst at Mintel.

Managing Financial Institutions

Despite advanced reliance on technology, college students do relatively little electronic banking beyond checking account balances and transferring money between accounts.

While over six in 10 students (64%) have downloaded their bank's mobile app, only 18% use their smartphone to conduct more than half of their transactions. Furthermore, only 39% of those who have downloaded their bank's app to their smartphone use it to deposit checks.

As financial institutions continue to expand their electronic services for all customers, 80% of students still feel it is important to bank with companies that have branch locations nearby.

Budgeting

"Although some college students don't use the word 'budget,' they seem to keep one, even if it isn't a formal exercise. The fact that 71% feel confident in their abilities to manage their day-to-day finances indicates that they generally stay on top of their spending even if there are a few slip-ups here and there.

Many use some type of technology to keep track of what they spend, whether it is an online function or a mobile one," Kaiserman continued.

Overwhelmingly, both men and women age 18-23 look to their family for information about financial services (56%).

However, data shows that women also tend to rely on friends (29%), while men look to classes in school (37%) for additional information.

Men and Women

While many male college students recognize that they will have to invest in the stock market if they want to build a large retirement account, few females do – and all are skittish about the market as a result of their and their families, negative experience with the recession.

Mintel data shows that males are more likely than females to have a checking or savings account in their own name at an online-only bank or have an investment account in their own name.

When it comes to saving money in the short and mid-term, males are more likely (38%) to do so in a bank or credit union every month than women (31%).

Additionally, men age 21-23 are much more likely (62%) to have a credit card in their own name as opposed to men age 18-20 (28%). Nearly 80% of men age 21-23 are confident their bank or credit union can meet all their financial needs versus men age 18-20 (54%).

Who's Picking up the Tab

Very few college students, a mere 14%, in fact, have all their college expenses paid for by their parents or guardians.

This number rises slightly to 17% for women. This indicates that college students have some responsibility for at least a portion of their own expenses, whether immediately, in the future (if they have taken out loans), or both. Most college students (60%) – and especially women (64%) – pay for their own entertainment without help from parents or guardians.

Furthermore, 27% have either some or all responsibility for paying for their own college expenses.

Debt over the Long Haul

While student debt continues its ascension, previous generations have been facing similar long-term effects that current students fear.

According to a Mintel report, 71% of respondents age 65 and over believe they will be able to live comfortably in retirement, but that number drops to 49% among those age 55-64, who are preparing to retire in the near future.

Nearly one third (32%) of U.S. consumers age 55-64 identify payments on educational loans as a major reason for not saving more to live comfortably upon retiring.

This number increases to 40% for ages 45-54. The greatest financial concerns for current college students include making enough money to live on their own (51%), making student loan payments (33%), and managing day-to-day finances (31%).

Millennials Emerge as the "Super-Saver" Generation

Saving money may be challenging for most Americans, but a new survey from **TD Bank** reveals that nearly half of Americans are feeling confident about their ability to save for the future.

The TD Bank Saving & Spending Survey questioned more than 1,600 U.S. consumers about their saving and spending habits. Given the current economy, the survey surprisingly found that nearly half of consumers (49%) described themselves as "good savers."

Millennials are leading the charge with 56% reporting that they are "good savers," compared with 43% of gen Xers and 48% of baby boomers.

Among those who wished they were saving more, 42% reported that unavoidable expenses and financial commitments impaired their ability to save.

"Conventional wisdom assumes Americans are spenders, rather than savers," said **Nandita Bakhshi**, Head of Consumer Bank, TD Bank. "So it's encouraging to see such a strong commitment to saving across the board, particularly among millennials. Only 4% of respondents stated that saving isn't a priority, regardless of their financial situations."

Retirement represents another key focus for most Americans, with 57% reporting that they are currently saving or investing money for retirement. Still, a majority of consumers are not confident that they will have the funds to retire comfortably.

Indeed, only 29% of respondents are very or extremely confident that they will save enough to retire comfortably, while 36% of Americans list saving for retirement as one of their main financial fears.

Millennials, once again, break away from the pack, feeling twice as confident as gen Xers in their ability to save for a comfortable retirement (42% versus 20%, respectively).

Where Do Americans Overspend?

While saving is a top priority, a majority of Americans still report that they are overspending in some areas. Frequently, restaurants were cited as the top culprit in overspending (40%), followed by coffee/lunches (23%) and clothing/shoes (15%).

When it comes to retail spending, one-half of all respondents and 69% of millennials surveyed admitted to indulging on impulse purchases. Among the generations, boomers were the least prone to binge-buying, with 49% noting that they "try not to spend outside their budget."

Minding Their Own Budget

Millennials are not only the best savers; they're also the most diligent about their budgets. According to the TD Bank Saving & Spending Survey, 44% of Americans check their budget once a week or more. This figure climbs to 53% for millennials, compared to 43% for gen Xers and 37% for baby boomers.

New technology is also changing the way Americans manage their finances. Today's American consumers are relying more heavily on banking/financial apps (40%), with conventional spreadsheets taking a secondary position (29%). Reliance on banking/financial apps is particularly prominent among millennials, at 59% versus 38% for gen Xers and 24% for baby boomers.

"Given the wealth of budgeting resources and technology available today, there's something for everyone for tracking financial habits," said Bakhshi. "Even if you don't actively budget today, the ease of these new financial apps can provide a great point of entry for controlling spending and managing savings."

Number of Millionaire Households In the U.S. Said to Hit New High

There were 10.1 million U.S. households with net worth of at least $1 million, last year, up from 9.6 million in 2013 and the highest level on record, according to the Spectrem Group's "2015 Market Insights Report."

That equates to 8.3% of all households, back on par with pre-recession levels of 8.2% in 2007.

Meanwhile, the number of households with at least $100,000 in net worth also climbed, to 39.6 million.

Some key numbers from the report include:

- There are 29 million Mass Affluent households with a net worth between $100,000 and $1 million, an increase of more than 500,000 from the year before;
- The number of Millionaire households with a net worth between $1 million and $5 million is approaching nine million, sitting now at 8,790,000; and
- There are 1,168,000 Ultra High Net Worth households with a net worth between $5 million and $25 million.

It's worth noting that last year; an Ipsos study noted that the number of US households with annual income of at least $100,000 has been growing, with 28% of the adult population living in such a household.

U.S. E-Commerce Conversion Rates, by Device, Q4 2013-Q4 2014

U.S. e-commerce conversion rates on smartphones (1%) distantly trailed comparable rates for tablets (3.11%) and traditional computers (3.78%) during Q4 2014, according to Monetate's latest quarterly analysis covering a random client sample.

Indeed, unlike tablets and computers, conversion rates on smartphones failed to keep pace with the year-earlier period. The study notes that, globally, top performers far outstripped the industry average (6.44% vs. 2.84%) in average conversion rates.

Meanwhile, in the U.S., smartphones ($113.10) topped tablets ($80.69) in average order value during Q4 2014, and also comprised a greater share of traffic (18.2% to 15.8%).

Attitudes Towards the Economy Show Both Month-Over-Month and Year-Over-Year Improvements

Americans are reporting positive economic sentiments in regards to their household, their region, and the nation as a whole, according to a recent study from The Harris Poll.

This month, a third (32%) of U.S. adults expect the economy to improve in the coming year, while 47% expect that it will remain the same and roughly two in ten (21%) expect it to get worse.

Expectations have improved since last month (only 28% were expecting improvement), as well as in comparison to January 2014 (when 26% indicated the same).

Interestingly, men (35%) are more likely than women (29%) to expect the economy to improve in the next year and nearly half of Democrats (48%) expect to see improvement, with three in 10 independents (30%) and only 15% of Republicans indicating the same.

Over Half of Consumers Gloomy on Economy

Asked to rate the state of their own personal finances, 36% surveyed for the National Restaurant Association's annual Restaurant Trends described them as only "fair" while 18% said they were "poor." That's virtually the same as in 2010, when the economy was just beginning to climb out of the Great Recession.

"This persistent recession is negatively impacting spending," NRA said, describing consumer spending as "lackluster."

"In the 21 quarters since the official end of the recession, personal consumption expenditures rose just 12.2% in inflation-adjusted terms, according to the Bureau of Economic Analysis, a until of the Commerce Department.

Just how punk the Obama "recovery" has been comes into stark focus when you realize that during the same period in the three previous recessions, consumer spending increased by an average of 21.8%.

Real spending on "services," which includes restaurants, rose just 8.8% during the last 21 quarters —less than half the average 19.6% gain during the previous three recessions.

Even now, a solid majority of American consumers are reluctant to spend, NRA says. Twenty-seven percent say they are "very concerned about the economy and are holding back significantly" while 47% say they are taking a "wait-and-see approach", holding back somewhat on spending until the economy improves.

What's really surprising, NRA notes, is that a majority of higher-income households are also cutting back. Among households with income of $100,000 or more, one in five say they are holding back significantly on spending, while 35% say they are holding back somewhat.

This explains why NRA projects table-service restaurant sale this year will grow a dismal 0.6%. But, some might say, when times are tough, people drink more so bars should be doing really well. NRA projects their sales to rise an anemic 1.1%.

Food/Beverages

Millennials' adult beverage choices evolve as they mature. Historically adventuresome in their drinking habits, Millennials continue to explore, especially in on-premise settings, as they mature. They transfer their new discoveries from restaurant experiences to their retail buying decisions while also balancing curiosity with loyalty to some tired-and-true brands. In 2014, monthly restaurant sales exceeded grocery store sales for the first time on record.

Hispanic food shoppers now represent a rapidly growing segment of the customer base of grocers throughout the country, with the growth coming largely from the continuing dispersal of Latinos into areas not traditionally known for having substantial Hispanic populations.

America's Favorite #Game Day Snacks, By State

You won't believe what people snack on while watching football.

To be sure, when most football loving Americans think of game day snacks, they imagine pizza, wings, and beef. But some states seem to prefer pancakes, pumpkin and even veganism, according to a new DirecTV study that analyzed more than 25,000 Instagram photos that used the hashtag #gameday featuring food.

It turns out Florida, Nevada, and South Dakota have exchanged typical gamed snacks in favor of goodies void of animal by-products.

And although the majority of football-crazed Instagramers prefer classics such as chicken and burgers, states like Montana, Kansas and Maine have begun chewing on less-traditional treats, such as eggs Benedict.

Cheeses are most popular in six states (South Carolina, New Hampshire, Pennsylvania, West Virginia, Maryland, and Hawaii, followed by pizza (Indiana, Missouri, Arizona, and Delaware), and eggs Benedict (Mississippi, Montana, Kansas, and Maine).

Unsurprisingly, Jambalaya is most popular in Louisiana — and surprisingly, New Jersey. While those living in the Natural State prefer pancakes.

Millennials' Adult Beverage Choices Evolve as They Mature

With nearly three in 10 U.S. adults being Millennials of legal drinking age, the Millennial generation (born between 1977 and 1992) is a crucial demographic for bev/al marketers.

Donna Hood Crecca, senior director at **Technomic**, calls them "ideal adult beverage consumers. They are open and willing to learn about new styles and flavors of beer, wine and spirits. They are frequent consumers in many retail and restaurant settings, where they balance exploration and trial with loyalty to a few favorite brands that deliver on flavor, quality and price."

Technomic's just-published Special Trends in Adult Beverages Report shows how catering to Millennials can boost profits for all in the bev/al chain. Key findings include:

Equal opportunity imbibers: Millennials are likely to purchase adult beverages at a variety of retail and on-premise venues. This group is also open to engaging in all three adult beverage categories—spirits, wine and beer—as well as a range of different types and flavors of alcohol drinks.

Age brings sophistication: As Millennials age, they are more inclined to buy craft beer and to have a more evolved palate for exploring different varietals and regions of beer and wine.

A propensity to drink multiple types of adult beverages on a single occasion: 30 percent of Millennials consumed more than one type of drink on their most recent on-premise occasion. Primary reasons for switching were a desire to experiment with different beverages or flavors or to try a new drink.

Balancing adventure and loyalty: Historically adventuresome in their drinking habits, Millennials continue to explore, especially in on-premise settings, as they mature. They transfer their new discoveries from restaurant experiences to their retail buying decisions while also balancing curiosity with loyalty to some tried-and-true brands.

Restaurant Sales Surpassed Grocery Store Sales for 1st Time

Monthly sales at restaurants exceeded grocery stores sales for the first time on record, the National Restaurant Association noted today.

In his latest Economist's Notebook commentary, the National Restaurant Association's Chief Economist Bruce Grindy breaks down industry sales trends:

For the first time on record in December, monthly sales at restaurants exceeded grocery stores sales, according to data from the U.S. Census Bureau. This development was hinted at through preliminary data releases in recent months, but was officially confirmed by today's annual benchmark of Census data.

The gap between monthly grocery store sales and restaurant sales started gradually shrinking in 2010 – a trend that was partially due to the increase in consumers buying their groceries at big box stores.

There has been a dramatic shift toward restaurants that occurred in the last 10 months. In June 2014, grocery store sales exceeded restaurant sales by $1.6 billion. By April 2015, the gap had essentially reversed, with restaurant sales moving out in front by $1.5 billion.

In fact, the $3.1 billion sales shift registered during the last 10 months is nearly as much as occurred during the previous 4.5 years.

Household Finances Getting a Boost from Lower Gas Prices

The reallocation of consumers' food dollar toward restaurants coincided with the sharp decline in gas prices in recent months, which suggests that the savings at the pump may have helped accelerate this change in consumer behavior. To investigate the impact of lower gas prices, the NRA commissioned ORC International to conduct a national telephone survey of 1,008 adults between April 30 and May 3.

Not surprisingly, 80% of car owners say the recent decline in gas prices positively impacted their household finances. This sentiment was generally consistent across all income levels, with individuals in lower-income households the most likely to say that lower gas prices had a 'very significant' positive impact on their finances.

Restaurants Are Likely Benefitting From Lower Gas Prices

Among car owners who say the recent decline in gas prices positively impacted their household finances, 49% say the lower gas prices have increased their willingness and ability to do things like purchase meals, snacks or beverages from restaurants, fast food places or coffee shops.

Individuals in lower-income households are even more likely to feel that way, with a majority of car owners in households with income below $50,000 saying the positive impact that lower gas

prices are having on their finances has increased their willingness and ability to patronize restaurants, fast food places or coffee shops.

Growing Consumer Confidence Boosting Restaurant Frequency

Overall, 33% of adults surveyed say they are patronizing restaurants more often now than they were one year ago. Within this group, the most common reason given is that they feel more confident in their financial situation – mentioned by 63% of consumers who are using restaurants more frequently.

Fifty-six percent of consumers say they increased frequency because gas prices are lower, while 46 percent say it's because their household income went up. Three in 10 consumers say they are using restaurants more often because they got a new job or because their home or investments are worth more.

Pent-Up Demand Remains Elevated

With gas prices likely contributing to the dramatic shift in consumer spending during the last several months, the question is if these spending patterns will hold when gas prices increase again.

To be sure, there appears to be even more room for growth in the months ahead. When asked about their current restaurant usage, a significant proportion of the American public say they would like to be patronizing restaurants more often.

Thirty-eight percent of all adults say they are not eating on the premises of restaurants as frequently as they would like, while 37% say they are not purchasing takeout or delivery as often as they would like.

Putting these results in a historical context, this measure of pent-up demand remains well above pre-recession levels.

On a consistent basis during the stronger restaurant business environment of the mid-2000s, typically only one-quarter of adults said they were not patronizing restaurants as frequently as they would like.

Debunking the Myth of the "Typical" Hispanic Food Shopper Is Key to Market Growth for U.S. Retailers

Spending on food at grocery and other food stores by Latino consumers has risen more than 80% over the past 10 years, a growth rate more than double that of U.S. consumers on average.

Hispanic food shoppers now represent a rapidly growing segment of the customer base of grocers throughout the country, with growth coming largely from the continuing dispersal of

Latinos into areas not traditionally known for having substantial Hispanic populations, Packaged Facts research director David Sprinkle says.

The in-store behavior of Hispanic food shoppers is the product of a complex interplay among a wide range of factors.

Including their national heritage, the extent of their affiliation with their original culture and the language they speak at home. In short, the most important lesson for marketers and retailers looking to learn about how individual Hispanic food shoppers fill their shopping carts is that there may be no such thing as a typical "Hispanic" food shopper.

Where Latinos have landed in their nationwide dispersal is a key factor influencing what they purchase and how retailers can best attract their patronage.

In Los Angeles, for example, stocking the shelves for the Hispanic food shopper means understanding the preferences and traditions of shoppers who are mainly Mexican but also include a substantial population of Salvadorans and Guatemalans.

In Miami food stores need to satisfy the expectations of Cubans, Colombians, Venezuelans, Hondurans and Nicaraguans. In New York they need to cater to Puerto Ricans and Dominicans along with shoppers from a wide variety of other countries in Central and South America.

Hispanic food shoppers react in different ways to Spanish-language labeling because of wide variations in language use and/or degree of acculturation. Puerto Ricans and South Americans are least likely to say Spanish-language labeling helps them in the store, while Cubans and Central Americans are most likely.

Food and beverage preferences can vary widely as well.

For example, the households of Spanish-dominant Latinos and those with a high degree of attachment to their original culture are nearly five times as likely as food shoppers on average and around four times more likely than bilingual/English dominant Latino food shoppers to have bought Cornish game hen in the past seven days.

Veal is another type of meat enjoying a much higher than average degree of meat enjoying a much higher than average degree of popularity among Spanish-dominant food shoppers.

Compared to households of food shoppers with a low degree of identification with their original culture, those who have a high degree of identification are more likely to drink sparkling water, still bottled water, and thirst quencher drinks.

Consumption of ground coffee is also closely related to language use and degree of acculturation. Households of bilingual/English dominant food shoppers are twice as likely as their Spanish-dominant counterparts to drink relatively large quantities of ground coffee.

While there can be significant differences in food preferences within the Hispanic population, a gap between the purchasing patterns of Hispanic and all food shoppers does persist.

There are a wide variety of food products that Latinos (with the exception of Puerto Ricans and, in a few cases, Mexicans) choose not to buy. These include traditional mainstream American foods such as peanut butter, pretzels and pickles.

Regional American eating habits can also have an impact on Hispanic food preferences.

Compared to all food shoppers throughout the country as well as other Hispanic food shoppers, Puerto Ricans and Dominicans living in NYC are more likely to live in a household that eats bagels.

So, when it comes to noshing on bagels, Puerto Ricans and Dominicans act more like New Yorkers than anything else.

Generations

Generational differences are nothing new and are certainly not uncommon, but the differences are major. Generation Z (ages 15-20) top three spare-time activities are listening to music (37%), reading (27%), and watching TV (23%). Perhaps somewhat surprising, among online U.S. adults, Baby Boomers (46-65) spend almost twice as much time on a daily basis with TV, radio and print as do Millennials (16-30).

Baby Boomers have generally positive attitudes towards their primary care doctors, as the vast majority agree that their doctor listens carefully to their questions and concerns (88%) and knows their name, history and medical issues (82%) as well as the medications and care they receive from specialists (79%). However, almost half report some frustrations with their doctor.

Gen Xers now outnumber Baby Boomers among affluents for the first time, with the former accounting for 37% of all affluents and the latter 32%. Both Millennials and Gen Xers say they're more likely to spread the word about their favorite brands and products face-to-face than via social media.

Increasing Amount of Gen Xers Own the Tech Trio: Smartphone, Computer and Tablet

Roughly 37% of adult in the United States own a smartphone, computer *and* tablet, according to survey results from the Pew Internet & American Life Project.

In looking at how the ownership of all three devices breaks out among demographic groups, the study indicates that it is highest among 30-49-year-olds (51%), college graduates (53%), and those coming from households with at least $75k in annual income (60%).

Last year, a survey from Deloitte found that 37% of Americans aged 14 and older owned the trio of devices, with that figure up to 51% among Millennials (14-30).

What Are Gen Z's Top Spare-Time Activities?

TV viewing is one of the more popular spare-time activities across generations, but for Gen Z consumers (ages 15-20) it takes a back seat to music listening and reading, per results from a Nielsen survey of more than 30,000 online consumers across 60 countries.

Indeed, a leading 37% of Gen Z respondents indicated that listening to music is one of their top-3 spare-time activities, ahead of reading (27%) and watching TV (23%).

Gen Z's affinity for music is supported by research into U.S. teens' preferred media habits. Recently, a study from Common Sense Media revealed that listening to music is the most common — and most enjoyed — media activity among U.S. teens (13-18).

TV viewing also emerged as a preferred media activity in that survey, although reading was further behind than in the Nielsen survey.

Interestingly, both pieces of research show that social media is further down the list. In the Common Sense Media survey, fewer than half (45%) of U.S. teens reported using social media everyday, while in the Nielsen survey, reviewing social media was only in the middle of the pack in terms of top spare-time activities, behind exercising and connecting with family and friends.

Several spare-time activities appear to be prominent across the other generations, according to the Nielsen research.

Watching TV, for example, is the leading spare-time activity for Millennials (31%), Gen Xers (38%) and Boomers (42%), while falling second only to reading among the Silent Generation. Reading, connecting with friends and family, and travel are also top-5 activities for those generations.

The popularity of TV viewing as a spare-time activity among Millennials (with social media not in the top 5) is backed by research published a couple of years ago by the Urban Land Institute, which found watching TV to be U.S. Millennials' top use of their free time.

Separately, Nielsen's "Global Generational Lifestyles" report also finds that:

While making money is the top future aspiration among Gen Z respondents, being fit and healthy is tops among Millennials and widens the gap with other aspirations alongside age, with family time also becoming more important with age;

Boomers appear to be the most distracted at mealtimes, being the generation most likely to say that they eat most of their dinner meals at home while doing something else and to say that meal times are not technology free;

Millennials (58%) are the most likely to eat out at least once a week, at twice the rate of Boomers (29%);

Millennials are the most apt to pay more for food with health benefits, citing fair trade benefits as their most important;

Boomers (74%) are slightly more satisfied with their occupations than Millennials (68%) and Gen Xers (69%), and are also more satisfied with their work environment/setting and work/life balance;

Given the choice, STEM emerges as the top career choice for Gen Xers, while IT is tops among Millennials and Gen Xers, Education & Training leads among Boomers, and Health Science would be the career choice of the largest share of those from the Silent Generation;

Although a majority of respondents from all generations say they save enough money each month, more are *not* confident than confident in their financial futures; and

Boomers are the most likely to say that their debt motivates them to be careful about spending.

Traditional Media Consumption Estimates, by Generation

Among online U.S. adults, Baby Boomers (46-65) spend almost twice as much time on a daily basis with TV, radio and print as do Millennials (16-3) per newly-released data from a TNS study.

In fact, while Baby Boomers report spending more than double the time with TV (3.4 hours per day) as with TV and video online (1.3 hours), Millennial estimate spending more time with digital than offline TV (2.7 vs. 1.9 hours per day).

For comparison, Nielsen figures suggest that while youth watch substantially less traditional TV than their older counterparts, traditional TV viewing among Millennials is in excess of 2 hours per day, surpassing 3 hours per day for the 25-34 demographic.

Baby Boomers Like Their Primary Care Doctors, But Have Some Concerns

Baby Boomers (51-69) have generally positive attitudes towards their primary care doctors, as the vast majority agree that their doctor listens carefully to their questions and concerns (88%) and knows their name, history and medical issues (82%) as well as the medications and care they receive from specialists (79%).

However, almost half report some frustrations with their doctor, and some have taken action as a result, according to a survey conducted by Ipsos on behalf of MDVIP.

Respondents to the survey – who were required to have a primary care doctor or to have seen one in the past 5 years – were asked to choose their top-three frustrations (if any) when seeing their primary care doctor over the last few visits. Waiting while in the office (32%) was the top irritant, followed by the limited time they actually have with the doctor (26%).

That's not too surprising, given that almost one-third of respondents report that, when going for a visit, they typically spend more time in the waiting room than they do with the doctor.

As a result, having visits that don't feel hurried and last as long as they need to (62%) is the quality Baby Boomers most value in a primary care doctor. Other qualities sought by Baby Boomers include a kind and compassionate bedside manner (50%) and same-day or next-day appointments (46%). These experience-driven factors appear to be more important than a doctor's strong credentials (29%) or price transparency (17%).

Meanwhile, more than one-third of respondents report taking some type of action due to their frustration with a doctor, with about 1 in 6 (16%) having stopped seeing a doctor and/or switched a doctor (20% women versus 12% men). Another 11% have considered switching doctors, but not followed through. Social media isn't an avenue for their frustrations, though, as only 1% have complained on social media.

Although relatively few Baby Boomers in the MDVIP and Ipsos Public Affairs survey have taken action as a result of their frustrations, that doesn't mean their current experiences match their ideal ones.

Asked to choose from a list of descriptions associating visits with other experiences, Boomers were most likely to describe their typical visit as being akin to shopping at the grocery store – going in, getting what's needed, and then being done. But the ideal experience for the largest share of respondents is similar to consulting a trusted financial advisor – that knows their personal situation, makes good recommendations and gives them peace of mind.

Gen X Now Reportedly Largest Generation of Affluents

Among affluent, Gen Xers (34-50) now outnumber Baby Boomers (51-69) for the first time, with the former accounting for 37% of all affluents and the latter 32%, according to Ipsos' latest annual survey of affluents in the U.S. The results are essentially switched from last year, leading Ipsos to declare this "a changing of the generational guard." Even so, Boomers continue to lead on one important front.

Indeed, Boomer respondents reported a median household net worth of $913K, almost twice the figure reported by Gen Xers ($552K). Millennials (18-33), who comprise one-quarter of affluents, reported a median net worth of $516K, not far behind Gen Xers; Seniors (70+), the smallest group (5% share) of affluents, reported the highest median net worth, of $1.42 million.

The Ipsos survey notes that affluent Gen Xers are far from being a monolithic group, a point that is often mentioned about Millennials, but less so with respect to Gen Xers. Younger Gen Xers (under 40), for example, tend to have similar tastes to Millennials in various areas (such as social media, entertainment trends and organic food), while older Gen Xers share more psychographic traits with Boomers.

That's interesting in light of other research on Gen Xers. Recently, the Pew Research Center revealed that 58% of Gen Xers identify with their generational label, compared to 78% of Boomers. An earlier study from MetLife, meanwhile, found that just 41% of Gen Xers related most to their own generation, while 28% related most to Baby Boomers.

When it comes to the various traits they ascribe to their generation, the Pew survey discovered that Gen Xers are roughly in the middle of Millennials and Baby Boomers (perhaps a function of using averages). The Ipsos survey, for its part, shows that while 54% of Gen Xers aged 34-41 agree that they "like to stand out from others," only 41% of those aged 42-50 agree.

Overall, the Ipsos study reveals that 23% of American households (and 28% of American adults) qualify as being affluent, on par with last year's results.

Among the $2.7 trillion in annual consumer spending by affluents (which represents an uptick from last year), the largest expenditure categories are:

- Automotive;
- Home and garden;
- Personal insurance;
- Travel;
- Education;

Those results signify a greater spending role for travel and electronics than in last year's survey.

Not surprisingly, affluents tend to live in urban areas, with 44% living in 10 major cities. The top 5 cities by share of affluents are:

- New York City (10% of affluents);
- Los Angeles (7%);
- Chicago (5%);
- San Francisco (4%); and
- Washington, DC (4%).

Affluents living in these cities tend to exhibit different characteristics, with those in New York City showing an above-average inclination to value their cultural or ethnic heritage and to have an interest in fashion and luxury. Affluents in San Francisco skew heavily Asian-American (29% of San Francisco affluents versus 8% nationally) and tend to be more liberal, with interests in hybrid vehicles and organic food.

By comparison, affluents in Los Angeles have stronger interests in automobiles, luxury, fashion and entertainment. (One wonders if these differences in interests are restricted to affluents, or are city-wide...)

In other highlights from the report, affluent Millennials spend 10.4 hours a week with social media, almost twice the affluent average of 5.5 hours per week.

Although Facebook and YouTube are the top social platforms for affluents overall and Millennials in particular, the youngest group is more heavily drawn to Instagram (54% using) and Snapchat (35%) than the affluent population as a whole (29% and 13%, respectively), with this likely a reflection of the traditionally younger audience of these platforms.

For Boomers, Packed Social Calendar Trumps Little Black Book

Nearly half of single female Boomers (45%) aren't interested in dating, but an active social life is a priority.

That's a key conclusion of a new study conducted by Harris Poll on behalf of Del Webb, a national brand of PulteGroup, Inc., one of the nation's largest homebuilders and the leading builder of communities for active adults.

Just 38% are looking for companionship or marriage, the study found.

The third in a series of newly released data from the 2015 Del Webb Baby Boomer Survey finds that 42% of respondents are just as socially active today (if not more) than they were at 35 years old. Two-thirds (67%) say they engage in social activities outside the home at least once a month, and nearly one-in-five (17%) are socially active outside the home a few times a week. The survey was conducted online among 1,020 single female U.S. adults ages 50-68.

They're Catching the Latest Movies, Traveling Abroad and Volunteering:

As dating takes a back seat, the calendars of single female boomers are instead filled with social, physical and mental activities, and include a wide range of hobbies and interests. In fact, just five percent prioritize pursuing a romantic relationship. Aside from spending time with family and friends, the survey found they rank a healthy lifestyle as their top priority (68%).

"Since we built the first Del Webb community in 1960, we've seen firsthand how staying active can keep you mentally and physically young," said Deborah Demos, Lifestyle Director at Sun City Mesquite about 90 miles north of Las Vegas. "Single Boomer women aren't slowing down as they are out with friends, hitting the gym, volunteering, furthering their education, and more. It comes as no surprise that our survey data also shows three quarters (76%) of single female Boomers feel younger than their age. The fact is, the women in this demographic are thriving."

Among those who engage in social activities, the most popular pastimes include dinners with friends (66%), trips to the movies (51%) and attending concerts (31%), according to the study.

Other top social activities include:

- ✓ Seeing plays and musicals (30%);
- ✓ Seeking formal and informal education (28%);
- ✓ Outdoor activities (e.g., hiking, canoeing, kayaking, etc.) (24%);

✓ Attending sporting events (22%);
✓ Happy hours (15%); and
✓ Dancing (14%)

The study also revealed that volunteer work is a top activity among single female Boomers, with nearly one-third (30%) citing this as a way they spend their time. Del Webb estimates that its 300,000 residents across the country contribute more than three million hours of time each year to work for nonprofit organizations, from mentoring and tutoring to fundraising and board membership.

"It is incredible to witness the willingness and enthusiasm of this generation to share their time and talents," added Demos. "Promoting a culture of volunteerism at Del Webb has long been a priority for us, and we are proud to see our single female Boomer residents spend thousands of hours each year doing work beyond our community walls."

Looking for Love?

For the single female Boomers who are interested in dating, many are ready to mingle – not marry. The survey found that 25% of respondents are seeking companionship, while others are just looking to meet people and socialize (3%). Just 13% want to find love and get married.

"This is a dynamic, powerful group of women with incredibly diverse interests," said Demos. "Whether furthering their education, making the world a better place, or just wanting to have fun, these women can – and do – have it all. By understanding this unique demographic we can make sure our Del Webb communities offer activities, clubs and amenities that meet the needs of the single female Boomer."

Face-to-Face Tops Social As W-O-M Vehicle

Both Millennials and Gen Xers say they're more likely to spread the word about their favorite brands and products face-to-face than via social media, according to results from a CrowdTwist study. Beyond those two leading word-of-mouth vehicles, though, email proves more popular among Gen Xers while texting is more apt to be used by Millennials.

The results are from a survey of 1,208 North American consumers ages 18-69, from which subsets of 403 Gen X consumers (born between 1965 and 1980) and 402 Millennials (born between 1981 and 1997) were examined in separately-released reports. (The report examining Boomers has yet to be released; presumably, face-to-face will also be a more popular W-O-M vehicle than social media among this group of respondents.)

Millennials (50.5%) and Gen Xers (49.6%) were equally as likely to say they are extremely loyal or quite loyal to their favorite brands. Of these two sets of respondents, though, Millennials appear to be the group more likely to switch brands.

With consumers increasingly modifying their shopping habits due to loyalty programs, preventing churn is paramount for those marketers using a loyalty or reward program. For both cohorts, the top reasons given for abandoning a loyalty program were:

- The rewards not being compelling or relevant;
- Being tired of waiting for points to accumulate; and
- Not having enough ways to earn points.

When it comes to earning those points through non-purchase activities, answering a survey is easily the favorite method for Gen Xers (78.2%) and Millennials (74.4%). Of note, among the various activities listed, checking-in at a location ranked higher for Gen Xers than Millennials, while the opposite was true for watching videos.

Finally, discounts/coupons and cash back/credit were the most important benefits (in that order) for both generations. While brand experiences ranked as one of the less important benefits, these were cited by significantly more Millennials (11%) than Gen Xers (1.7%).

American Adults' Feelings of Financial Responsibility, by Age

Three-quarters of American Millennials (18-34) feel that they are financially responsible and generally do not spend beyond their means, according to results from an Ipsos and Wells Fargo survey.

However, Millennials are less likely than adults ages 55 and older (87%) to feel financially responsible, and are about twice as likely to say they tend to spend their money and not think twice about it (36% vs. 19%).

The survey also finds that Millennials (69%) are significantly less likely than adults aged 55 and up (87%) to know and understand the financial process involved in the purchase of a home, presumably as they're less likely to have been through that process.

Millennials Emerge as the "Super-Saver" Generation

Saving money may be challenging for most Americans, but a new survey from **TD Bank** reveals that nearly half of Americans are feeling confident about their ability to save for the future.

The TD Bank Saving & Spending Survey questioned more than 1,600 U.S. consumers about their saving and spending habits. Given the current economy, the survey surprisingly found that nearly half of consumers (49%) described themselves as "good savers."

Millennials are leading the charge with 56% reporting that they are "good savers," compared with 43% of gen Xers and 48% of baby boomers.

Among those who wished they were saving more, 42% reported that unavoidable expenses and financial commitments impaired their ability to save.

"Conventional wisdom assumes Americans are spenders, rather than savers," said **Nandita Bakhshi**, Head of Consumer Bank, TD Bank. "So it's encouraging to see such a strong commitment to saving across the board, particularly among millennials. Only 4% of respondents stated that saving isn't a priority, regardless of their financial situations."

Retirement represents another key focus for most Americans, with 57% reporting that they are currently saving or investing money for retirement. Still, a majority of consumers are not confident that they will have the funds to retire comfortably.

Indeed, only 29% of respondents are very or extremely confident that they will save enough to retire comfortably, while 36% of Americans list saving for retirement as one of their main financial fears.

Millennials, once again, break away from the pack, feeling twice as confident as gen Xers in their ability to save for a comfortable retirement (42% versus 20%, respectively).

Where Do Americans Overspend?

While saving is a top priority, a majority of Americans still report that they are overspending in some areas. Frequently, restaurants were cited as the top culprit in overspending (40%), followed by coffee/lunches (23%) and clothing/shoes (15%).

When it comes to retail spending, one-half of all respondents and 69% of millennials surveyed admitted to indulging on impulse purchases. Among the generations, boomers were the least prone to binge-buying, with 49% noting that they "try not to spend outside their budget."

Minding Their Own Budget

Millennials are not only the best savers; they're also the most diligent about their budgets. According to the TD Bank Saving & Spending Survey, 44% of Americans check their budget once a week or more. This figure climbs to 53% for millennials, compared to 43% for gen Xers and 37% for baby boomers.

New technology is also changing the way Americans manage their finances. Today's American consumers are relying more heavily on banking/financial apps (40%), with conventional spreadsheets taking a secondary position (29%). Reliance on banking/financial apps is particularly prominent among millennials, at 59% versus 38% for gen Xers and 24% for baby boomers.

"Given the wealth of budgeting resources and technology available today, there's something for everyone for tracking financial habits," said Bakhshi. "Even if you don't actively budget today, the ease of these new financial apps can provide a great point of entry for controlling spending and managing savings."

U.S. Multitasking Behavior, by Generation

Nine in 10 Americans age 14 and older claim to always or almost always multitask while watching TV, up from 81% a couple of years ago, per Deloitte's latest Digital Democracy survey.

In fact, 96% of Leading Millennials (26-31) are now regularly multitasking while watching TV, with their most common activities being browsing the web (45%) and text messaging (41%).

Among the youngest crowd (14-25), 94% of whom at least almost always multitask, text messaging (53%) and using a social network (47%) are the most common activities.

Meanwhile, 1 in 5 respondents report almost always browsing for products and services online, with this behavior most common among the 26-31 bracket (30%).

Overall, respondents estimated that only 22% of their multitasking activities on average are directly related to the program they are watching, with this figure highest among trailing (25%) and leading (28%) Millennials.

Health and Beauty Aids

Americans are conflicted about sleep. A large majority understand that sleep is necessary to recharge, restore and refresh, however, when asked about their feelings towards sleep, their answers become more complex.

More than half of Americans are unable to sleep throughout the night. Sixty-two percent of Americans regularly suffer from symptoms of insomnia, yet only 20% believe they actually have the condition and just 12% have been diagnosed by a doctor.

Americans Are Torn on Feelings About Sleep

Research recently conducted by the Better Sleep Council (BSC) shows Americans are conflicted about sleep. The survey found that a large majority of people understand that sleep is necessary to recharge, restore and refresh.

However, when asked about their feelings toward sleep, their answers become more complex and polarized.

The survey, administered during April 2015 in support of the BSC's annual "May is Better Sleep Month" campaign, shows that the way sleep is framed influences the way people feel about it.

When asked about how important sleep is, only 2% view sleep as a waste of time. But negative feelings become more prominent when people are told how much of their lives are spent asleep.

For example, when told they will spend an average of one-third of their lives sleeping, 15% of respondents felt negatively about the amount of time spent "wasted" on sleep – despite the fact that this is the typical biological requirement.

And when told that they will have slept for roughly 20 years by the time they reach age 60, a total of 33% of respondents were dismayed that they were "about to waste 20 years" of their life or said they "never want to sleep again."

"The research clearly shows that what we understand about sleep versus how we feel about it is polarizing – and that has profound ramifications on how Americans treat the importance of sleep," said Mary Helen Uusimaki, BSC vice president of marketing and communications. "Spending one-third of your life sleeping is not a negative; it's a biological need. Those that feel time is being wasted on sleep will more likely cheat themselves of the seven to nine hours they need to make their waking hours more healthy, productive and enjoyable."

According to the research, Millennials are significantly more likely to feel that spending 20 out of 60 years sleeping is a waste of time (30%), compared to Generation X (23%) and Baby Boomer (21%) respondents.

That number rises when examining male responses only – 34% of Millennial males feel the time is wasted, compared to Generation X males (18%) and Baby Boomer males (20%). A possible reason for this difference is the desire for younger people to experience the here and now to its fullest, as captured by the popular slogan, "I'll sleep when I'm dead."

"Negative attitudes about sleep can be linked to what other experts have concluded – that a primary cause of excessive sleepiness among Americans is self-imposed sleep deprivation," said Terry Cralle, R.N., certified clinical sleep educator and BSC health and wellness spokesperson. "Health professionals should be concerned that Americans may think of sleep as a waste of time, when in fact, chronic sleep deprivation can lead to serious health issues, including heart disease, obesity, stroke and dementia."

There is some hope, however, as 33% of respondents have no concerns about spending one-third of their lives sleeping – the statement evokes positive feelings, and they consider sleep worthy of that much of their time. Another 24% feel it's necessary to recharge. However, half of respondents struggling to fall asleep, unfortunately, turn to the television for help – a method sleep experts discourage. What should they try instead? The Better Sleep Council recommends starting with these five tips:

1. **Make sleep a priority.** Keep a consistent sleep and wake schedule – even on the weekends. If necessary, try adding sleep to your to-do list. And don't be late.
2. **Maintain a relaxing sleep routine.** Create a bedtime routine that relaxes you. Experts recommend reading a book, listening to soothing music or soaking in a hot bath.
3. **Create a sleep sanctuary.** Your bedroom should be a haven of comfort. Create a room that is dark, quiet, comfortable and cool for the best sleep possible. Consider a bedroom makeover.
4. **Evaluate your sleep system.** Your mattress and pillow should provide full comfort and support. Your bed and your body will naturally change over time, so if your mattress is seven years old (or older), it may be time for a new one. Pillows should generally be replaced every year.
5. **Banish technology.** Television, smartphones, tablets, laptops and computers should be kept out of the bedroom. Intense backlighting of electronics triggers stimulating chemicals in the brain that tell your body it's time to be awake.

More Than Half of Americans Are Unable To Sleep Throughout the Night

New survey results are waking Americans up to a widespread health issue — insomnia.

Even though 62% of Americans regularly suffer from symptoms of insomnia, only 20% believe they actually have the condition and merely 12% have been diagnosed by a doctor, according to the America: Insomnia Nation survey supported by Pernix Therapeutics Holdings, Inc.

Contrary to popular belief, insomnia is not just the inability to fall asleep. One of the most enlightening findings from the study was that over 50% of Americans are unable to stay asleep throughout the night.

The new survey, which sheds light on the nation's behavior and attitudes toward insomnia and sleeplessness, also uncovered that:

- On average, nearly three-quarters of Americans (72%) are missing out on almost three weeks of sleep per year (470 hours);
- Many Americans (51%) feel that sleeplessness is glamorized and that successful people like CEOs and government or business leaders get less sleep than the average person. However research proves that a good night's sleep can actually improve performance and spur creativity;
- A good night's sleep can positively impact mood (74%) and productivity (70%); and
- When it comes to health, happiness and wellbeing, Americans rank getting a good night's sleep second in importance (46%)—just behind spending time with their family (69%).

Thankfully, there are ways to help achieve a good night's sleep, according to Dr. Adam Sorscher, Assistant Professor of Community and Family Medicine at The Geisel School of Medicine at Dartmouth.

"Following a regular shut-eye strategy like staying away from your cell phone before bed or blocking out light is one of the most critical ways to help you achieve a full night's sleep," said Dr. Sorscher. "But while most Americans acknowledge the importance of a good bedtime routine, only half regularly follow one. And for people with insomnia, practicing a good bedtime routine alone may not even be enough."

Growing Global Health Awareness
Could Mean Big Business For Manufacturers

Nearly half (49%) of the global respondents in Nielsen's Health &Wellness Survey believe themselves to be overweight.

That spells opportunity for marketers, Nielsen says

Fifty percent of consumers are actively trying to lose weight and 88% are willing to pay more for foods with healthy attributes, but only to a degree.

Obesity rates around the world are rising rapidly and not just in developed countries. In fact, 62% of the world's 671 million obese individuals live in developing markets, according to the 2013 Global Burden of Disease Study.

The study estimated that 2.1 billion people (nearly 30% of the global population) were overweight or obese.

The obesity crisis and consumer aspiration to be become healthier could be a growth driver for manufacturers who better align their offerings to consumer needs and desires for healthier food.

Around 75% of global respondents believe they "are what they eat" and nearly 80% are actively using foods to forestall health issues and medical conditions, such as obesity, diabetes, high cholesterol and hypertension.

Dividing global respondents into four buckets of spending intent, the highest percentages are only moderately willingly to pay a premium for health claims — an average of 38% across 27 attributes included in the study.

About one-quarter of global respondents are very willing to pay a premium (27%), followed by 23% who are slightly willing and 12% who are not willing.

While there was not one health attribute that swayed dramatically from these spending intention buckets globally, a few regional differences prevail.

A willingness to pay a premium for health benefits is higher in developing markets than elsewhere; more than nine- in-10 respondents in Latin America (94%), Asia-Pacific (93%), and Africa/Middle East (92%) say they are willing to pay more for foods with health attributes for some degree.

Compare that to eight-in-10 in Europe (79%) and North American (80%).

For most attributes, there is also a gap between the percentage of respondents that say a health attribute is very important and the percentage that are very willing to pay a premium.

For example, 43% of global respondents say the absence of GMOs is very important in the foods they purchase, but only 33% are very willing to pay a premium for these products — a 10-percentage point difference.

One notable exception is organic foods.

Consumers are expressing their "sentiments with their wallets," said Susan Dunn, executive vice president, Global Professional Services, Nielsen. "As Millennials' purchasing power increases, manufactures and retailers that make the effort to understand and connect with this generation's need increase the odds of success."

The generation gap is particularly pronounced for functional foods that reduce disease risk or promote good health and for socially/environmentally responsible foods.

For example, 41% of Generation Z and 32% of Millennial respondents are very willing to pay a premium for sustainably sourced ingredients, compared to 21% of Baby Boomer and 16% of Silent Generation respondents.

Generation Z and Millennials are also leaders in the gluten-free movement.

Thirty-seven percent of Generation Z respondents and 31% of Millennials are very willing to pay a premium for gluten-free products, while only 22% of Baby Boomer and 12% of Silent Generation respondents are willing to do so.

Thirty- three percent of respondents say organics are very important and the same percentage is also very willing to pay a premium for these products.

A willingness to pay a premium for health attributes declines with age.
Generation Z (under 20) and Millennials (21-34) are more willing to pay a premium for all attributes, even those that are more important to Generation X (35-49) and Baby Boomers (50-64).

Percentages believing that they are very important are lowest among the Silent Generation (aged 65+) for all 27 attributes.

Attributes gaining the most favor included products that are GMO-free, have no artificial coloring/ flavors and are all natural.

Healthcare/Medical

Baby Boomers have generally positive attitudes towards their primary care doctors, as the majority agree that their doctor listens carefully to their questions and concerns (88%) and knows their name, history and medical issues (82%) as well as the medications and care they receive from specialists (79%). However, almost half report some frustrations with their doctor.

For teens (13-18), parents are the top source of health information not the internet. While one-quarter get a lot of health information from the internet (including 1 in 10 from social media), digital remains behind health classes in school (32%) and doctors/nurses (29%) as a top source of information. 30% of California parents don't vaccinate their kids and doctors blamed them for the measles outbreak in 2015.

Baby Boomers Like Their Primary Care Doctors, But Have Some Concerns

Baby Boomers (51-69) have generally positive attitudes towards their primary care doctors, as the vast majority agree that their doctor listens carefully to their questions and concerns (88%) and knows their name, history and medical issues (82%) as well as the medications and care they receive from specialists (79%).

However, almost half report some frustrations with their doctor, and some have taken action as a result, according to a survey conducted by Ipsos on behalf of MDVIP.

Respondents to the survey – who were required to have a primary care doctor or to have seen one in the past 5 years – were asked to choose their top-three frustrations (if any) when seeing their primary care doctor over the last few visits. Waiting while in the office (32%) was the top irritant, followed by the limited time they actually have with the doctor (26%).

That's not too surprising, given that almost one-third of respondents report that, when going for a visit, they typically spend more time in the waiting room than they do with the doctor.

As a result, having visits that don't feel hurried and last as long as they need to (62%) is the quality Baby Boomers most value in a primary care doctor. Other qualities sought by Baby Boomers include a kind and compassionate bedside manner (50%) and same-day or next-day appointments (46%). These experience-driven factors appear to be more important than a doctor's strong credentials (29%) or price transparency (17%).

Meanwhile, more than one-third of respondents report taking some type of action due to their frustration with a doctor, with about 1 in 6 (16%) having stopped seeing a doctor and/or switched a doctor (20% women versus 12% men). Another 11% have considered switching doctors, but not followed through. Social media isn't an avenue for their frustrations, though, as only 1% have complained on social media.

Although relatively few Baby Boomers in the MDVIP and Ipsos Public Affairs survey have taken action as a result of their frustrations, that doesn't mean their current experiences match their ideal ones.

Asked to choose from a list of descriptions associating visits with other experiences, Boomers were most likely to describe their typical visit as being akin to shopping at the grocery store – going in, getting what's needed, and then being done. But the ideal experience for the largest share of respondents is similar to consulting a trusted financial advisor – that knows their personal situation, makes good recommendations and gives them peace of mind.

Teens Trust Parents More Than Internet for Health Information

Parents are the top source of health information for teens (13-18), 55% of whom say they get "a lot" of health information from them, according to a study from Northwestern University.

While one-quarter get a lot of health information from the internet (including 1 in 10 from social media), digital remains behind health classes in school (32%) and doctors/nurses (29%) as a top source of information.

Satisfaction rates with information derived from the internet are relatively low, with 24% "very satisfied" with the information found online, versus 57% very satisfied with information from their parents and 54% from doctors and nurses.

Still, more than eight in 10 are at least somewhat satisfied with the information they find.

Among those who are not, the main reasons are too much conflicting information (42%), the information not appearing reliable (40%) and the information found not being relevant to their particular situation (35%).

According to the study, teens are heavily reliant on search to find health information online. Among the 84% who have looked for health information on the internet, 58% report "often" beginning their search by Googling a topic, and an additional 14% say they often begin their search by using a different search engine.

Top rank matters to teens: half of those who use search engines to find information online typically click on the first link that comes up.

Overall, almost one-third of teens say they have changed their behavior because of digital health information.

Customers Less Satisfied with Energy Utilities, Shipping and Healthcare

Following yet another harsh winter, customer satisfaction with gas and electric service providers is down 2.7% to an ACSI score of 74.3 on a 0-100 scale, according to the American Customer Satisfaction Index (ACSI).

"Higher cost tends to weaken customer satisfaction, particularly when spending is not discretionary, as is the case with commodities such as energy," says Claes Fornell, ACSI chairman and founder. "It is not as much the cost of energy per se, but that usage was high and took a bigger bite out of household income."

The ACSI report covers customer satisfaction with three utility categories (cooperative, investor-owned and municipal) and two health care service industries (hospitals and ambulatory care), along with consumer shipping and the mail services of the U.S. Postal Service (USPS).

Investor-Owned Utilities: Rising Cost of Electricity, Natural Gas Dampens Satisfaction

Household satisfaction with investor-owned utilities falls 1.3% to an ACSI score of 74.

Among the largest investor-owned utilities, the highest-scoring companies are both natural gas suppliers – Atmos Energy (ACSI score of 82) and CenterPoint Energy (81).

FirstEnergy is next at 79 and posts the largest gain (+8%); it now ties Sempra Energy. Dominion Resources, PPL and NiSource all come in at 78, followed by Southern Company, Entergy (+1%) and NextEra Energy (+1%) at 77. The only other providers to improve are Xcel Energy (+1% to 76), Public Service Enterprise Group (+3% to 72), and PG&E (+1% to 71).

Most utilities have moved in the opposite direction, with DTE Energy and Exelon deteriorating the most (-8%). Duke Energy (-6%) also declines, while Eversource Energy (formerly Northeast Utilities), hurt particularly hard by winter storms, falls 7% to the industry low of 66.

Municipal Utilities: Smaller Companies Hit Hardest; Salt River Project Maintains Lead

 Most large municipal utilities improved from a year ago, but smaller providers, which make up a majority of the market, dropped to a combined ACSI score of 73.

The Salt River Project (SRP) leads in customer satisfaction for a fifth straight year, edging up 1% to 80, and CPS Energy advances 3% to 77.

Meanwhile, the Los Angeles Department of Water & Power (LADWP) slips 1% and scores far below for customer satisfaction at 68.

Cooperative Utilities: Best in Category

Smaller rural cooperative utilities hold a strong lead over the other utility categories, but slip 1.2% to an ACSI score of 80. Despite a 1% downturn, Touchstone Energy Cooperatives remains one of the Index's top-scoring energy utilities at 80, followed by the aggregate of smaller co-ops (-3% to 78).

Health Care & Social Assistance: Patient Satisfaction Continues to Fall

Patient satisfaction is down 3.2% to an ACSI score of 75.1, the lowest level in nearly a decade.

According to patients, ambulatory care such as office visits to doctors, dentists and optometrists (76) is better than hospital services (74) by a significant margin, but quality of care is less satisfactory and both categories weaken from a year ago.

Demand for health care services is rising, with preliminary figures on household health care spending up nearly 6% in 2014 – the largest increase since before the recession.

This is probably in part a result of growth in the number of Americans with health insurance. During the same period, the rate of growth in the health care workforce slowed, which likely contributed to less efficient access to care.

However, since the middle of 2014, the health care sector has been adding workers at a significantly faster pace, which may lead to higher levels of patient satisfaction in the near future.

"Health care is a non-discretionary expense that consumers delay at their own risk," says ACSI Managing Director David VanAmburg. "While consumers might postpone a vacation or the purchase of a new pair of shoes, they rarely have the flexibility to put off healthcare regardless of cost or quality of care.

The influx of the newly insured is putting pressure on a system that is still playing catch up. Rising demand that is outpacing supply, coupled with increasing healthcare costs, is a formula for lower satisfaction."

Outpatient hospital care shows improvement (+5% to 80), but considerably lower satisfaction with inpatient services and poor emergency room service (-10% to 64) has caused overall patient satisfaction with hospitals to worsen.

Consumer Shipping: Steady from a Year Ago

Customer satisfaction with shipping is stable at an ACSI score 81.

Both FedEx and UPS are steady with identical ACSI scores of 82, while the USPS gains for its Express and Priority Mail delivery business (+3% to 75).

However, regular mail service falls for a second straight year. With a tightening budget, higher postage rates and shrinking mail volumes, satisfaction with USPS regular mail service sinks to 69, its lowest level in nearly 20 years.

Survey Reveals One in Five Insured Americans Avoid Seeing a Doctor Due to Fear of Cost

Approximately two in five insured Americans (38%) do not have a good understanding of which healthcare services are covered under their current plan, according to an online survey by Harris Poll on behalf of SCIO Health Analytics.

One in five insured Americans, or roughly 44 million people, have avoided visiting a doctor for a general health concern within the past 12 months because of cost concerns.

The online poll surveyed more than 2,000 U.S. adults aged 18 and older about their general sentiments around the Affordable Care Act (ACA) or Obamacare, healthcare costs and their overall understanding of the healthcare system, as well as services covered under their plan.

Approximately half the U.S. adults (117 million) have at least one chronic condition, of which 14% of (or 16.4 million) have avoided a doctor's visit in the past 12 months because of cost concerns. While chronic conditions such as heart disease, asthma, and diabetes are generally incurable, they can be managed through early detection, improved lifestyle and treatment.

"These findings are particularly relevant at this time as millions of Americans are once again deciding their annual healthcare benefit options through Open Enrollment," said Siva Namasivayam, CEO, SCIO Health Analytics. "While Americans are spending more time researching health plans, the survey reveals a significant knowledge gap in the specifics of their health care options that may eventually lead to unnecessary risks and costs."

Namasivayam warned that the implications of these findings are even more staggering when you consider treatment costs for Americans with chronic conditions are already around $277 billion annually.

Avoiding medical treatment for these conditions can lead to an increased risk of complications, emergency room visits, hospitalizations, readmissions, work absenteeism and disability that could potentially drive healthcare costs even higher and cripple an already over- burdened system.

When asked how their healthcare situation has changed since the introduction of the Affordable Care Act:

- 41% of Americans say they have spent more time researching what is covered by insurance plans (either in their own plan or other plans);
- 60% of Americans say they do not have a better understanding of the healthcare system despite the media coverage and public/political discourse around Obamacare; and Among those insured, 44% did not know the out of pocket costs/co-pay for prescription drugs, and 61% did not know the costs for urgent care/walk-in clinic visits.

The survey also discovered that age and gender play a role in understanding healthcare costs and services.

Among insured adults, 48% of those aged 18-34 say they lack a good understanding of what healthcare services are covered under their plan, compared to 27% of those aged 65 and older.

Younger insurance holders, especially men, are also much more likely to be cost-conscious when visiting the doctor.

When asked if they avoided visiting the doctor for a general health concern in the past 12 months because of cost concerns, 40% of insured men aged 18-34 answered yes, compared to 27% of insured women in the same age group responded the same (compared to an overall average of 20% for all adults age 18+).

How do Americans want to receive health plan information? According to the survey:

- 62% (the majority) say they would likely be better able to understand their health plan information using the websites offered by their healthcare plan provider;
- 41% would be likely to better understand their health plan information using member phone support offered by their healthcare plan provider;
- 37% of U.S. adults say they get information about healthcare costs and services from their insurance company; and
- 31% get information about healthcare costs and services from their doctor.

30% of California Parents Don't Vaccinate Kids; Docs Blame Them for Measles Outbreak

Ninety-two percent of physicians think the current measles outbreak is directly attributed to parents not vaccinating their children, according to the latest poll from SERMO, the leading U.S. social network for doctors.

According to USA TODAY, the unvaccinated rate in some California schools is as high as 30%. Currently 19 states allow parents to skip vaccines for their children due to personal beliefs or philosophical reasons. "I will not accept a child in my practice if they do not vaccinate," said Dr. Linda Grigis, a family practitioner based in New Jersey. "Measles kills one or two out of every 1,000 persons who become ill with it in the U.S. No child will die from a vaccine-presentable disease on my watch."

The sentiment against "anti-vaxxers" is strong among SERMO participants, many of whom remain anonymous on the platform.

One internist wrote, "It is dangerous for every other patient in your practice. An anti-vac kid brought in by a parent for a rash sitting in the waiting room of a busy pediatric practice could spread measles to countless others in a matter of minutes."

Yet some doctors believe seeing a non-vaccinated patient is an opportunity to educate. An OBGYM wrote, "We have a large community of anti-vaxxers in my state and it would be difficult to refuse them outright. Instead I use persuasion to try to educate them and make my advocacy position very clear. I have had some limited success with this tactic."

An ER doctor contributed to the conversation in strong words, "If you, intelligent, right-minded doctors, who know and can articulate the value of childhood immunization, exclude non-immunizers from your practice, what will happen to them? They will go to the quacks. The quacks will benefit. The patients will suffer. Everyone will suffer as these ideas continue to spread and herd immunity drops."

Since initial reports, measles has spread to over 80 people in 11 states with the likelihood that more patients will be diagnosed soon.

Customer Service Pain Points Still Driving Consumers Away

Some 53% of U.S. customers surveyed last year reported having switched providers during the prior year due to poor service, according to a recently-released Accenture Strategy study.

That 53% figure is up from 51% in 2013 and 46% in 2012, though the most recent study tracked switching behavior in an additional industry (health care providers), which may have had an impact on the results.

Of the 11 industries tracked, customers in the retail sector were the most prone to switching (most likely due to the ease of doing so), with 30% reporting having switched providers due to poor service.

Next on the list, 11% of cable/satellite TV service customers reported having switched providers, likely related to providers' chronically low customer satisfaction ratings.

The overall poor quality of the customer experience was providers' biggest culprit, cited by 72% of those who switched in at least one industry as a main reason for doing so.

Lost trust in the company (44%) and customer service representatives' lack of knowledge (36%) were also significant pain points for switchers.

Significantly, some 73% of those who switched said they would not consider switching back to their original provider or doing business with them again.

Among those who would consider switching back, pricing or other deal (56%) would be the most likely to draw them back, with many also saying they would consider a move back if the original provider introduced a superior product or offering (47%) or the new provider failed to deliver on their expectations (42%).

Even so, 51% of those who would consider returning to their original provider said at least one year would have to pass before they would give the company another chance.

Meanwhile, eight in 10 respondents who switched said that their previous service provider could have done something that would have kept them as a customer.

A majority also said that being recognized and rewarded for doing more business with the provider would have had an impact.

Respondents overall (not just switchers) reported the following negative customer service experiences to be their most frustrating:

- Contacting customer service multiple times for the same reason (86%);
- Being put on hold for a long time (85%);
- Customer service agents who cannot answer the questions (84%);
- Repeating the same information to multiple customer service agents (83%);
- The company delivering something different than what they promised up front (83%); and
- Unfriendly or impolite customer service agents (82%).

Respondents were unlikely to keep bad experiences to themselves: 70% said they had told people about a bad customer service or support experience they had had during the prior year.

And beyond the 46% who said they quit doing business with a company immediately following a bad experience, another 44% said they shifted a portion of their spending to another provider, suggesting that outright switching isn't the only negative outcome from poor experiences.

Holidays/Seasonal

The majority of Canadians surveyed feel giving cash is an appropriate gift for their children (60%) or grandchildren (60%), yet fewer people (39%) are comfortable giving cash to other family members, and even fewer to their spouse (23%) or a friend (23%). Holiday shoppers planned on spending an average of $805 on holiday merchandise in 2015, up from $802 in 2014.

Sixty-two percent of Americans who set a holiday budget go over their limit by an average of $140, marking a 20% increase from what people estimated they would overspend in 2014. Cyber Monday surpassed $3 billion in total digital sales to rank as the heaviest U.S. online shopping day in history. U.S. holiday digital commerce spending via desktop and mobile devices grew 14% in 2015 with total sales reaching around $70.1 billion. Americans spent an average of #173 on Mother's Day in 2015, up almost $10 (6%) from 2014's total. Total consumer spending on Easter in 2015 was projected to grow to $16.4 billion, slightly higher than 2014's projected $15.9 billion but still below 2012-2013 levels.

Holiday Etiquette: Is It Appropriate to Give the Gift of Cash?

They say "money can't buy happiness," but does that mean it's not a suitable holiday gift?

The answer is yes — depending on the recipient, according to a new poll conducted by Edward Jones.

The majority of Canadians surveyed feel it is appropriate to give cash as a gift to their children (60%) or grandchildren (60%). However, fewer people (39%) are comfortable giving cash to other family members, and even fewer to their spouse (23%) or a friend (23%).

When asked who's likely to see the biggest windfall this season, not surprisingly the survey revealed that children are named most often (41%) followed by spouses/partners (27%). Fewer than one in ten mentions Mom (8 %) and even fewer list a sibling (5%). The biggest loser is poor old Dad – only one out of a hundred people say he tops their gift giving list.

"Canadians tend to spend the most on their children, and cash makes for an easy, acceptable and often desired present," says Patrick French, director of financial and retirement planning with Edward Jones. "However, parents and grandparents may want to consider taking this gift a step further, and give children some practical advice when handing over an envelope of money."

For those planning to give children or grandchildren cash this holiday season, Edward Jones suggests the gift should be accompanied by some advice:

- **Teach children how to save** – When giving children cash, help them understand the difference between saving and spending. Many suggest dividing money into three pools – one for spending, one for saving, and one for giving.
- **Explain principles of investing** – Even fairly young children can comprehend what it means to invest in stocks, if it's carefully explained to them. Use examples of the companies with which they may be familiar, like entertainment companies, consumer packaged goods, or fast food restaurant chains— and stick to the basics.
- **Align a monetary gift with a child's future goal** – For example, if attending college or university is a goal for your child, consider making a contribution to a Registered Education Savings Plan (RESP). With an RESP you can put aside money for your child's or grandchild's post-secondary education, and RESP owners are eligible for the Canada Education Savings Grant, which, at a minimum, provides 20% on every dollar of the first $2,500 contributed to RESP each year.
- **Encourage them to save for the future** – It's not just youth that benefit from monetary gifts this time of year. For adult children, it is worth a discussion around setting up a Registered Retirement Savings Plan (RRSP), as this is a great way to encourage them to think long-term. Your children might also consider a Tax-Free Savings Account (TFSA). Every Canadian resident who has reached the age of majority can contribute to a TFSA, which serves as a convenient tax shelter.

Retail Sales Expected to Rise 3.7% This Holiday Season

Retailers have their work cut out for them during the 2015 winter holiday season. In 2014, retailers experienced one of the strongest holiday seasons in recent years, according to a report by Mintel International provided by MarketResearch.com.

And this year, the continued economic growth, improving job market, and lower gas prices are all positive factors contributing to high sales in 2015.

Holiday shoppers plan on spending an average $463 on family members. This year, a common theme many merchandisers are seeing is self-shopping. With gifts for family and friends and themselves, consumers are planning to spend $805 on holiday merchandise, up from $802 in 2014.

The holiday season, November and December, is one of the most important times of the year for retailers. Many companies account for nearly 30% of their annual business during the holidays. Retail sales are expected to increase by 3.7% this year, which will hit an estimated $630.5 billion.

Holiday Cheer in the Workplace in Waning

The National Retail Federation (NRF) predicts consumers will spend more in November and December. But, more American workers are likely to leave their office colleagues off their shopping lists this holiday season, a new study finds.

According to the "WorkSphere" survey from national staffing company Spherion and conducted online in November 2015 by Harris Poll among more than 1,000 adults employed full or part time, employees plan to give less and spend less on workplace gifts this year.

Fewer workers this year than last plan to give gifts to nearly everyone in their workplace, with only 31% planning to give gifts to their co-workers at their level (down from 38% in 2014), 28% planning to give gifts to their boss (down from 34% in 2014), and 19% planning to give gifts to other colleagues (down from 24% in 2014).

The number of workers planning to give gifts to their direct reports remained steady at 17%, down only slightly from 18% last year.

Further, those who do still plan to give gifts in the workplace will likely spend less in 2015 than they did in 2014.

American workers anticipate spending an average of $17 less on gifts for their immediate colleagues this year than last. Direct reports, bosses and other office mates also should expect to receive less, with the amount workers plan to spend on these groups decreasing by an average of $10-$14 this season.

"While many offices and their workers want to acknowledge the holiday season within the workplace, many are struggling to find the right balance in making sure all employees feel comfortable and can enjoy celebrating," said Sandy Mazur, Division President, Spherion. "As the holiday season draws closer, it's important for companies and their workers to be transparent and set ground rules for gift giving, decor and events that match their office culture, while also promoting the fun and camaraderie that this time of year is all about."

Overall, about half of companies are planning to celebrate the holiday season as an office (51%), with 58% of workers noting their company typically acknowledges specific holidays during the period between Thanksgiving and New Year's Day.

However, this practice seems to go against the opinions of a significant number of American workers. Forty-four percent think their company should host a general end-of-year celebration, not specific to religious or cultural beliefs, while 19% of companies already have plans to host a non-denominational "holiday party" this year.

The survey found several other interesting trends surrounding how companies and their employees are planning to approach the holiday season:

The Office as a Home for the Holidays?

- Companies who host a seasonal celebration are almost as likely to bill it as a "Christmas" party (22%) as they are a "holiday" party (19%, respectively). Similarly, an even number of companies display holiday-specific decorations for different holidays (16%) as they do for just one specific holiday (15%). One-in-five also do not typically acknowledge specific holidays at all during the holiday season.

'Tis the Season of Appreciation

- 55% of workers think the reason their company is planning to celebrate the upcoming holiday season is to thank employees and show appreciation for their work throughout the year.
- More than half (53%) of workers would give their company a grade of "B" or higher for their success in making all employees feel included and appreciated during the holiday season.
- Among those who plan to buy gifts for people at work, 44% would give gifts anyway to people who do not celebrate Christmas, Hanukkah or Kwanzaa to make them feel included.

Unwrapping Workplace Gift-Giving Challenges

- The pressure of having to buy something for everyone is a detractor again this year for those who do not plan to buy gifts, with 41% of workers saying it's just too much. Nearly one in five workers who won't buy gifts are concerned with perceptions of trying to gain favoritism.
- As the structure of the traditional workplace shifts, 18% of workers say one reason their company isn't planning to celebrate the upcoming holiday season is because employees are too spread out and there is no central location for everyone to celebrate.

Americans Expect to Go $140 Over Budget for Holiday Gifts

Sixty-two percent of Americans who set a holiday budget go over their limit by an average of $140, marking a 20% increase from what people estimated they would overspend last year, according to a new holiday shopping survey released by Coinstar.

In order to buy gifts for everyone on their list, 66% of shoppers find they need to cut back on things they enjoy like dining out (43%) and entertainment (42%), or even take on credit card debt (27%) or purchase an item on layaway (22%).

Not only do people have to sacrifice before the holidays, but this overspending leads to post-holiday money issues, too. Americans reported they find themselves saving less money (20%), having to set a budget (19%) or dealing with debt (18%) in the first few weeks after the holidays.

"The holidays can be a stressful time of the year, particularly when it comes to money," said Andrea Woroch, a nationally recognized consumer and money saving expert. "Fortunately, there is hidden money throughout most homes in the form of coins and gift cards that can help people avoid taking on debt because of their over-spending."

Additional survey findings include:

- **Credit card use grows:** Gifters are nearly 20% more likely to use credit cards instead of cash or gift cards to pay for their holiday gifts this year (49% in 2015 vs. 41% in 2014);
- **Budgeting needs for the younger crowd:** More than twice as many people ages 18-34 admit they need to set a budget after the holidays when compared to people over the age of 35 (30% vs. 14%); and
- **Millennials are making sacrifices:** Eighty percent of people ages 18-34 admitted to needing to make trade-offs to ensure they can purchase gifts for everyone on their list, while 47% of people that age need to use credit cards to pay for their presents.

Cyber Monday Surpasses $3 Billion in Total Digital Sales To Rank as Heaviest U.S. Online Spending Day in History

For the holiday season-to-date, $27.9 billion has been spent online, marking a 6% increase versus the corresponding days last year, according to comScore.

Cyber Monday reached $2.28 billion in desktop online spending, up 12% versus year ago, representing the heaviest online spending day in history and the first day of the 2015 season to surpass $2 billion in sales.

The weekend after Thanksgiving also reached a major milestone as it saw its first ever billion-dollar online shopping day on Sunday, while Saturday sales reached the $1 billion mark for second year in a row.

The two days combined posted particularly strong growth online, raking in $2.169 billion for an increase of 8% compared to the same weekend last year.

For the five-day period from Thanksgiving through Cyber Monday, online buying from desktop computers totaled $7.201 billion, up 10% versus last year.

Mobile Commerce Brings Total Cyber Monday Spend to More Than $3 Billion

Total digital spend on Cyber Monday, when inclusive of comScore's preliminary mobile commerce estimates, reached $3.118 billion, a 21-percent annual gain vs. $2.586 billion spent on Cyber Monday 2014.

This marks the first time in history that total digital spending surpassed the $3 billion milestone in a single day. Mobile commerce is estimated to have accounted for 27% of total digital commerce on Cyber Monday 2015, with $838 million spent via smartphones and tablets.

Amazon Ranks #1 Among Online Retailers on Cyber Monday

Some 107.8 million Americans visited online retail properties on Cyber Monday using a desktop computer, smartphone or tablet, representing an increase of 23% versus year ago. Amazon ranked as the most visited online retail property on Cyber Monday, followed by Wal-Mart, eBay, Target and Best Buy.

"Cyber Monday maintained its reputation as the most important online spending day of year, exceeding $3 billion in total digital spending and once again becoming the heaviest online spending day of all-time," said comScore chairman emeritus Gian Fulgoni.

"Despite some talk of Cyber Monday declining in importance, the day's historical highs and continued strong growth rates confirm it is still a hugely important shopping event."

Fulgoni added, "It comes as no surprise that Amazon led all online retail properties in Cyber Monday traffic, but several multi-channel retailers such Wal-Mart and Target also had very strong showings. Although some web sites experienced unfortunate server problems on Cyber Monday that appear to have been caused by heavy mobile traffic, it's not yet clear what the impact was for those retailers. What is clear is that the consumer economy is still healthy, and it's looking optimistic that the success of Black Friday weekend and Cyber Monday will carry on throughout the rest of the season."

Shopping at Work Accounts for More Than Half of Cyber Monday Spending

More than half of desktop e-commerce dollars spent in the U.S. on Cyber Monday originated from work computers (52.2%), while buying from home computers comprised of the remaining share (47.8%), despite more buyers opting to make purchases from this location. Consumers between 35 and 54 years old accounted for 46.5% of total dollars spent on Cyber Monday, while females (61.6%) spent significantly more than males (38.4%).

U.S. Holiday Digital Commerce Spending Via Desktop And Mobile Devices Expected to Grow 14%

The 2015 holiday season forecast is that total online retail spending for the November–December period will reach $70.1 billion, representing a 14% gain versus year ago, according to comScore.

Spending using desktop computers for that period is expected to reach $58.3 billion, up 9% year-over-year.

Mobile commerce is predicted to account for $11.7 billion of retail spending, representing 17% of total digital commerce and growing at a rate of 47% vs. last season. In total, digital commerce is expected to account for about 15% of consumers' discretionary spending.

"The 2015 online holiday shopping season is expected to surpass $70 billion in spending, representing a year-over-year growth rate of 14 % across desktop, smartphones and tablets, and once again far outpacing the growth of brick-and-mortar retail during the most important stretch of the year for retailers," said Gian Fulgoni, Executive Chairman Emeritus of comScore.

"Although we anticipate a marginal slowdown in the digital commerce growth rate from last year's 15% level, the overall economic outlook is positive, which bodes well for consumers and retailers," he said. "Importantly, there's one additional shopping day between Thanksgiving and Christmas this year, which when coupled with low gas prices means that consumers will have more cash on hand to take advantage of the slightly longer holiday season."

Added Fulgoni, "Last year, many retailers opened stores on Thanksgiving Day with unexpected results, as some consumers shifted their store visits from Black Friday to Thanksgiving Day but reduced their spending rate.

The good news is that online buying more than compensated for the softness of in-store sales, with growth rates of more than 25% during those two days. We anticipate that happening again this year. In addition, we expect Cyber Monday – the first Monday after the Thanksgiving Holiday weekend – to surpass $3 billion in online sales and become the heaviest online spending day in history for the sixth straight year, with roughly half a billion of those dollars coming from mobile devices."

Black Friday is Better Online

Consumers will spend a record $630.5 billion during the 2015 shopping season, the National Retail Federation predicts.

Nearly half of these people will either browse or buy online, spending $105 billion and using multiple devices in the process, including desktops, laptops, tablets and smartphones, according to Criteo, a performance marketing technology company, which released original data on Black Friday, Cyber Monday and "Bounceback Tuesday" shopping trends to help marketers navigate the consumers' evolving path to purchase.

Findings are based on an analysis of nearly 200 retailers and 63.7 million online transactions during the 2014 holiday season, and provide actionable insight for retail brands to effectively plan for this year's shopping rush.

Because four in 10 eCommerce sales in the U.S. include a cross-device journey, every device and platform counts for retailers as they strategically invest significant resources to engage and convert consumers through promotion and advertising.

Criteo's deep-dive into consumer browsing and buying activity uncovers two trends:

First, Black Friday is increasingly turning into an online sales event as consumers are more frequently using mobile devices to make purchases, and online shopping is extending further into the work week.

Second, For companies focused on attracting and retaining consumers during this time period, online advertising campaigns should be fully optimized across all devices.

Black Friday is Becoming Cyber Monday

While Black Friday has historically been an in-store, discount-driven event, Criteo data based on last season's transactions reveals that for many retailers' online sales on Black Friday were nearly equal to those of Cyber Monday. Driving the growth of eCommerce during Black Friday is the adoption and use of mobile devices to browse and buy online.

- Mass merchants experienced online sales 275% higher on Black Friday than during non-holiday periods—nearly equivalent to Cyber Monday sales.
- Sales volumes on smartphones and tablets on Black Friday were 18% higher than on Cyber Monday.
- On Black Friday, 32% of eCommerce transactions occurred on a mobile device (tablet or smartphone), compared to 24% on Cyber Monday.

"Bounceback Tuesday" Sees Strong Online Sales

Online shopping peaks are spreading further into the week, with sales remaining steady on the Tuesday after Black Friday and Cyber Monday—defined by Criteo as "Bounceback Tuesday."

- In 2014, sales across all key retail categories were 159% above the average on Bounceback Tuesday.
- Specific retail sectors, such as sporting goods, experienced 224% above average online sales on Bounceback Tuesday, which were higher than Black Friday, despite the rise of online sales on that date.
- The toys and gadgets (+223%) and computers and technology (+190%) retail sectors also saw a sales lift on Bounceback Tuesday.

- "The path to purchase for today's consumer has evolved and, as a result, people are doing a tremendous amount of online shopping across all devices on Black Friday. Sales on mobile especially have hit record numbers, according to 2014 data. Retail companies have a huge opportunity to engage consumers through personalized and relevant online advertising during the entire spending period, including Black Friday, Cyber Monday and Bounceback Tuesday," said James Smith, EVP, Americas at Criteo.

Hispanics Expect to Spend More Money this Holiday Season

Hispanics will be spending more on holiday shopping this year and are more likely to buy gifts online than in the past, according to a national survey by the Florida Atlantic University Business & Economic Polling Initiative (FAU BEPI).

Numbers were up across the board from last year's survey, with 30.7% saying they expect to spend more on holiday shopping this year, compared with 28.9% in 2014. The number of respondents who said they would not be doing any holiday shopping dropped nine points from 20.1% in 2014 to 11.1% in 2015, suggesting Hispanics are doing better financially.

The number of Hispanics who plan to shop on Black Friday went up four points from last year (56% to 60%), while those who plan to shop online on Cyber Monday increased from 52% in 2014 to 58% this year. Females are more likely than males (67% to 54%) to shop on Black Friday, while Hispanics in the highly prized 18 to 34 age brackets (72%) are most likely to surf the web for deals on Cyber Monday.

Additionally, more Hispanics expect to do most of their holiday shopping before Thanksgiving, increasing from 21.5% in 2014 to 27.7% this year.

Overall, spending appears to be on the rise in 2015 with 13% of respondents saying they will spend more than $1,000 compared with 8% in 2014.

"With the buying power of Hispanics, retailers should be more focused than ever on attracting this lucrative segment of the population to their brands," said Monica Escaleras, Ph.D., director of the BEPI.

Another indication of an improving economy, Escaleras noted, can be found in the 5% increase among Hispanics who said they would use cash for their purchases, up to 64% from 59% in 2014. Females are more likely to use cash than males (69% to 58%), while Hispanics in the northeast are significantly more likely to pay for their holiday purchases with credit (45% compared to 25% nationally).

Mother's Day Spending Set for Growth

American consumers were expected to spend an average of $173 on Mother's Day this year, up almost $10 (6%) from last year's total and the highest figure in the survey's 12-year history, according to the latest survey for the National Retail Foundation conducted by Prosper Insights & Analytics.

Total spending is projected to reach $21.2 billion, representing a 6.6% rise from last year's $19.9 billion. The survey finds greeting cards to be the most popular planned gift (with 80% planning a purchase), followed by flowers (67.2%) and special outings (54.2%).

Department stores (33.4%) top the list of shopping destinations, ahead of specialty stores (28.2%), online (25%) and discount stores (24.8%).

Other research also supports growing spending this year, though to different degrees.

IBISWorld expected average household spending to be $169.21, a 3.8% increase from last year, with total spending reaching $20.8 billion, a modest 1.7% year-over-year increase.

Total spending was expected to be highest for special outings ($4 billion), though the largest year-over-year growth in spending is projected to be for flowers (+4.2% to $2.5 billion).

Like IBISWorld, Brand Keys comes to a total spending figure similar to that of the NRF, with total spending predicted to reach almost $20 billion.

The average per-celebrant spending in Brand Keys' survey is $193, representing a 5% increase from 2014's average. As with the NRF survey, men are expected to significantly outpace women in spending, with cards (95%), brunch/lunch/dinner (88%) and flowers (86%) emerging as the most popular gifts.

The largest increase in gift popularity this year is for meal occasions, up 8% year-over-year in planned purchases.

Easter Spending Expected to Grow Slightly

Total consumer spending on Easter is projected to grow to $16.4 billion this year, slightly higher than last year's projected $15.9 billion but still below 2012-2013 levels, according to the National Retail Federation (NRF).

Eight in 10 adults will celebrate, consistent with last year, but celebrants are expecting to spend a little more this year ($140.62 vs. $137.46).

Candy (87.1%) and food (85.7%) are the items that most celebrants expect to buy this year, as with years past.

Also consistent with prior surveys, discount (58.6%) and department (40.7%) stores are the most likely destinations again this year.

Home/Housing

Americans remain positive about home buying, but are slightly less optimistic than they were in 2013 and 2014. National mover rate remains steady and is still highest among youth, as 21.4% of 18-24-year-olds and 20.7% of 25-30-year-olds did so during the 2013-2014 period.

American renters are growing more confident in the housing markets with more than 12% of current renters (roughly 5.2 million) saying they were planning to buy a house in the next year, an almost 25% jump from the same time last year when 4.2 million renters said they had plans to buy within 12 months. More than half of homeowners (57%) planned to spend money on home improvement projects, with the most popular focusing on the outdoors (43%). Bathroom remodels (29%) and kitchen remodels (26%) also remain popular.

Homeowners Wary of Housing Market's Future

Homeowners feel great about the current state of the housing market, but for the first time are less optimistic about the future, according to the Zillow Housing Confidence Index (ZHCI).

The survey asked 10,000 renters and homeowners about the condition of their local real estate market, their expectations for home value growth and affordability in the future, and their aspirations for homeownership. Past surveys found homeowners feeling exuberant about the future, with 5.2 million renters saying they planned to buy this year.

The percentage of renters who say they plan to buy a home in the next year fell from 12.1% to 11.4% in the first six months of this year, and a smaller percentage of those surveyed said it was a good time to buy. The percentage of those surveyed who believe people who have recently bought a home will be better off in 10 years fell from 61% to 59%.

"The housing market is slowing down, and Americans' confidence in the future of the market is understandably fading a bit, too," said Zillow Chief Economist Dr. Svenja Gudell. "Despite remaining quite confident overall, homeowners are less confident about the future than they are about the present. Seeing still stronger than normal home value appreciation in markets like San Francisco and Seattle might remind them of the last housing bubble. But the good news is things are leveling off with no crash in sight. If incomes rise to keep up with home values – and that's a big if – people can count on homeownership in their future, even in hot markets."

Home value growth has slowed in almost all housing markets this year, giving homebuyers some breathing room.

In those markets with marked slowdowns, many more buyers are looking to buy their first home. For example, eight percent of Philadelphia renters said they planned to buy within a year in the January survey, when home values were rising at a 3.1% annual rate.

In July, when Philadelphia home values were flat, 18% said they planned to buy within a year. And many of those new potential buyers are millennials. Just one percent of 18- to 34-year-old Philadelphia renters surveyed in January planned to buy within a year, but that had increased to 23% in the July survey.

The opposite occurred in markets where home value growth, despite having slowed overall, is still well above national norms. Here, renters are less optimistic about their buying prospects. In San Francisco, 18% of 18- to 34-year-old renters planned to buy a home within a year when asked in January.

At that point, San Francisco home values were rising at a 7.9% annual rate. In July, home values were up 11% year-over-year, and only 5% of millennial renters surveyed then said they planned to buy within a year.

In January, 45% of all households surveyed in San Francisco said it was a good time to buy a home, and 40% said it was a bad time. In July, the numbers had flipped: 40% said it was a good time, and 46% said it was a bad time to buy.

Similar patterns played out in technology boom towns Seattle, San Jose and Denver as home values there kept soaring.

Despite high home values in San Jose, the Silicon Valley market was ranked first among 20 markets for housing confidence. Homeownership aspirations there, however, ranked behind more affordable metros: Atlanta, Miami, and Las Vegas.

Seattle rose from number 10 to number two for housing confidence overall, and those surveyed expressed higher expectations for the housing market in the future. Denver, too, rose from number eight to number three, fueled by both renters and owners feeling great about the market and expecting growth, even if they are less confident about their own ability to buy.

The ZHCI is derived from the U.S. Housing Confidence Survey (HCS), which polls 10,000 homeowners and renters about housing market conditions, expectations for the future and their attitudes toward homeownership in general, across 20 of the large metro areas in the United States.

"In the eyes of households in 17 of the 20 metropolitan areas, the outlook for the real estate market has dimmed since the start of 2015," said Terry Loebs, Founder of Pulsenomics. "Given the out-sized impact of homeownership on personal balance sheets and its interplay with the aspirations and behaviors of U.S. consumers, if this downshift in housing expectations persists, it could portend a longer period of price deceleration and more sluggish consumer spending than some people are currently expecting."

Views of Home Buying Climate Slightly Less Positive in U.S.

Americans remain positive about home buying, but are slightly less optimistic than they were in 2013 and 2014.

Presently, 69% believe it is a good time to buy a house, down from an average 74% during the two years prior, but similar to what Gallup measured from 2009-2012.

Americans are more confident about purchasing a house now than they were between 2006 (when home values stopped rising and interest rates increased) and 2008 (after the housing bubble burst). In those years, just over half endorsed home buying.

The most recent results are based on Gallup's annual economy and Personal Finance survey.

The slightly less positive views of buying a home may have been influenced by lackluster home sales earlier this year, as many parts of the country experienced unusually cold weather.

The newest data on home sales, released last week, show there was a surge in sales of existing homes in March.

Since 1978, Americans have generally been optimistic about the home-buying climate, with majorities saying it is a good time to buy even in times when the economy struggles, including after the housing bubble burst.

Thus, the measure likely reflects the value Americans put on homeownership in addition to their views of the prevailing housing market.

Although Americans' perceptions of real estate as the best long-term investment sank considerably during the recent recession, prior to that it was the clear leader of four possible choices, and more recently, it has returned to the top spot.

Confidence that it is a good time to buy a home has dropped the most since 2013-2014 among Americans residing in the Western part of the country, with 64% now saying this, down from an average 75%.

There were smaller drops among those living in the East and South, while views in the Midwest are steady if not up slightly.

National Mover Rate Remains Steady; Still Highest Among Youth

The national mover rate between 2013 and 2014 was 11.5%, or 37 million people aged 1 and older, according to the latest data from the US Census Bureau.

That figure is in line with recent years, hovering between 11.5 and 12.5% since 2008, and is down from about 1 in 5 people when the survey began in 1948. Youth continued to be the most likely to move, as 21.4% of 18-24-year-olds and 20.7% of 25-34-year-olds did so during the 2013-2014 period.

The Census Bureau notes that suburban migration continues, with suburbs having a net gain of 2.2 million movers, while principal cities had a net loss of 1.7 million.

As expected, renters also continued to be the most likely to move, with almost one-quarter (24.5%) living elsewhere the year period.

By contrast, the mover rate among those living in owner-occupied housing units was 5%.

Confidence in U.S. Housing Market On The Rise, Especially Among Renters

American renters are growing more confident in the housing markets, and more than 5 million are planning to buy a home this year, according to the Zillow Housing Confidence Index (ZHCI).

More than 12% of current renters nationwide – roughly 5.2 million – said they plan to buy in the next year, an almost 25% jump from the same time last year, when 4.2 million renters said they had plans to buy within 12 months.

Thanks to historically low mortgage interest rates and home values below peak levels, buyers can expect to spend about 15% of their monthly income on a mortgage payment, compared to 22% historically, according to Zillow research.

Typical renters should expect to pay 30% of their income to rent, compared to 25% a generation ago.

"As home affordability continues to look great and rental affordability looks abysmal, many current renters clearly seem to be re-thinking their attitudes toward homeownership, and are expressing more confidence in the overall housing market as a result," said Zillow Chief Economist Dr. Stan Humphries. "But while this confidence is heartening, it's important to inject a note of reality here: Not all renters who want to buy this year will be successful. Saving a down payment, qualifying for a mortgage and finding an affordable home to buy all remain formidable challenges for many."

Among all renters surveyed nationwide, 59.7% said they think buying a home is the best long-term investment a person can make, compared to 56.9% at the same time last year. This improved long-term outlook was especially evident among younger renters. Among all 18- to 34-year-old renters, 66.2% said owning a home was the best long-term investment, compared to 61.4% last year.

The index is measured on a 100-point scale, with readings more than 50 indicating general confidence.

Overall, housing market confidence is rising more quickly among renters than homeowners. Among only homeowners, headline confidence rose 3.7 points year-over-year, to 70.6 in January.

Among renters only, overall confidence rose 4.4 points in the past year, to 62.4. Confidence among all owners and renters rose 3.6 points, to 67.4.

Although survey respondents in most markets said they expected home value appreciation to slow in 2015, in all areas they also said they expected home value growth to exceed the rate of inflation by an average of more than 2%.

During the past year, consumer expectations for long-term home value growth have increased. Consumers now expect homes to appreciate over the next 10 years by slightly more than what is expected by experts – and at a faster rate than before the housing bubble.

"This latest increase in The U.S. Housing Confidence Index confirms that prevailing sentiments and expectations among consumers concerning their local real estate market–important economic factors not reflected in widely-followed consumer confidence indexes–continue to improve and bode well for the U.S. economy," said Terry Loebs, Founder of Pulsenomics.

"Renter aspirations for homeownership are on the rise in most cities. More homeowners are recognizing restoration and growth in the value of what for most of them is their largest asset by far–their home. In every market surveyed, both renters and homeowners expect the annual growth rate of local home values to handily beat the rate of inflation within the broader economy over the coming decade. These insights should remove any lingering doubt that the U.S. housing market's foundation is now solid enough to withstand The Fed's monetary policy liftoff."

Homeowners Ready to Spend on Renovations in 2015

The home improvement industry continues to regain strength as many homeowners are looking to complete home remodeling or maintenance projects this year. In fact, more than half of homeowners (57%) plan to spend money on home improvement projects, according to an annual survey by LightStream, an online lending division of SunTrust Banks, Inc.

The most popular projects will focus on the outdoors, with 43% investing in improvements including decks, patios, or landscape remodels. Bathroom remodels (29%) and kitchen remodels (26%) also remain popular.

Updating a home's look, features and technology are driving 52% of renovation plans, followed closely by repairs (49%). Interestingly, family needs across generations are also motivating change: five percent say they are remodeling to suit a growing family and three percent are accommodating aging parents.

But just how much are homeowners willing to spend on enhancements?

More than one third (36%) plan to invest $5,000 or more, with a solid 18% spending more than $10,000.

When it comes to paying for these projects, more than half of homeowners say they will tap savings (59%). Many plan to use credit cards (30%).

Seven percent will look to secure a home improvement loan. Home equity lines of credit are also cited as a financing option (9%).

According to the second quarter *2014 Zillow Negative Equity Report*, nearly 35% of homeowners do not have sufficient equity in their homes to leverage.

Some homeowners, even when using savings, choose to finance part of their renovations if it makes financial sense. Like four percent of those surveyed who are planning pools this year, Michael and Michelle Flick had long anticipated enhancing their backyard and had saved for a pool.

They planned to add an enclosure as a "phase two project," once they rebuilt their savings.

New Movers' Most Common Service Provider Changes

One-third of all internet (33%) and cable TV (32%) subscribers who move change their provider, according to an Epsilon survey of 963 households that recently moved.

That's not as bad as the number who change their water provider (41%) but consumers don't have a choice as to whom their water provider is, while they clearly have a choice about which internet and cable TV service to use.

The most popular reasons for moving are to have more space (22%), be in a new neighborhood (18%) and be closer to family (18%).

Movers' present opportunities for marketers, as 75% of owners and 57% of renters reported making purchases related to their move, with furniture the most popular type.

Interestingly, almost 1 in 10 cell phone owners said they had switched providers.

Insurance

While some people decide what insurance to get based on reputation, some people are turning to reviews on social media. Some 21% of property and casualty insurance holders surveyed across 14 countries say they have read reviews posted by other people on social media regarding their insurance claims experiences.

Customers continue to report significantly higher satisfaction rates with credit unions than with banks. One in five insured Americans avoid seeing a doctor due to fear of cost.

1 in 6 Insurance Policy Holders Base Buying Decisions On Claims Found on Social Media

Some 21% of property and casualty insurance holders surveyed across 14 countries say they have read reviews posted by other people on social media regarding their insurance claims experiences.

Another 22% plan to do so in the next two years according to a new report from Accenture.

Furthermore, 17% say they've based their buying decisions on a comparison of others' claims experiences.

An additional 24% will do so in the next two years.

Separately, the report finds that 30% of respondents are very (5%) or quite (25%) likely to switch providers in the next 12 months.

That figure is far higher (65%) among those who have been dissatisfied with a claim they've filed

Customer Satisfaction with Finance and Insurance Sector

Customers continue to report significantly higher satisfaction rates with credit unions (an index score of 85 on a 100-point scale) than with banks (76), according to the ACSI's latest report on the industry.

As for insurance, life (80) and property and casualty (79) carriers outperform health insurance carriers (70) in satisfaction.

The health insurance industry has the 4th lowest index score of the 43 industries tracked.

Survey Reveals 1 in 5 Insured Americans Avoid Seeing Doctor Due to Fear of Cost

Approximately two in five insured Americans (38%) do not have a good understanding of which healthcare services are covered under their current plan, according to an online survey by Harris Poll on behalf of SCIO Health Analytics.

One in five insured Americans, or roughly 44 million people, have avoided visiting a doctor for a general health concern within the past 12 months because of cost concerns.

The online poll surveyed more than 2,000 U.S. adults aged 18 and older about their general sentiments around the Affordable Care Act (ACA) or Obamacare, healthcare costs and their overall understanding of the healthcare system, as well as services covered under their plan.

Approximately half the U.S. adults (117 million) have at least one chronic condition, of which 14% of (or 16.4 million) have avoided a doctor's visit in the past 12 months because of cost concerns. While chronic conditions such as heart disease, asthma, and diabetes are generally incurable, they can be managed through early detection, improved lifestyle and treatment.

"These findings are particularly relevant at this time as millions of Americans are once again deciding their annual healthcare benefit options through Open Enrollment," said Siva Namasivayam, CEO, SCIO Health Analytics. "While Americans are spending more time researching health plans, the survey reveals a significant knowledge gap in the specifics of their health care options that may eventually lead to unnecessary risks and costs."

Namasivayam warned that the implications of these findings are even more staggering when you consider treatment costs for Americans with chronic conditions are already around $277 billion annually.

Avoiding medical treatment for these conditions can lead to an increased risk of complications, emergency room visits, hospitalizations, readmissions, work absenteeism and disability that could potentially drive healthcare costs even higher and cripple an already over- burdened system.

When asked how their healthcare situation has changed since the introduction of the Affordable Care Act:

- 41% of Americans say they have spent more time researching what is covered by insurance plans (either in their own plan or other plans);
- 60% of Americans say they do not have a better understanding of the healthcare system despite the media coverage and public/political discourse around Obamacare; and
- Among those insured, 44% did not know the out of pocket costs/co-pay for prescription drugs, and 61% did not know the costs for urgent care/walk-in clinic visits.

The survey also discovered that age and gender play a role in understanding healthcare costs and services.

Among insured adults, 48% of those aged 18-34 say they lack a good understanding of what healthcare services are covered under their plan, compared to 27% of those aged 65 and older.

Younger insurance holders, especially men, are also much more likely to be cost-conscious when visiting the doctor.

When asked if they avoided visiting the doctor for a general health concern in the past 12 months because of cost concerns, 40% of insured men aged 18-34 answered yes, compared to 27% of insured women in the same age group responded the same (compared to an overall average of 20% for all adults age 18+).

How do Americans want to receive health plan information? According to the survey:

- 62% (the majority) say they would likely be better able to understand their health plan information using the websites offered by their healthcare plan provider;
- 41% would be likely to better understand their health plan information using member phone support offered by their healthcare plan provider;

- 37% of U.S. adults say they get information about healthcare costs and services from their insurance company; and
- 31% get information about healthcare costs and services from their doctor.

Millennials

Millennials tend to get grouped together in one category, but it turns out that the regions in which they live may play a part in how they act. More than 75% of American Millennials would classify themselves as financially responsible and generally do not spend beyond their means.

However, there are some affluent Millennials (those living in households with annual income of at least $100,000). Those Millennials are loyal to their financial institutions. Even though Millennials are usually considered to be more tech-savvy, the majority of smartphone-owning Millennials say most of their retail browsing occurs in store.

Different Regions Splurge On Different Things

Millennials living in Maine, New Hampshire, Massachusetts and Connecticut spend the most on coffee, with those in Maine – the most caffeine-addicted state – spending a remarkable $307 a year on average.

According to the study, which analyzed user data from the past year to see exactly how people born between the late eighties and early 2000 spend their money on things considered 'vices', the Northeast is also home to the millennials who drink the most alcohol.

Mississippi, Iowa, Alabama, South Dakota and West Virginia spend the least on alcohol.

When it comes to fast food, however, the geographic trends are completely opposite.

Twenty-somethings in Oklahoma are the biggest spender on fast food by far, shelling out around $1,194 a year. In fact, more than two-thirds of Oklahomans buy fast food at least once a week.

In second place is Kansas, where millennials spend $1,040 a year at fast food chains, followed by Texas, Virginia and Maryland.

Adversely, nearly all of the states that spend the least on fast food are located in the Northeast.

Vermont is on the very bottom of the list, where millennials only spend about $431 a year. Rounding out the bottom five are Connecticut, New York, Pennsylvania and Montana.

American Adults' Feelings of Financial Responsibility, by Age

Three-quarters of American Millennials (18-34) feel that they are financially responsible and generally do not spend beyond their means, according to results from an Ipsos and Wells Fargo survey.

However, Millennials are less likely than adults ages 55 and older (87%) to feel financially responsible, and are about twice as likely to say they tend to spend their money and not think twice about it (36% vs. 19%).

The survey also finds that Millennials (69%) are significantly less likely than adults aged 55 and up (87%) to know and understand the financial process involved in the purchase of a home, presumably as they're less likely to have been through that process.

45% of 18-24-Year-Olds in U.S. Are Part of a Minority Group

Asian-Americans were the fastest-growing minority group in the U.S. last year for the third consecutive year, according to the Census Bureau in newly-released estimates.

Indeed, Asian-Americans' population growth rate increased from the prior year, up 3.2% to 20.3 million as of July 1, 2014. The Hispanic population grew by a relatively smaller 2.1% (equal to the previous year's growth rate), but to a much larger 55.4 million.

In fact, Hispanics accounted for almost 17.4% of the population as of July 2014.

Other race or ethnic groups also grew between July 2013 and 2014:

- The African-American population grew by 1.3% to 45.7 million;
- The number of Native Americans and Alaska Natives increased by 1.4% to slightly more than 6.5 million; and
- The Native Hawaiian and Other Pacific Islanders population grew by 2.3% to 1.5 million.

As a result of those figures, the U.S.' minority population (all groups other than non-Hispanic single-race whites), climbed to almost 121 million people, accounting for 37.9% of the total population.

The non-Hispanic white-alone population was the only one to have more deaths than births between 2013 and 2014. That population is much older than the minority population; the median age of the non-Hispanic white-alone population was 43.1 years, while it was 28.5 for Hispanics and under 35 for all other races save non-Hispanic Asians (36.4).

The relative youth of the minority population means that for the first time, a majority (50.2%) of children under 5 belong to a minority group. Looking at various age groups, the data indicates that:

- Some 48.1% of Americans under the age of 18 are minorities (any group other non-Hispanic single-race whites);
- Minorities represent 45.5% of 14-17-year-olds;
- Minorities comprise 44.9% of the 18-24 bracket;
- Some 42.3% of Americans aged 25-44 belong to a group other than non-Hispanic whites;
- Fewer than one-third (31%) of Americans aged 45-64 are minorities; and
- About 1 in 5 Americans aged 65+ (21.7%) or 85+ (17.7%) are minorities.

Affluent Millennials Say They're Loyal To Their Financial Institutions

Affluent Millennials are open to non-financial brands, finds a report from LinkedIn conducted by Ipsos that looks specifically at affluents in the U.S. At the same time, once they become customers with a financial institution, they're considerably more likely than their Gen X counterparts to claim loyalty to it.

The subset of affluents examined, were defined as those living in households with investable assets in excess of $100,000.

(A separate definition of affluents – those living in households with annual income of at least $100,000 – finds that 28% of the U.S. adult population qualifies, with 22% of these being Millennials aged 18-32. Two-thirds of those qualified on the basis of their parents' income rather than their own.)

Affluent Millennials in particular provide both opportunities and challenges for traditional financial brands, according to the LinkedIn study results.

For example, 69% of affluent Millennials reported being open to financial offerings from non-financial brands, compared to 47% of affluent Gen Xers.

At the same time, 47% of affluent Millennials said they are "very" loyal and plan to do more business with the financial institutions they work with (compared to 27% of affluent Gen Xers), and another 48% claim to be "somewhat" loyal to them (versus 59% of affluent Gen Xers).

It's worth noting that as a subset of the 1,500+ survey population, affluents may be a relatively small sample, so while the results are thought-provoking, the comparisons may not be statistically significant.

Nevertheless, affluent Millennials are also more likely than their older counterparts to consider their financial institutions a one-stop shop, per the study's results.

Among those with multiple checking accounts, 54% hold them all with the same institution, versus 33% of affluent Gen Xers. Similarly, among multiple account holders, affluent Millennials are more likely than affluent Gen Xers to keep their retirement accounts (42% vs. 24%), brokerage accounts (37% vs. 23%) and savings (39% vs. 23%) accounts with the same brand.

While that may present opportunities for traditional brands, the report also suggests that there is a "very high risk" of traditional brands losing out to outsider brands.

Trust can be a differentiator, as the report's authors link affluent Millennials' higher degree of loyalty to their higher level of trust in their current financial institutions.

LinkedIn has some other suggestions for the factors that matter to affluent Millennials: a strong and positive social presence; a relationship with the company; influence of family and friends' relationship with the company; and the company's purpose (such as a social mission).

In other interesting study results:

- Affluent Millennials appear to want to perform their own research, make investment decisions and execute trades (in comparison with Gen Xers), but at the same time are more likely to consider a financial advisor a must-have.
- Affluent Millennials (27%) are more likely than Millennials or Gen Xers (18-19%) to believe that in the future banks will no longer be primary financial institutions. They're also more likely to predict a cashless society and a sharing-based economy.
- Affluent Millennials have loftier goals than affluent Gen Xers, being 3 times more likely to want to start a charitable foundation (19% vs. 6%) and start a business (30% vs. 11%). They're also 50% more likely to want to buy a second home (27% vs. 18%).

Smartphone-Owning Millennials Say Most Of Their Retail Browsing Occurs In-Store

With all the hype about e-commerce, it's sometimes easy to forget that it remains a fraction of total retail spending.

Now, new survey results from Adroit Digital show that the retail store is also Millennials' preferred place to browse for retail purchases, even among smartphone owners. Among the 1,000 U.S. and Canadian Millennial smartphone owners surveyed, a majority (57%) reported spending most of their time browsing for retail purchases in-store rather than on a mobile device (15%) or PC (28%).

Also of interest, Millennials were twice as likely to say they *never* (34%) browse online before buying in-store as to say they always (16%) do so.

Millennial Moms Expected to Add $750 Billion to U.S. Economy

With a tap, swipe or click, 13 million Millennial Moms will spend over $750 billion in the U.S. this year. And their economic impacts will only increase as the number of Millennial Moms is expected to at least double over the next decade, according to just-released research by BSM Media.

With the top of the curve still to be reached, knowing the demands and expectations of Millennial Moms will drive even more business growth, likely to historic levels.

Technology use, purchasing behaviors, social trends, voting power and much more are detailed in a new book by marketing to moms expert Maria Bailey, *Millennial Moms, 202 Facts To Help Drive Brands and Sales*. Debuting as an Amazon #1 PR and Marketing "Hottest New Release", the book features an in-depth look at the background and influence of these moms, plus tactics to empower companies that want to tap in to this lucrative consumer group.

What makes Millennial Moms tick?

Social shopping is standard for Millennial Moms. 90% say they take a picture from a store's fitting rooms to garner friends' opinions on a potential clothing purchase.

Millennial Moms carry at least two wireless devices. In fact, the majority totes between three and four devices and over 10% say they always carry five or more tech gadgets.

Millennial Moms are pragmatic. 90% will not purchase a product without reading a review first.

Transparency is a must. More than half of these young mothers rate transparency as "extremely important", trusting brands that are open about their products.

Education and healthcare are the most important political issues for Millennial Moms. Politicians will do well to tap in to the Millennial Mom vote, with an estimated 85% saying they will cast their ballots in the election.

In an easy-to-read format with charts, quick insights and interviews with Millennial Moms, Bailey's new book is a must-read for anyone interested in this unique generation that is the largest cohort in history.

"They are uber-spending, hyper-connected moms who exert massive influence on everything they touch, from push presents to half birthdays and customized everything," explains Bailey, the author of this latest book based on five years of research on Millennial Moms.

"Everyone needs to understand these high tech, value-seeking mothers who are constantly raising the bar and changing the rules."

Millennials' Adult Beverage Choices Evolve as They Mature

With nearly three in 10 U.S. adults being Millennials of legal drinking age, the Millennial generation (born between 1977 and 1992) is a crucial demographic for bev/al marketers.

Donna Hood Crecca, senior director at **Technomic**, calls them "ideal adult beverage consumers. They are open and willing to learn about new styles and flavors of beer, wine and spirits. They are frequent consumers in many retail and restaurant settings, where they balance exploration and trial with loyalty to a few favorite brands that deliver on flavor, quality and price."

Technomic's just-published Special Trends in Adult Beverages Report shows how catering to Millennials can boost profits for all in the bev/al chain. Key findings include:

- **Equal opportunity imbibers:** Millennials are likely to purchase adult beverages at a variety of retail and on-premise venues. This group is also open to engaging in all three adult beverage categories—spirits, wine and beer—as well as a range of different types and flavors of alcohol drinks.
- **Age brings sophistication:** As Millennials age, they are more inclined to buy craft beer and to have a more evolved palate for exploring different varietals and regions of beer and wine.
- **A propensity to drink multiple types of adult beverages on a single occasion:** 30 percent of Millennials consumed more than one type of drink on their most recent on-premise occasion. Primary reasons for switching were a desire to experiment with different beverages or flavors or to try a new drink.
- **Balancing adventure and loyalty**: Historically adventuresome in their drinking habits, Millennials continue to explore, especially in on-premise settings, as they mature. They transfer their new discoveries from restaurant experiences to their retail buying decisions while also balancing curiosity with loyalty to some tried-and-true brands.

Millennial Viewers Most Likely to Feel
TV Show Quality is Improving

Millennials (18-35) may be watching less traditional TV, but those who watch TV tend to be more excited than other generations about shows in general, according to results from a Harris Poll. In fact, among TV viewers, more than three-quarters of Millennials said that there is at least one new/upcoming show that they're really excited about (versus the adult average of 62%), and 61% agreed that shows are getting better and better (versus the average of 47%).

TV viewers who stream shows also tended to be more excited about upcoming shows and the quality of programming.

Separate results from the survey indicate that comedies and sitcoms are easily Millennials' favorite type of programming, while Boomers (51-69) and Matures (70+) tend to prefer news and detective/crime shows.

Half of the adults surveyed said they watch TV via streaming, including 18% who reported watching most (12%) or all (6%) of their TV shows via streaming.

How Are Millennials Using Their Phones?

Roughly 58% of American adults consider themselves addicted to their phone, and that figure rises to 76% among Millennials (18-34), finds Invoca in a recently-released study.

The report shows that amid the numerous activities being performed on phones, calls remain popular – and frequent text messaging remains the most frequent activity performed on a mobile phone by Millennials, with two-thirds using their phone to send messages more than 5 times a day.

The second-most frequent activity is making calls, which 37% of Millennials do more than 5 times a day. After that, one-third update social media with that frequency, while slightly more than one-quarter watch videos (27%), take pictures (27%) and send emails (26%) more than 5 times a day using their phone.

Interestingly, Millennials are more likely than their older counterparts (45+) to make calls with that regularity, as fewer than one-third (29%) of respondents aged 45 and older said they make calls using their mobile phone more than 5 times a day

Overall, respondents to the Invoca survey identified calling as the single most valuable function of their phone, ahead of messaging, social media, email and video.

This has some implications for businesses; in comparing mobile purchases to calls to businesses, the study notes that "sometimes a call is just easier than a click."

In fact, 59% of respondents report calling businesses at least a few times a month, and 42% call a business at least once a week. Additionally, respondents are more than twice as likely to have called a business in the past month (65%) than to have used their phone to fill out a form (24%), and Millennials are three times more likely to call a business (66%) than to use social media to contact one (22%).

What Are Millennials' Most Important Life Aspirations?

Starting a family or spending time with family ranks as the most important of six life goals for a leading 29% of young Americans aged 22-35, closely followed by being happy, which is the top goal for 28% of Americans of this age, according to a study from Navient, the nation's largest student loan provider.

Being debt-free (24%) is also a much greater goal than home ownership or career advancement, per the survey, though the financial health of the respondent appears to have an impact on the ranking of these goals.

The study was based on a survey, conducted by Ipsos, of 3,006 young Americans aged 22-35.

Navient constructed a "financial health index" based on 15 objective and behavioral indicators, then segmented the sample into three groups of financial health based on those index scores. One in 5 respondents were classified as being in "excellent" financial health, with a majority 63% falling in the "good" category and the remaining 17% determined to be in "poor" financial health.

Interestingly enough, Millennials with "excellent" financial health were the most likely to say that being debt-free is their most important life goal, with a leading 32% saying that this is the case.

This group was less likely than average to say that being happy (20% vs. 29%) and being with family (23% vs. 29%) are their most important goals, but put more emphasis on owning a home (20% vs. 12%).

By contrast, for those in "poor" financial health, being happy (33%) is the leading aspiration, followed by being with family (31%) and then being debt-free (27%).

For those in "good" financial health – the largest group – being with family (31%) and being happy (29%) were the top goals, with fewer pointing to being debt-free (20%) or owning a home (11%).

The study also examined respondents' satisfaction with various aspects of their lives. Measured on a 10-point scale (with 10 being the highest level of satisfaction), respondents reported being most satisfied with life (7) and health (7), and least satisfied with their jobs (6.1) and current income (5.6).

However, they appear to be more optimistic about their future in those latter areas, with a 6.6 satisfaction rating for future earnings and a 6.3 rating for career advancement.

Once again, there were some interesting discrepancies when the study segmented satisfaction ratings, this time by the respondent's "most important" goal.

For example, the group of respondents who said that home ownership is their most important goal were more satisfied with all aspects of their lives (including their health, job, income and future prospects) than any other group. Perhaps counting home ownership as one's most important goal requires a general satisfaction with other facets of life?

On the opposite end of the spectrum, those who said that "being happy" is their most important goal rated all aspects of their lives (life, job, health, income, future prospects) lower than any other group, suggesting a link between greater satisfaction in those areas and overall happiness.

Satisfaction with different areas of life also differed by respondent demographics:

Satisfaction with life and health (top-3 box score on the 10-point scale) tended to be above-average for those with an advanced degree, males, those with income of at least $100k, and those employed full-time; and

Not too surprisingly, satisfaction with job- and income-related areas tended to be highest for those with advanced degrees, those working full-time, and those with at least $100k in income.

Amid a host of other data, the study also tracked Millennials' agreement with various financial attitudes and behaviors, finding that the highest level of average agreement was with the following statements:

- "I need time to save up before attending big events (such as a wedding, anniversary, or family reunion)" – average of 3.77 on a 5-point scale;
- "I use a grocery list so as to not overspend" – 3.75;
- "Even if it's a small amount, I can put money away each month" – 3.69;
- "I don't eat out as often as I would like because I don't want to spend the money" – 3.59; and
- "I subscribe to online streaming services (i.e. Netflix, Hulu) rather than cable because they are less expensive" – 3.59.

By contrast, the lowest levels of agreement were for the following statements:

- "I am a member of various clubs in my community" – 2.6;
- "I only buy name-brand clothing" – 2.67;
- "If I have money left over at the end of a pay period, I just have to spend it" – 2.77;
- "I regularly volunteer in my community" – 2.95; and
- "I own the newest model/make of my gadgets; such as smart phones and wearable technology" – 2.96.

Are Brands Getting More Trustworthy?

More than 7 in 10 American adults aged 18-34 agree that the number of visionary brands has increased, according to a recent study from PricewaterhouseCoopers (PwC), and a majority of adults aged 35-54 (64%) and 55-79 (57%) agree, according to the survey results.

However, there is less agreement with trustworthiness, as only a minority (42%) of adults aged 55-79 agree that the number of trustworthy brands has increased.

Still, a majority (56%) of 18-34-year-olds feel there are more trustworthy brands now, an important result given prior research indicating that trustworthiness is the brand attribute most important to Millennials around the world.

In fact, the word "trustworthy" was the one most associated with leader brands among U.S. respondents in PwC's report.

Mobile Devices

Thirty-nine percent of people expect pages to load equally fast on a mobile or laptop/desktop, as opposed to 35% who would wait longer on a mobile device and 26% who would wait longer on a laptop or desktop. Daily time spent by adults with mobile internet grew by 11.3% in 2014.

Ninety percent of U.S. mobile internet time was said to be spent in apps in 2015. Ninety percent of mobile devices have represented the majority of email opens for some time now, but more recent studies have shown that PC users tend to click more than mobile users.

Mobile Accounted For Nearly One-Sixth Of Retail E-Commerce Spending in Q3

Meanwhile, a separate study by comScore found U.S. retail e-commerce spending grew by 15% year-over-year in the third quarter, marking the 20th consecutive quarter of double-digit growth.

Mobile continued to grow at a much faster clip (70%) than desktop (8%), with the latter seeing growth below 10% for the third consecutive quarter.

In sum, mobile accounted for slightly more than 16% of the total retail e-commerce sales of $69.7 billion, up from 14.7% share in Q1.

Consumers Still Value Performance Over Content in the Website Experience

A high-performing website is once again more important to consumers than fresh and updated content, a consistent cross-screen experience and personalized content, finds Limelight Networks in its latest annual "State of the User Experience" study.

Somewhat surprisingly, though, consumers appear to have more patience this year for site load times, with 51.6% willing to wait more than 5 seconds before they get frustrated or leave the site.

That's no longer true for mobile devices, though, as 39% share expect pages to load equally fast on a mobile or laptop/desktop, as opposed to 35% who would wait longer a mobile device and 26% who would wait longer on a laptop or desktop computer.

In other results, one-third of respondents said they leave a page and buy the product from a competitor if they have to wait too long for a page to load when shopping online.

U.S. Adults' Daily Major Media Consumption Estimates

Daily time spent by adults with the mobile internet will grow by 11.3% this year, predicts eMarketer, but growth rates will then drop below the double-digits for the first time, with this attributed to fewer new mobile device users and a limit to the number of activities possible on mobile.

Still, with time spent with traditional media generally declining, by the end of next year adults are projected to spend more time solely with mobile social media than they are with print.

90% of U.S. Mobile Internet Time Said Spent in Apps

Apps continue to dominate U.S. time spent with mobile, says Flurry, reaching 90% of mobile minutes in June 2015, up from 86% share in Q2 2014.

Breaking down mobile internet consumption by app and browser categories, the data shows Facebook's app by itself occupies 19% share of time spent, meaning that it alone accounts for almost twice as much time spent with mobile as browsers.

The study also finds that time spent with gaming apps has shrunk, while mobile users are spending more time with entertainment and messaging/social apps.

It's worth noting that a recent study of mobile programmatic, this time from Smaato, found that mobile web usage is growing quickly on a *global* level and is eating up a greater share (38%) of mobile ad spend.

And another study, from Adobe, indicates that in the US, preference for apps versus the mobile web depends on the task.

Top Reasons for Abandoning a Mobile Transaction

A majority (56%) of U.S. smartphone owning adults have abandoned a mobile transaction, according to Jumio, though this figure is down from 66% in a similar survey conducted in 2013.

Among those who have abandoned a mobile transaction, purchase uncertainty (45%) was the top reason cited, followed by slow load times (36%) and difficulty with navigation (31%).

These usability concerns appear to outweigh security concerns around payment (27%) and personal (26%) information, per the survey's results.

Mobile Email Engagement Grows

Mobile devices have represented the majority of email opens for some time now, but studies have shown that PC users tend to click more than mobile users. That may now be changing, according to the latest quarterly report from Yesmail.

The study demonstrates that what had been a wide gap in click-to-open (CTO) rates between mobile and desktop users has shrunk this year.

For the better part of the past two years, mobile click-to-open rates were roughly 50% lower than comparable rates on desktops, but that gap has halved in recent quarters.

That's the culmination of a trend that has seen mobile CTO rates grow by almost 30% over the past 2 years, while desktop CTO rates have declined by 18%.

Yesmail notes that the growth in mobile CTO means that consumers may not feel the need to re-open a message on a desktop, contributing to the decline in desktop CTO rates.

Indeed, a recent BlueHornet survey of adults aged 18-64 found that, faced with an email on their mobile device that does not display correctly, one-third of consumers would save it until they could read it on a computer.

Data from the Yesmail study suggest that increasing engagement with mobile email is indeed tied to fewer emails lacking mobile optimization.

In Q2, half of all emails sent were responsive, up from 28% a year earlier. Yesmail has previously shown that mobile email CTO rates are significantly higher for brands using responsive emails.

Add all of those trends up, and Yesmail reports that mobile clicks accounted for 46% of all email clicks in Q2, up from 35% share during the year-earlier period, and 27% of email-driven orders (up from 22% in Q2 2014).

Tellingly, smartphones for the first time accounted for the majority of all mobile revenue (53%) and mobile orders (54%) for Yesmail's clients. This shift may be due to the increase in responsive design adoption, as Yesmail has noted in the past that tablets had assumed the lead in mobile email revenue given that they were a more responsive-agnostic device.

It's not just mobile engagement that has grown; Yesmail notes that overall, audiences appear more engaged, even as volume has grown.

Indeed, Yesmail recorded 8 opens per opener in Q2, representing a 17% increase over the past 2 years.

Moreover, the proportion of "never active" subscribers (those who have never opened or clicked on an email) dropped to 68.9%, an all-time low for Yesmail.

One-Quarter of Premium Video Ad Views Occurred on Mobile Devices in Q1

Premium digital video ad views continue to migrate to devices outside of desktops and laptops, according to FreeWheel's latest quarterly report, with strong growth in particular coming from smartphones, which accounted for 17% of overall views, more than double a year earlier.

OTT Devices also demonstrated rapid growth year-over-year, though their 8% share was consistent with the previous quarter.

In other study results:

- Authenticated viewing accounted for 57% of long-form and live monetization for programmers (MVPDs) in Q1, more than double the 25% share from a year earlier;
- OTT devices continue to represent the second-largest share of authenticated ad views, at 19% in Q1;
- Overall video views grew by 40% year-over-year and video ad views by 43%, driven by live and long-form viewing;
- Tablets and OTT devices continue to be used primarily for long-form (20+ minutes) and live viewing, with the opposite true for desktops/laptops and smartphones; and
- Ad completion rates were almost as high for post-roll (72%) as for pre-roll (73%) videos.

Mobile Media Drive Phone Calls to Businesses But Calls Driven By Offline Sources Last Longer, Are Higher Quality

Mobile-only media such as mobile search and display are the source of a majority of phone calls to businesses, according to an Invoca analysis of 32 million phone calls throughout 2014.

But are these media referring high-quality calls?

Looking at the top marketing channels driving calls, the study indicates that mobile search was by far the largest source of calls, referring 45% of the study's sample over the yearlong period.

While the results may be specific to Invoca's platform and therefore not necessarily broadly applicable, it isn't surprising that mobile search is such an influential driver of calls given its convenience and the popularity to click-to-call functionality in search results.

Beyond mobile search were desktop display (11% share of calls) and desktop search (9%), followed by mobile display (8%).

So while mobile trumps desktop by a large margin in search-driven calls, display-referred calls were slightly more the realm of desktop than mobile.

In looking at the discrepancy between search- and display-referred calls, it's worth noting that research released several years ago found that mobile local search ad clicks were most often followed by a phone call, while display ad clicks were most frequently followed by accessing maps and directions.

Returning to the Invoca study, the analysts note that call durations are an indicator of high buyer-intent, such that the duration of a call is a key indicator of call quality.

Mobile trails on this front, with mobile search-referred calls lasting 3 minutes and 58 seconds on average and mobile display-driven calls 2 minutes and 58 seconds, both shorter than the overall average of 4 minutes and 7 seconds.

That may not necessarily reflect low-quality calls, though, instead perhaps being indicative of the on-the-go mentality of mobile callers, whose searches often convert quickly.

Nevertheless, offline channels – which drove just 16% of the calls analyzed – generally averaged longer durations.

Newspaper-referred calls, for example, averaged 6 minutes and 10 seconds, more than a minute longer than desktop display, the best-performing online source.

Calls driven by magazines, direct mail and directories also saw durations higher than the average. As the study authors note, the level of effort in calling from a print ad reflects high buyer intent.

In other interesting study results:

- Tuesdays received the highest volume of phone calls, 48% more than Sundays, which had the lowest;

- One-quarter of calls came from landlines;
- The recreation and leisure and insurance industries had the highest call volume;
- The home services industry had the longest average call duration (6 minutes and 48 seconds), followed by the insurance industry (5 minutes and 26 seconds);
- Notably, while 79% of automotive calls came from offline channels (with TV a prime source), automotive calls lasted just 1 minute and 52 seconds on average;
- Offline sources also accounted for an above-average share (44%) of financial services calls, although mobile search was the single largest source of calls (21%); and
- Radio accounted for 7% of insurance calls (versus 6% of calls overall), with insurance being a key advertising vertical on radio.

Mobile Email CTO Rates 40% Higher
For Brands Using Responsive Design

Mobile email clicks accounted for almost 40% of all email clicks in Q4 2014, according to the latest quarterly report from Yesmail.

Mobile's click share was buoyed by a 20% year-over-year increase in click-to-open rates, from 10.3% in Q4 2013 to 12.6% in Q4 2014.

Yesmail ties that result to an increase in the number of emails using responsive design, as brands exclusively using responsive design in their emails enjoyed a 40% higher mobile CTO than those who didn't use responsive design in any of their campaigns (14.1% vs. 10.1%).

Even so, mobile CTOs continued to trail their desktop equivalents in Q4 (12.6% and 21.6%, respectively), as has been the case for some time. Nevertheless, a mobile email click returned more than double the average revenue as a desktop email click (40 cents and 19 cents, respectively).

In other study results covering year-over-year trends (using a consistent set of marketers):

Mobile conversion rates (purchases resulting from an email click) grew by 70%, while desktop conversion rates dropped by 4%;

Mobile revenues comprised one-fifth of all email-generated revenue, up by one-third from a year earlier;

The share of orders completed on a mobile device increased by 21% to almost one-quarter of all email-generated orders; and

Mobile's average order value (AOV) grew by 28%, twice the rate of growth for desktop AOV.

Estimated Mobile Share of U.S. Organic Search Traffic

Mobile search traffic reportedly grew by 54% year-over-year in Q1 and now represents an estimated 45% share of U.S. organic search traffic, according to a Merkle I RKG analysis of a cross-section of its clients (most heavily represented by the retail sector).

The iPhone (18%) and iPad (12%) alone contributed a combined 30% of organic search traffic, per the report, more than double the share (13%) from Android devices.

Separately, mobile's share of Yahoo search traffic dropped from 50% in Q4 2014 to 43% in Q1, mainly due to increased desktop traffic resulting from the Yahoo-Firefox deal.

At the same time, mobile grew to represent almost half – 47% – of Google organic search traffic, per the study. In fact, Google represented 88.2% of mobile search traffic in Q1 2015, versus about 8 in 10 organic search visits overall.

Desktop search traffic was up 14%. Organic search overall contributed slightly less than 33% of site visits.

Music

Music may be considered universal, but what it's listened to may vary based on ethnicity and age. Roughly 44% of Americans aged 12 and up listen to online radio on a weekly basis, and the percentage of those listening on a monthly basis (53%), cracked the majority threshold for the first time. Music streaming revenues were up 29% in 2014 and surpassed CD sales in the process.

For in-car audio, however, AM/FM Radio is still consumers first choice.

Where Consumers Listen to Music

Multicultural consumers (Hispanics, African-Americans and Asian-Americans) are more digitally connected to music than the total market, per Nielsen data.

They are more likely to typically listen to internet/streaming radio services, on-demand audio and video streaming, and less likely to tune in to regular AM/FM radio.

Yet they spend more annually on CDs ($13) than digital albums ($10) and reserve the largest share of their music-relate budgets for live events – spending an average of $50 on live music annually.

Results of the study also suggest brands can engage with multicultural consumers via music sponsorships.

Online Radio's Reach Continues to Grow

Some 44% of Americans aged 12 and up listen to online radio on a weekly basis, up from 36% last year and 33% the year prior, according to the latest annual "Infinite Dial" report from Edison Research and Triton Digital.

Moreover, the percentage of survey respondents listening to online radio (defined as listening to AM/FM radio stations online and/or listening to streamed audio content available only on the internet) on a monthly basis cracked the majority threshold for the first time, reaching 53% of the 12+ population, up from 47% last year.

No surprise, then, that a recent report from the Radio Advertising Bureau found optimism surrounding radio's digital ad sales growth, expected to be in the double-digit range again this year.

Unlike in years past, though, online radio's rising reach isn't accompanied this year by growing consumption, the Edison Research study finds. Weekly time spent tuned in to online radio averaged 12 hours and 53 minutes among weekly listeners, down almost a half-hour from last year's average of 13 hours and 19 minutes.

That suggests that new weekly listeners this year are lighter consumers than average, though not to a large extent.

While online radio continues to appeal most to youth, this year's increase in reach owes much to the 25-54 demographic. Half of respondents in that group reported having listened to online radio during the prior week, up from 37% in the prior year's survey.

By comparison, 69% of 12-24-year-olds (up from 64%) and 18% of those aged 55 and older (up from 13%) reported having listened during the prior week.

Other findings:

- Pandora remains the clear internet audio leader in terms of brand awareness (75% of respondents aged 12 and up), although iTunes Radio (62%) and iHeartRadio (59%) grew rapidly in awareness from last year;
- Some 34% of survey respondents (54% of those aged 12-24) tuned in to Pandora during the month prior to the survey, compared to 11% each for iHeartRadio and iTunes Radio;
- Among weekly online radio listeners, Smartphone's (73%) have moved ahead of desktops and laptops (61%) to become the clear leader among devices commonly used for listening, with tablets (32%) a ways behind;
- 63% of respondents have at some point used YouTube to watch music videos or listen to music, and 41% did so in the week prior to the survey, up from 55% and 33% last year, respectively;
- Among respondents aged 18 and up who had driven or ridden in a car in the month prior to the survey, AM/ FM radio was the top medium for listening (81%, down from 86% last year), followed by a CD player (55%, down from 61%), MP3 player/owned digital music (38%, up from 31%), online radio (21%, up from 14%) and satellite radio (17%, flat);
- One-third of respondents have never listened to an audio podcast, up from 30% last year, and roughly half of those have listened in the past month;
- Among respondents who say it is "very important" or "somewhat important" to keep-up-to-date with music, AM/FM radio is viewed as the most important source, although YouTube is more important among 12-24- year-olds; and
- This year the internet has supplanted radio as the medium used by the largest share of respondents to first learn about new music.

Music Streaming Revenues Up
29% in 2014, Surpass CD Sales

Digital subscription and streaming revenues grew almost 29% last year to reach roughly $1.87 billion, surpassing sales of CDs ($1.85 billion) in the process, according to a report from the Recording Industry Association of America (RIAA).

Streaming revenues comprised 27% of all industry revenues, up from 21% a year earlier. Physical shipment revenues (of which CDs represented 82%) accounted for 32% share and digital downloads a leading 37% share.

The report notes that paid streaming subscriptions grew by 26% year-over-year to reach 7.7 million.

Separated by $2 billion in revenues as recently as 2011, streaming revenues have closed the gap with digital download revenues and are now just $0.7 billion behind ($1.9 billion and $2.6 billion, respectively).

Overall, music industry revenues dropped by 0.5% to slightly below $7 billion.

AM/FM Radio Still Consumers' First Choice For In-Car Audio

Among American adults who use audio players in the car, two-thirds first turn on the AM/FM radio when listening to music, reports Ipsos in a newly-released study, while roughly 1 in 7 (14%) tune in to Sirius XM and about 1 in 10 (11%) turn on their CD player.

Preference for AM/FM radio is consistent across age groups, gender, and household income levels, though appears to be higher among females and older consumers.

Interestingly, 18-34-year-olds are more likely to first play a CD (15%) than to listen to streaming digital audio services or a digital music collection (10%).

How American Spend on Music

A slight majority (52%) of Americans' spending on music goes to live events, says Nielsen in reporting the results of a recent survey. Admission to live music concerts represents the largest share of music-related expenditures; at almost one-third (32%) of all spending, concert admissions alone are on par with combined spending on physical forms of music (13%), digital tracks/albums (11%) and music gift cards (7%).

While there's roughly an equal weight in overall spending between live events and recorded music, Millennials (18-34) and Hispanics skew more towards live events. For Millennials, 64% of all music-related spending goes to live events, while for Hispanics events account for 61% of all expenditures. Both groups over-index in share of dollars spent on music festivals and admission to DJ events, while under-indexing on satellite radio subscriptions and gift cards.

(That doesn't necessarily mean they spend less on those formats when considering absolute dollars. After all, Hispanics report spending 50% more on music than the average consumer, per the report.)

As the results show, music festivals are a particularly influential part of Millennials' music-related spending, and the survey indicates that Millennials comprise 44% of all festival goers. In examining the reasons why fans (not just Millennials) choose a festival, the report reveals that the line-up (86%), proximity to where they live (68%) and price (62%) are the chief influencers, though half choose based on where their friends and about half go to the same festival each year.

Previous research from Nielsen has shown that music sponsorships can provide opportunities for marketers: 43% of music fans surveyed said they notice when a brand or product sponsors an artist or brand. A significant share of fans also said they would be persuaded to try a product based on the brands' promotional activities.

Live events, performances and concerts appear to be a growing source of music discovery for Americans. This year about 1 in 8 (12%) respondents aged 13 and older said they discover music from live events, up from 7% last year. Still, radio (AM/FM or satellite) continues to be the most common method by which Americans discover music, cited by 61% of respondents. Word-of-mouth is also popular, as friends and relatives are a source of music discovery for 45% of respondents, including 65% of teens (13-17).

In other highlights from the Nielsen report:

- ✓ Three-quarters of survey respondents said they listen to music online during a typical week;
- ✓ Almost half – 44% – listen to music on a Smartphone during a typical week;
- ✓ Cost (83%) and ease of use (82%) rank as the most important factors when selecting a streaming music service;
- ✓ The top reasons respondents are unlikely to subscribe to music streaming services is that they are too expensive (46%) and they can stream music for free (42%); but
- ✓ Almost 1 in 10 of those who don't currently pay for streaming indicate that they are likely to subscribe within the next 6 months.

Netflix

Since becoming a streaming service, Netflix has become increasingly popular. The amount of people watching on TV and the streaming hours are rising consistently.

The way people watch is changing, too. The number of U.S. households relying on dedicated set-top/plug-in devices (a.k.a. digital media players) continues to grow.

Streaming hours are also rising, up 350% since 2011. Unsurprisingly, Netflix is the top brand among Millennials (Amazon might be No. 1 overall, but you don't hear the phrase Amazon and [insert verb here]like you do Netflix and chill). Netflix did top Amazon in one category though brand loyalty.

How People Watch Netflix on TV

The number of U.S. households relying on dedicated set-top/plug-in devices (a.k.a. digital media players) to watch Netflix on a TV set continue to grow, according to a new GfK study.

By contrast, videogame systems — while still the most common hardware for Netflix viewing on a TV screen — are used much less than they were three years ago.

The study shows that 28% of those who stream Netflix on a TV used a digital media payer (such as Chromecast, Apple TV, or Roku) to do so; nearly double the 2013 level (15%) and about five times the 2011 statistic (6%).

The spike comes as ownership of the players among all homes has increased tenfold — from 2% to 21% — since 2010.

Some of today's higher-end TV sets, which have streaming capabilities built in, have also become popular — with use of buy-in streaming reported by 28% of those who watch Netflix on TV — up from 20% a year ago and 13% in 2011.

Conversely, reports of watching Netflix on TV through a videogame system have dropped to 43% — down 5 percentage points from 2013 and almost 20 point below the 2011 level (62%).

The new reports shows far-reaching generational differences in how people access Netflix.

Generations X and Y are twice as likely as Baby Boomers to use a video game system to watch Netflix on TV.

Capabilities built into TV sets are highly preferred by Gen Y Netflix viewers, and both Generations X and Y show strong use of digital media players.

Netflix Streaming Hours Up 350%

Netflix streaming has increased 350% during the last 10 quarters, according to new research from The Diffusion Group (TGD).

Netflix subscribers' total streaming hours have almost tripled in the United States from 1.8 billion in Q4 2011 to 5.1 billion in Q2 2014, and subscriber streaming internationally has increased from 28.3 to an estimated 46.6 hours per month.

U.S. consumption remains responsible for the majority of total worldwide streaming hours, even though the rate of international streaming growth has outpaced that of domestic streaming.

In Q3 2011, U.S. Netflix subscribers made up 94% of the worldwide total, while in Q2 2014 the U.S. stake of total worldwide subscribers fell to 72%, a direction expected to extend as Netflix executes its international expansion strategy.

"When Netflix first launched in 1998 as an innovative DVD-by-mail subscription service it would have been difficult to imagine that, not only would it pass HBO to become the largest premium TV/movie subscription in the U.S., but that it would be ramping up a formidable international streaming business," notes Bill Niemeyer, TDG Senior Adviser and author of the new report.

Niemeyer says this is all the more remarkable given that Netflix launched its streaming service in 2007.

...But Among Millennials, Netflix is No. 1

While amazon.com topped the brand buzz rankings among US adults overall last year, Netflix topped the charts among Millennials; according to YouGov's, the online pollster, segment rankings.

Of note, while Nike didn't crack the top 10 among the adult population at-large, it came in fifth among Millennials while taking the top ranking among African- Americans and the second spot with Hispanics.

Also interesting: YouTube's ranking among the Millennial generation (#4) was actually 2 spots lower its overall standing among adults.

Meanwhile, Samsung enjoyed strong buzz scores among minority groups, coming in first for Hispanics and second for African-Americans.

The top five brands for Millennials:

1. Netflix (35.2);
2. Amazon.com (34.5);
3. Google (34.4);
4. YouTube (34.0);
5. Nike (32.6);

The top buzz for African Americans:

1. Nike (41.3);
2. Samsung (37.2);
3. Google (37.0);
4. YouTube (36.0);
5. Dove (35.8)

The top buzz for Hispanics:

1. Samsung (33.4);
2. Nike (34.0);
3. YouTube (33.9);
4. Netflix (33.5);
5. amazon.com (32.7)

Top U.S. Markets by SVOD Penetration

Washington, DC and San Francisco are the leading U.S. markets by subscription video-on-demand (SVOD) penetration, with 52% of households in each having access to Netflix, Amazon Instant Video or Hulu Plus as of November 2014, according to a recent study from Nielsen.

The study notes that 42% of U.S. households have access to at least one service, with Netflix remaining easily in the lead (36% of households), ahead of Amazon (13%) and Hulu (6%).

Some services are more popular in some markets than others: San Francisco (48%) edges Washington DC (47%) in Netflix penetration, while Washington, DC (24%) takes the lead over Seattle (23%) in Amazon Instant prime penetration, with San Francisco further back (18).

Seattle, meanwhile, has the largest share (9%) of homes with access to Hulu Plus.

Netflix Tops Amazon in Brand Loyalty

Netflix is this year's brand loyalty leader, rising 11 spots from last year's results to take the mantle from Amazon, reports Brand Keys in its latest annual loyalty study, which ranked customer engagement and loyalty for 753 brands across 65 categories of loyalty engagement.

Amazon (for tablets), Apple (for both smartphones and tablets) and Facebook (for social networking) rounded out the top 5, with these brands among the ones most likely to meet consumer expectations for their respective categories. Of the top 20 brands, 17 (or 85%) are related to digital technology or social networking.

Indeed, social networking is the most highly represented category among the top 100 brands (with 13), followed by automotive (10) and traditional retail (9). That's a dramatic change from 5 years ago, when personal care led with 13 brands in the top 100, followed by cosmetics (13) and traditional retail (10).

Among brands new to the top 100 this year are Uber (#21) and HBO GO (#78). KIA generated the biggest improvement in ranking (up 19 spots), while HTC suffered from the biggest free fall (down 66 spots).

Online Line Radio

Listening to music has definitely gotten easier with the birth of online radio such as Spotify, Pandora, and Apple Music. And it only continues to grow.

Some 44% of Americans aged 12 and up listen to online radio on a weekly basis, up from 36% last year and 33% the year prior.

Online Radio's Reach Continues to Grow

Some 44% of Americans aged 12 and up listen to online radio on a weekly basis, up from 36% last year and 33% the year prior, according to the latest annual "Infinite Dial" report from Edison Research and Triton Digital.

Moreover, the percentage of survey respondents listening to online radio (defined as listening to AM/FM radio stations online and/or listening to streamed audio content available only on the internet) on a monthly basis cracked the majority threshold for the first time, reaching 53% of the 12+ population, up from 47% last year.

No surprise, then, that a recent report from the Radio Advertising Bureau found optimism surrounding radio's digital ad sales growth, expected to be in the double-digit range again this year.

Unlike in years past, though, online radio's rising reach isn't accompanied this year by growing consumption, the Edison Research study finds. Weekly time spent tuned in to online radio averaged 12 hours and 53 minutes among weekly listeners, down almost a half-hour from last year's average of 13 hours and 19 minutes.

That suggests that new weekly listeners this year are lighter consumers than average, though not to a large extent.

While online radio continues to appeal most to youth, this year's increase in reach owes much to the 25-54 demographic. Half of respondents in that group reported having listened to online radio during the prior week, up from 37% in the prior year's survey.

By comparison, 69% of 12-24-year-olds (up from 64%) and 18% of those aged 55 and older (up from 13%) reported having listened during the prior week.

Other findings:
• Pandora remains the clear internet audio leader in terms of brand awareness (75% of respondents aged 12 and up), although iTunes Radio (62%) and iHeartRadio (59%) grew rapidly in awareness from last year;

• Some 34% of survey respondents (54% of those aged 12-24) tuned in to Pandora during the month prior to the survey, compared to 11% each for iHeartRadio and iTunes Radio;

• Among weekly online radio listeners, smartphones (73%) have moved ahead of desktops and laptops (61%) to become the clear leader among devices commonly used for listening, with tablets (32%) a ways behind;

• 63% of respondents have at some point used YouTube to watch music videos or listen to music, and 41% did so in the week prior to the survey, up from 55% and 33% last year, respectively;

• Among respondents aged 18 and up who had driven or ridden in a car in the month prior to the survey, AM/FM radio was the top medium for listening (81%, down from 86% last year), followed by a CD player (55%, down from 61%), MP3 player/owned digital music (38%, up from 31%), online radio (21%, up from 14%) and satellite radio (17%, flat);

- One-third of respondents have never listened to an audio podcast, up from 30% last year, and roughly half of those have listened in the past month;
- Among respondents who say it is "very important" or "somewhat important" to keep-up-to-date with music, AM/FM radio is viewed as the most important source, although YouTube is more important among 12-24- year-olds; and
- This year the internet has supplanted radio as the medium used by the largest share of respondents to first learn about new music.

Facebook Offers Draw Youth to Local Businesses

Local deals and offers on Facebook have a strong pull with youth says G/O Digital in a new survey fielded among 18-29 year-olds who own at least a smartphone or tablet and a desktop computer, who have an interest in making purchases from local/small businesses.

Of the various Facebook marketing tactics identified, respondents were most likely to attribute influence to Facebook offers that can be redeemed at a local store.

When presented with seven Facebook marketing tactics and asked which would be more likely to impact them to make an in-store purchase from a local or small business, a majority 40% of respondents cited Facebook offers which can be redeemed at a local store, distantly trailed by promoted posts (12%); photos/videos that encourage choice of favorite products, styles and colors (11%); and loyalty app promotions (10%), among others.

Similarly, the largest share of respondents cited Facebook offers when asked which marketing tactic would most influence them to visit the website, mobile site or app of a local/small business.

Overall, 84% of those surveyed said that local deals and offers on Facebook have some impact on their decision to make a purchase in-store.

Aside from offers, the study demonstrates that customer reviews and ratings are an influential element when it comes to respondents' decision to interact with local businesses on Facebook.

Asked which of five factors they care more about when engaging with a local or small business online, 41% of those surveyed cited customer reviews/ratings, far outweighing others such as "featured products/services relevant to your needs" (19%) and "number of page 'Likes'" (15%).

Furthermore, eight in ten said they would be more likely to purchase products or services in-store from a local/small business if there were more positive customer reviews/ratings on the brand/s website, mobile site or Facebook page.

A recent study from BrightLocal similarly demonstrated the power of customer reviews for local business, discovering that 88% of those who responded claimed to regularly (39%) or occasionally (49%) read online reviews to determine the quality of a local business.

G/O Digital's study focused on Facebook marketing merits special attention, given that 62% of respondents indicated that it is the most useful social channel to research products and services before visiting a local/small business, far ahead of Pinterest (12%), Twitter (11%), Instagram (9%) and others (6%).

Motivations for Going Online Vary Across Cultures

There are 4 primary motivations for going online, according to a new A.T. Kearney study: interpersonal connections; self-expression; exploration; and convenience.

Yet the extent to which those factors motivate consumers can differ quite widely across various countries, with few connected consumers in the U.S., for example, motivated by the potential to express their opinions and be heard.

Overall, 95% of respondents (consumers who go online at least once a week) across 10 markets studied agreed with statements related to the motivation of exploring new subjects.

There was also strong agreement among connected consumers that convenience is a motivator for going online, with this measure along 3 lines:

- Accessing products and services and making purchases (92%);
- Flexibility choosing entertainment when it's wanted (83%); and
- Finding locations when walking or driving around (82%).

While there was not much variation in agreement with those motivations among the countries studied, the extent to which consumers agreed with other drivers of connectedness did vary.

For example, while 94% of respondents in India agreed with questions related to connecting with friends and family as a motivator, just 34% in Japan concurred.

Similarly, while 89% in China agreed with questions related to motivations of self-expression, only 30% in Japan feel the same way.

(The U.S. also under-indexes the global average in this regard, with just 38% being motivated by self-expression.)

The analysts note that these motivations mean that brands should address consumers' needs by "building communities, holding conversations, entertaining, and educating consumers."

The results also suggest that the relative weight given to each of these should vary by target country.

Meanwhile, consumers' motivations translates into how they allocate their time online.

For example, in Japan where few are motivated to go online in order to connect socially, consumers reported spending more time shopping online than social networking.

Meanwhile, consumers in China reported spending more time with online entertainment than respondents in other countries.

Separately, Chinese respondents were more motivated than any others to go online by the ability to flexibly choose their entertainment.

On a separate note, the study finds a strong — and not entirely unexpected — correlation between age and the influence of social networks on buying decisions.

While 32% of those aged 16-25 said that they frequently base their buying decisions on their social network, only 5% of respondents over 65 agreed.

SOURCE: Connected Consumers Are Not Created Equal: A Global Perspective

Social Media Is Not Number One

Social media is the preferred customer service channel for just 2% of customers, far behind other channels such as phone (43%) and email (22%), this according to a Parature survey of roughly 1,000 United States adults.

Yet, respondents are not shy about using social media to interact with brands: 35% claim to have asked a customer service question on social media, while 35% have complained about a brand and 52% have praised a brand. Fifty-one percent among those that got a response said it gave them a somewhat or much more favorable view of the brand.

The survey does not detail whether the response was for a question, praise, or complaint. Research from Bazaarvoice has shown that brands can benefit from responding to negative reviews. Even so, a recent survey found that 1 in 5 brands rarely, if ever, respond to complaints on social media.

It is interesting to note, however, that survey respondents are more likely to take to social to praise rather than complain about a brand, as previous research has found that consumers are more likely to share bad than good service experiences.

Nevertheless, recent research from NewVoiceMedia suggests that half of US consumers will tell friends and colleagues not to use a business following an inadequate customer service experience – while 7 in 10 will recommend a company following a positive experience.

Overall, 59% of the Parature survey respondents who interacted with a brand on social media (be it praising, complaining, or asking a question of it) said they received a response from the brand. By comparison, Socialbackers data indicates that US Brands responded to just 38% of Facebook users' wall posts in June, down from February's high of 59%.

When looking for a rapid response, however, social media is not the preferred choice. When asked which channel they would use if they needed a fast or immediate response, a dominant 57% of respondents cited the phone, followed by live chat (24%). Just 1% of respondents said they would use social media.

Pay-TV

Pay-TV penetration stands at 83% of U.S. households in 2015. That's down from 87% in 2010, but up from the 81% registered in 2005. Digital streaming now represents an estimated one-quarter of time spent watching TV, closing the gap with live TV, which occupies a leading 39% of all time spent using TV content. Roughly two-thirds of U.S. adults pay for the majority of TV content that they watch in their home, and two-thirds use a monthly subscription service via a cable or satellite provider, but the chorus calling for a-la-carte pricing appears to be growing louder.

The top broadband providers representing roughly 94% of the market added about 3 million subscribers in 2014, bringing their total to 87.3 million. For U.S. adults, internet TV services are a more likely future content source than satellite pay-TV.

Pay-TV Penetration Rates, 2010-2015

Pay-TV penetration stands at 83% of U.S. households this year, reports Leichtman Research Group (LRG), based on its latest survey of 1,000+ adults.

Pay-TV penetration has been on the decline this decade, down from 87% in 2010, although it remains up from the 81% registered in 2005.

The total number of subscribers this year is in fact on par with the number in 2010, but occupied housing additions over the past 5 years means that the penetration rate is down.

In other highlights from the report:

- Renters living in TV households are about twice as likely as owners to not subscribe to a pay-TV service (23% vs. 12%);
- Roughly 1 in 5 respondents who moved in the past year do not subscribe to a pay-TV service;
- More than 6 in 10 (62% of) households not subscribing to a pay-TV service subscribe to a subscription video-on-demand service.

TV Content Streaming Growing;
Pay-TV Adoption Relatively Steady

Digital streaming now represents an estimated one-quarter of time spent watching TV, says GfK MRI in recently-released data, closing the gap with live TV, which occupies a leading 39% of all time spent using TV content.

Streaming is on par with time-shifting via DVR, which also captures an estimated one-quarter of viewing time, per the report. Interestingly, the study indicates that content viewers are spending almost one-tenth of their TV viewing time streaming through a traditional TV set.

Indeed, when consumers were separately asked about the devices on which they watch TV shows, they estimated spending 28% of their TV time streaming content to various devices:

- Online streaming through a traditional TV set accounts for 9% of time spent watching TV;
- Accessing subscription or free online platforms via a computer or mobile device accounts for 16%; and
- The remaining 3% comes from other methods for accessing content, such as portable game consoles.
- In a separate study released earlier this year, Horowitz Research revealed that among adult heads of household who live in urban (population of 50k+) markets, 45% of Black TV viewers, 46% of Asian viewers and 51% of Hispanic viewers spend more than 20% of their total TV viewing time streaming video content to a computer, mobile device, or directly to a TV.
- By comparison, fewer White viewers – 39% – devoted that much time to over-the-top (OTT) options.

- Still, traditional live TV remains consumers' favorite means of consuming TV viewing, per the GfK study, which also found less than one-third of TV viewers reporting having watched a program on a smartphone (30%) or tablet (29%) during the prior 30 days.

Pay-TV, Broadband and Subs Continue Moving in Opposite Directions

Although the pay-TV subscriber market continues to be larger than the broadband subscriber market, that gap continues to narrow, per the latest data from Leichtman Research Group (LRG).

The results indicate that the top broadband providers – representing roughly 94% of the market – added about 1.2 million subscribers in Q1 2015, bringing their total to 88.5 million. Cable companies had a particularly strong quarter, with a net gain of slightly more than 1 million subscribers, their largest net add since Q1 2008.

By comparison, they didn't fare so well with pay-TV subscribers. Indeed, the top 9 cable companies shed roughly 60,000 video subscribers in Q1, though that wasn't much worse than in Q1 2014, when they lost around 50,000.

Overall, though, the top pay-TV providers (representing about 95% of the market) had a weak first quarter, adding only around 7,000 subscribers overall. That's despite this being traditionally a strong quarter: last year, these providers added more than 250,000 video subscribers in Q1.

Indeed, the top telephone providers (+140,000) had the fewest net adds since Q4 2006, while the top DBS companies (+52,000) had the fewest of any first quarter since LRG began tracking the pay-TV market.

Consumers Value Pay-TV, but Want Changes

Roughly two-thirds of U.S. adults pay for the majority of the TV content that they watch in their home, according to results from an Irdeto survey conducted by YouGov, and two-thirds of those mainly use a monthly subscription service via a cable or satellite provider.

While pay-TV continues to enjoy wide penetration albeit gradual subscriber losses, the chorus calling for à-la-carte pricing appears to be growing louder.

Indeed, among the total sample (regardless of their main service type), 58% said they would consider changing their current TV service to a "pick and choose" TV service in the future, with only 1 in 5 saying they would not do so.

(The survey defined a "pick and choose" service as one where subscribers could select the specific channels or content accessible to them rather than having a standard bundle of TV channels.)

Not surprisingly, among those that would consider such a service, cost is the main reason, with three-quarters saying they don't want to pay for lots of channels they don't watch, although fewer (53%) said they think it would be cheaper.

Among those that would not consider switching, the most common reason cited was liking having lots of channels to choose from (38%), with fewer (20%) feeling that channel bundles offer the best deal.

With recent news items about "skinnier" bundles and standalone streaming offerings, there have been numerous analyses about the cost-effectiveness of à-la-carte packages as opposed to the standard bundle, with some analysts suggesting that paying even for just a few channels could add up quickly.

(On that front, 40% of consumers responding to a new Ipsos survey indicated that they would pay up to $10 a month for ESPN, which is suing Verizon for allowing consumers to opt out of its channels for its custom TV offering.)

Nevertheless, recent research from Deloitte likewise finds that more consumers want à-la-carte pricing.

In its latest study, Deloitte found that 52% of consumers with a pay-TV service would prefer to subscribe only to the channels they watch regularly, as opposed to 40% who would subscribe to a package of channels even if they don't watch them all and 8% who would prefer to purchase only individual shows and events they want to watch.

That was the first time that a majority had chosen à-la-carte pricing, with the figures essentially flipping from two years earlier, when 50% preferred the bundle and 42% the à-la-carte option.

This may be the results of consumers watching fewer channels: respondents in the latest study reported regularly watching an average of 11 channels, down from 15 a couple of years earlier.

(For its part, Nielsen last year reported that despite an increase in the number of available channels, the average U.S. TV household watches 17-18 channels, unchanged since 2008. Other survey data suggests that most TV viewers estimate maxing out at 10 channels.)

As such, consumers appear to be making the calculus that pay-TV (notorious for its low customer satisfaction ratings) is too expensive and would represent greater value if they could choose their channels and presumably pay less.

Indeed, some 77% of the Ipsos survey respondents prefer the value of à-la-carte pricing as opposed to tiers of bundled channels.

But buried in the Deloitte report is perhaps the most surprising statistic of them all: so-called Leading Millennials (those aged 26-31) were *more* likely to consider their pay-TV service a top-3 most valued service than their mobile data plan (75% and 65%, respectively), suggesting that despite all of the changes brewing, pay-TV retains a good deal of value.

While trailing Millennials (14-25) in that report value a host of services over pay-TV, including streaming video, mobile data plans and gaming, the perceived value of pay-TV rises alongside the age of the respondent, almost matching the value of the home internet subscription among the oldest group.

Overall, those results suggest that despite the growing numbers of cord-cutters and "cord-nevers," most consumers value their pay-TV subscriptions, but just want more value for their money and see that in à-la-carte.

After all, in a new survey from Limelight Networks, consumers were far more likely to cite increasing prices (38%) as a reason for cutting the cord than the ability to directly subscribe to the channels they want online (16%).

Broadband Subs Closing Gap With Pay-TV

The top broadband providers — representing roughly 94% of the market — added about 3 million subscribers in 2014, bringing their total 87.3 million, according to data from Leichtman Research Group.

That equates to a total broadband subscriber base of around 93 million. By comparison, the top pay-TV providers – representing about 95% of the market – shed close to 126,000 subscribers, bringing their total down to 95.2 million.

That equates to a total pay-TV subscriber base of roughly 100 million. The resulting subscription gap between broadband and pay-TV – of roughly 7 million – compares with a roughly 16-million gap in 2011.

While pay-TV net losses have remained small – having lost just 0.2% of all subscribers over the past 2 years, (so much for cord-cutting?) – it's worth noting, as had TDG Research, that the latest net loss comes during a period of soaring household formation.

Few Consumers See Pay-TV as Their Dominant Source for Video Content Source in 2020

For US adults, internet TV services are a more likely future content source than satellite pay-TV, according to a newly released study from Irdeto.

Interestingly, user experience was cited as one of the key factors by those planning to watch mostly internet TV and by those seeing pay-TV as their primary viewing source in 2020.

The study asked respondents which type of service they plan to watch most of their TV/movies/sports content through in 2020, with 27% citing internet TV (a TV enabled with Netflix, Amazon Prime, Hulu Plus, etc.) and 18% pointing to satellite pay-TV.

The plurality of respondents — 33% — said they would likely watch a mixture of services so they can pick and choose the content they want.

(The remaining respondents don't plan to watch content on either service.)

There were — predictably — varying attitudes when sorting by demographic.

Among youth (aged 18-34), internet TV was the leading future source for 40%, more than triple the share who see pay-TV (12%) as being their dominant service.

But those aged 55 and older (who watch the most tradition TV) were more likely to plan for a mixture of services (26%) or primarily pay-TV (23%) than for internet TV (17%).

Focusing on internet TV, other demographic variables reveal that:

- Men (30%) are more likely than women (25%) to see it as their primary viewing source in 2020;
- There is little discernible difference when sorting by race;
- Respondents with a post graduate education (36%) were significantly more likely to see it as their primary source than those with lesser education levels (25-27%); and
- Those with children under 18 were more likely to see internet TV as the dominant source than those without kids of that age (24% vs. 25%).

Among respondents who plan to use internet TV for the majority of their viewing, the three identified reasons for doing so were all given equal weight — 41% cited the user experience and recommendations being better; 41% cited the user experience and recommendations being better; 40% cited the ability to watch content on more devices as a reason; and 29% pointed to a preference to be able to watch multiple episodes at once as a factor.

Among adults planning to use satellite TV, 56% said it was because the quality and user experiences better, while 32% said it was because there is more content available.

Pets

Many people are very conscious about what they put in their bodies, and pet owners are no different about what they feed their precious pups. Purina Pro Plan has been fed to the last eight Westminster Best in Show Champions.

8 of Last Westminster Dog Show Winners All Ate Same Food

The last eight Westminster Best in Show Champions, and six of the last seven 2014 group winners, all ate the same brand of dog food… Purina Pro Plan.

Purina thinks so many show dog handlers and owners choose to feed their dogs Purina Pro Plan is because of their commitment to delivering nutrition that performs. Each Purina Pro Plan formula is very bioavailable – allowing for optimal nutrient absorption, resulting in benefits like sustained energy, resilience, a healthy coat and lean muscle mass.

In addition to eight of the last eight Best in Show champions and six of the seven group winners, 94 of the top 100 all-breed show dogs in the country are fed Purina Pro Plan.

When It Comes to Gifts, Pets Outrank Spouse, Others

Pet owners are far more likely to buy a gift for their pet (69%) than for their significant other or spouse (61%), their kids (42%), friends (10%) or co-workers (3%), according to VetIQ, which asked its community just how much they loved their pets.

Furthermore, if given the choice, the majority of pet owners would prefer to stay home on Valentine's Day and cuddle with their pet (63%) than go on a romantic date with their significant other or spouse (35%).

Additional highlights from the survey include:

- More than 60% of pet owners say that their pet sleeps in bed with them;
- Nearly 83% of pet owners say that they receive the most unconditional love from their pet, vs. their significant other or spouse (9%), their kids (7%), or their best friend (1%);
- More than 80% of pet owners say their pet gets more kisses on a daily basis than their significant other;
- More than 83% of pet owners say that their pet is better at cuddling than their significant other;
- 73% of pet owners consider their pet to be a "Sweet Angel" vs. a "Little Devil" (27%); and
- 47% of pet owners selected "soul mates" as the best way to describe their relationship with their pet.

Rising Pet Ownership Forges Fresh Opportunity for Pet Food

The global pet food ingredients market is gaining momentum with the number of pet-owners having significantly increased in recent years. With higher disposable incomes and strong bonds between companion animals and people, heightened spending on pets will ensure the pet food ingredients market continues growing at a steady pace.

New analysis from Frost & Sullivan, Analysis of the Global Pet Food Ingredients Market, finds that the market earned revenues of $969.3 million in 2014 and estimates this to reach $1,426.3 million in 2021.

"Pets are considered indispensable for the well- being of aging population, thus expanding opportunities in the market," said Frost & Sullivan Chemicals, Materials & Food Industry Analyst, Dr. Nandhini Rajagopal. "Since most of the pet food in the market is similar, manufacturers should offer innovative and multi-functional ingredients to enable pet food suppliers to differentiate products from competitors. They must also develop customized formulations and natural ingredients, which owners prefer for high-breed pets."

However, if pet food becomes contaminated during storage due to the combination of ingredients, poor downstream processing or packaging failures, product recalls and decreased consumer confidence may occur.

Contaminated pet food can cause food poisoning to owners, and thus customers are cautious when buying these products, adversely impacting opportunities for ingredient manufacturers.

Strict regulations for pet food, its ingredients, packaging, storage and labeling will curb contamination rates and sustain market growth. Once pet owners are educated on the quality of different ingredients used in pet food, manufacturers will be more likely to use high- performing ingredients sought by customers globally.

"Safety, reliability and customization are key attributes pet food manufacturers must focus on to develop product lines that will be easily accepted by the market," noted Dr. Rajagopal. "Pet food ingredients manufacturers must thus invest in developing ingredients that can enable their customers to achieve these ends."

Radio

Despite the reach that online radio has, AM/FM continues to be the preferred medium among core radio listeners, with 81% of weekly radio station listening taking place on an AM/FM radio in a vehicle (51%) or at home, work, or school (30%).

Radio Listeners: AM/FM Still Strong;
Digital Platforms Key for Youths' Music Discovery

AM/FM radio continues to be the preferred medium among core radio listeners, with 81% of weekly radio station listening taking place on an AM/FM radio in a vehicle (51%) or at home, work, or school (30%), according to the latest annual TechSurvey from Jacobs Media.

Consistent with recent research, AM/FM radio continues to benefit from the in-car environment, with roughly half of respondents saying that most or all of their radio listening takes place in the car.

Overall, survey respondents were almost twice as likely to say they had increased (18%) than decreased (10%) their AM/FM radio listening (on any device) over the previous year.

Interestingly, the share of listening attributed to digital platforms didn't rise from last year, although the survey authors note that this year's sample skews older than last year.

Interestingly, though, recent research from Edison Research and Triton Digital found that while online radio's reach continues to grow, consumption this year is flat.

Meanwhile, as in previous years, the Jacobs Media survey finds that emotional connections are a primary driver of radio listening. Among the main reasons given for listening to AM/FM radio, 55% said they enjoy working with the radio on, 45% said it keeps them company, and 40% said they listen to get in a better mood.

The top reason, though, continue to be a desire to hear favorite songs/artists, cited by two-thirds of respondents.

Fewer respondents (34%) reported that a main reason for listening is to discover new music.

Even so, among those interested in new music and new artists, AM/FM radio is not only the most widely used discovery source (56%), but also the primary source for the most respondents (40%).

Still, there are wide generational gaps in music and artist discovery, with Gen Z respondents about half as likely as the survey average to cite AM/FM radio (on any device) as their primary source for finding out about new music and new artists (23% vs. 40%).

Instead, Gen Z respondents are more likely to turn to Facebook (11% vs. 5%), iHeart Radio (9% vs. 2%) and Spotify (5% vs. 2%). (The report's authors caution that the Gen Z sample size is small.)

Pandora, meanwhile, is particularly more influential than average among Gen Y respondents (12% vs. 5%) for music discovery.

The platform continues to lead all radio applications among respondents who own mobile devices, two-thirds of whom download radio-centric apps.

Regional

Where you live can obviously have an effect on what you call certain things (soda or pop or coke), your accent, and way of life. But perhaps surprisingly can also make a difference in what you splurge on.

Oklahoma spends the most on fast food, while those in Maine spend the most on coffee in a year.

Different Regions Splurge on Different Things

Millennials living in Maine, New Hampshire, Massachusetts and Connecticut spend the most on coffee, with those in Maine – the most caffeine-addicted state – spending a remarkable $307 a year on average.

According to the study, which analyzed user data from the past year to see exactly how people born between the late eighties and early 2000 spend their money on things considered 'vices', the Northeast is also home to the millennials who drink the most alcohol.

Mississippi, Iowa, Alabama, South Dakota and West Virginia spend the least on alcohol.

When it comes to fast food, however, the geographic trends are completely opposite.

Twenty-somethings in Oklahoma are the biggest spender on fast food by far, shelling out around $1,194 a year. In fact, more than two-thirds of Oklahomans buy fast food at least once a week.

In second place is Kansas, where millennials spend $1,040 a year at fast food chains, followed by Texas, Virginia and Maryland.

Adversely, nearly all of the states that spend the least on fast food are located in the Northeast.

Vermont is on the very bottom of the list, where millennials only spend about $431 a year. Rounding out the bottom five are Connecticut, New York, Pennsylvania and Montana.

Religion

Church attendance is highest in the state of Utah (unsurprisingly) and lowest in Vermont.

Church Attendance Highest in Utah, Lowest in Vermont

A little more than half of Utah residents say they attend religious services every week, more than any other state in the union, according to Gallup.

Residents in Southern states Mississippi, Alabama, Louisiana and Arkansas are the next most likely to be frequent church goers, with 45% to 47% reporting weekly attendance.

Vermont comes in on the other end of the spectrum, with only 17% of residents saying they attend religious services every week.

Top 10 States for church attendance:

1. Utah (51%);
2. Mississippi (47%);
3. Alabama (46%);
4. Louisiana (46%);
5. Arkansas (45%);
6. South Carolina (42%);
7. Tennessee (42%);
8. Kentucky (41%);
9. North Carolina (40%);
10. Georgia (39%)

Bottom 10 States for church attendance:

1. Vermont (17%);
2. New Hampshire (20%);
3. Maine (20%);
4. Massachusetts (22%);
5. Washington (24%);
6. Oregon (24%);
7. Hawaii (25%);
8. Colorado (25%);
9. Connecticut (25%);
10. Alaska (26%)

Ten of the 12 states with the highest self-reported religious service attendance are in the South, along with Utah and Oklahoma (39%).

The South's strong religious culture reflects a variety of factors, including history, cultural norms and the fact that these states have high Protestant and black populations — both of which are above average in their self-reported religious service attendance.

Utah's No. 1 position on the list is a direct result of that state's 59% Mormon population, as Mormons have the highest religious service attendance of any major religious group in the U.S.

Five of New England's six states rank among the bottom 10 states for church attendance.

Of these, Vermont, New Hampshire, Maine and Massachusetts have the lowest average attendance rates in the nations, with Connecticut not far behind.

The remaining states in the bottom 10 are all in the West, including the three states that are as far as one can go in the northwest corner of the country — Alaska, Washington and Oregon. States with average religious service attendance tend to cluster in the middle of the country.

In some states — Utah and the South — nearly half of residents report attending religious services weekly, while in others — mostly in the Northeast and the West — a fourth or less of residents attend weekly.

The state-by-state variations in church attendance are significant because attendance is a powerful indicator of underlying religiosity, which in turn is related to Americans' views on life, culture, society in general and politics.

For most segments of U.S. society — blacks being the exception — those who are the most religious are also most likely to be Republican, which helps explain the significant relationship between states with the highest church attendance and those that are traditionally red states.

Retail-Promotion

The types of digital promotions most likely to influence purchase decisions are coupons by a wide margin, not sales and daily deal vouchers.

Eight in 10 Americans who read promotional emails from retailers find it helpful when retailers send emails featuring products based on past purchases. Local deals and offers on Facebook have a strong pull with youth.

Facebook Offers Draw Youth to Local Businesses

Local deals and offers on Facebook have a strong pull with youth says G/O Digital in a new survey fielded among 18-29 year-olds who own at least a smartphone or tablet and a desktop computer, who have an interest in making purchases from local/small businesses.

Of the various Facebook marketing tactics identified, respondents were most likely to attribute influence to Facebook offers that can be redeemed at a local store.

When presented with seven Facebook marketing tactics and asked which would be more likely to impact them to make an in-store purchase from a local or small business, a majority (40%) of respondents cited Facebook offers which can be redeemed at a local store, distantly trailed by promoted posts (12%); photos/videos that encourage choice of favorite products, styles and colors (11%); and loyalty app promotions (10%), among others.

Similarly, the largest share of respondents cited Facebook offers when asked which marketing tactic would most influence them to visit the website, mobile site or app of a local/small business.

Overall, 84% of those surveyed said that local deals and offers on Facebook have some impact on their decision to make a purchase in-store.

Aside from offers, the study demonstrates that customer reviews and ratings are an influential element when it comes to respondents' decision to interact with local businesses on Facebook.

Asked which of five factors they care more about when engaging with a local or small business online, 41% of those surveyed cited customer reviews/ratings, far outweighing others such as "featured products/services relevant to your needs" (19%) and "number of page 'Likes'" (15%).

Furthermore, eight in 10 said they would be more likely to purchase products or services in-store from a local/small business if there were more positive customer reviews/ratings on the brand/s website, mobile site or Facebook page.

A recent study from BrightLocal similarly demonstrated the power of customer reviews for local business, discovering that 88% of those who responded claimed to regularly (39%) or occasionally (49%) read online reviews to determine the quality of a local business.

G/O Digital's study focused on Facebook marketing merits special attention, given that 62% of respondents indicated that it is the most useful social channel to research products and services before visiting a local/small business, far ahead of Pinterest (12%), Twitter (11%), Instagram (9%) and others (6%).

Digital Coupons Build Loyalty

The types of digital promotions most likely to influence purchase decisions are coupons by a wide margin, not sales and daily deal vouchers, according to a survey of 500 US consumers who used a digital coupon, offer, or online promotion code in the prior three months.

Forrester Consulting, on behalf of RetailMeNot, conducted the study, which also found consumers professing to word-of-mouth and loyalty benefits for brands offering online coupons or promotion codes.

Around 68% of respondents agreed they are likely to tell a friend about a company that uses online coupons or promotion codes.

An equal 68% agreed that they are more likely to be loyal to a brand that offers online coupons or promotion codes.

The survey also indicates that half are more likely to buy a product or service at full price later from a company that offers online coupons or promotion codes.

Digital coupons can also drive consumers to try new brands – and even induce some to switch brands, per the study.

Almost half of those surveyed reported being very (20%) or somewhat (27%) likely to try a new brand if they received a digital coupon, offer or online promotion code on their smartphone while shopping in a store.

Respondents were less likely to say that they would switch brand in this scenario, although 36% professed to being very (13%) or somewhat (23%) likely to do so.

Past research has found a compelling portion of consumers attributing keen influence to coupons (not just digital coupons) when making brand decisions, although two-thirds of those influenced by coupons said they use them to buy familiar brands rather than to try new ones.

Other results from the RetailMeNot survey:

- retailer emails are the primary source of digital coupons, offers or online promotion codes among those who had used a computer to find one (this finding true for tablet users also);
- social media was a lesser source of digital coupons, with this likely to fall even further given Facebook's decision not to allow Pages to incentivize likes through rewards;
- the vast majority of digital coupon users used them within days of finding them; half of respondents say they're more likely to visit a store if they receive a coupon for that store; and
- a slight majority of those who had used a smartphone to find a coupon spent even more money during their visit (online or in-store) than they had originally anticipated.

The study began in May 2014 and was completed in June 2014. Six in ten respondents were female and 37% are under 35. About two-thirds had made 1-10 purchases online during the prior 3 months, and 7 in 10 had used a digital coupon, offer or online promotion code 1-5 times during that time span.

Consumers' Most Popular Product Recommendation Types

Eight in 10 Americans who read promotional emails from retailers find it helpful when retailers send emails featuring products based on past purchases, according to a Listrak survey conducted by Harris Interactive.

Other research has similarly found product recommendations based on purchase history to be influential to shoppers.

The Listrak survey finds that the product recommendations (on websites or in emails) of most interest are on-sale items (81%).

Discounts are trailed distantly in the popularity stakes by the following types of recommendations:

- Organized by price (40%);
- New (39%);
- Highest-rated (38%);
- Top-sellers (31%); and
- Most "pinned" (8%).

Retail-Service Sector

Almost half (45%) of shoppers do not trust retailers to keep their credit and debit cards information safe from potential hackers. China predicted to pass the United States as the world's top retail market in 2018 is back on top as the leading emerging market for retail opportunities.

Security Breaches Affect Shopping Behavior

Almost half (45%) of shoppers do not trust retailers to keep their credit and debit card information safe from potential hackers, according to a report from Interactions, which noted that up to 44% of respondents have had their personal information stolen as a result of a security breach.

A new report from Retail Perceptions offers insight into how the loyalty to brands of consumers changed following highly publicized data breaches. Up to 12% of shoppers said they stopped shopping with retailers that experienced a breach, with another 36% indicating they shopped at the retailer less frequently.

With debit and credit cards being the top targets for hackers, shoppers may be inclined into making purchases via other means, namely cash. The majority (79%) of respondents said they were more likely to use cash as opposed to credit cards to purchase products in-store.

Buyers have varied opinions regarding their comfort levels shopping with retailers after they experience a security breach.

Roughly one-fifth (19%) of those surveyed feel comfortable going back to the same retailer to shop immediately, while another 19% said they would prefer to hold off for three to six months. Conversely, some people do not care as long as the breach is corrected quickly (22%).

Shoppers provided four key stipulations retailers would have to adhere to in order to regain their trust after a breach:

- provide free credit monitoring capabilities;
- offer additional incentives or discounts;
- provide clear and honest explanations to shoppers regarding the breach; and
- increase security measures and communicate the changes that have been made.

China Ranked Top Developing Market For Retail Investment

China — predicted to pass the U.S. as the world's top retail market in 2018 — is back on top as the leading emerging market for retail opportunities, says A.T. Kearney, which bases its Global Retail Development Index (GRDI) score on a mix of market attractiveness, country risk, market saturation, and time pressure (how fast retail is growing).

China (GRDI of 65.3) scored particularly well in "time pressure" (96.6 on a 100-point scale), enough to edge it past Uruguay (65.1) for the top spot.

Rounding out the top 5 this year are Chile (62.3), Qatar (59.1) and Mongolia (58.8), with the latter scoring highly for market saturation and time pressure.

Shopping & Spending

Forty-five percent of Americans are spending more today than they were a year ago, while 18% are spending less. Millennials are the groups most likely to say they have increased their spending, while members of Gen X are least likely to say they are spending more. Many consumers look to the price tag when calculating quality of a product, but they may not be getting what they are paying for.

Spending Trends in Data-Driven Marketing and Advertising

Data's role will expand considerably in the future, according to more than three-quarters of marketers, advertisers, service providers, technologists and publishers surveyed by the Winterberry Group and the GlobalDMA across 17 markets.

The study found broad agreement across those markets that the value of data-driven marketing and advertising (DDMA) is growing, and almost three-quarters expect to increase their spending on DDMA next year.

Looking at expected changes in spending on DDMA channels over the next year (measured on a 5-point scale where 1 represents a significant likely decrease and 5 a significant likely increase), the study found that the channels set for the largest increases in data-driven spend are:

- Mobile apps, messaging and user experience — 4.15;
- Social media engagement (apps, gamification, customer service, etc.) — 4.11; and
- Website/e-commerce (content and user experience) — 4.06.

The only channel not tabbed for an increase in data-driven spending is direct mail, for which spending should remain flat (2.99 average).

And while the spending outlook for teleservices/contact centers (3.23) and addressable TV (3.26) is more modest, those channels also see a small rise in data-driven spending.

Also worth noting is that for almost all of the channels identified, expectations for spending next year are greater than reported spending increases over the past year, another indication that this remains a growing field.

In many cases, spending expectations are following performance trends.

For example, the performance of mobile apps, messaging and user experience saw the largest reported improvement over last year, with website/e-commerce and digital display advertising performances also among those seeing the largest gains.

Meanwhile, the campaign execution functions tabbed for the greatest spending hikes next year are:

- Digital campaign execution — 4.02;
- Audience analytics, measurement and attribution — 4.01; and
- Data/database management (CRM and *DMP* technology) — 3.99.
- Looking at the factors most responsible for driving investments in data-driven marketing and advertising, respondents were most apt to point to demands to deliver more relevant communications to customers and be more "customer-centric" (52.7%) and a desire to maximize effectiveness and efficiency of marketing investments (49.3%).
- It is notable that the bisects inhibitor to investments in DDMA is a limited availability of the necessary budget (47.1%) rather than a poor understanding of DDMA and its contribution (30.4%).

Americans Spending More Today Than Year Ago

Forty-five percent of Americans are spending more today than they were a year ago, while 18% say they are spending less. The percentage of people who say they are spending more is relatively stable across several demographic categories.

Millennials are among the groups most likely to say they have increased their spending. Members of Generation X are least likely to say they are spending more.

Among the generations, millennials (the youngest Americans) are more likely than traditionalists (the oldest Americans) to report spending more this year than the previous year on rent or mortgage (39% for millennials vs. 24% for traditionalists), leisure activities (38% vs 21%), and clothing (31% vs. 16%). The spending of the other generational groups fall midway between these two.

Despite a majority of baby boomers saying they are *less willing to spend* this year in general, they are spending well more than they did a year ago compared with millennials on household essentials such as utilities (53% for baby boomers vs. 37% for millennials), healthcare (50% vs. 37%), home maintenance (39% vs. 23%), and household goods (37% vs. 26%). Again, the other generational groups fall between these two.

The generations also differ in the ways they try — or fail — to cut expenses. Not surprisingly, members of Gen X and millennials are both significantly more likely than the older generations to go online to compare prices (70% for members of Gen X and millennials). Baby boomers, meanwhile, are much more likely than other generations to say they shop at more than one store for similar items to get the best deals (24%), while traditionalists are much less likely than any of the others to purchase more at the store than they intend to (44%), to go shopping for fun (19%), and to make an impulse purchase (26%).

The data also suggests that millennials are more freewheeling and impulsive in their shopping behavior.

Significantly fewer millennials strongly disagree with the statement, "When I get some money, I spend it right away" (42%) than any of the other generations.

Furthermore, fewer millennials strongly agree with the statement "I only shop for exactly what I need" (21%), compared with the other generations.

Price Check: Cost Doesn't Signal Quality

While many consumers look to the price tag when calculating quality of a product, they may not get what they paid for, according to new research from the University of Chicago Booth School of Business.

The study is written by Ann McGill of Chicago Booth, Bart de Langhe of the University of Colorado at Boulder Leeds School of Business, Stijn M.J. Van Osselear of the Cornell University Journalism School of Management and Stefano Puntoni of the Erasmus University's Rotterdam School of Management.

For some products, like wines, there is greater variation in quality among lower-priced bottles, so it is possible to get a good bottle of wine for a good price, though basing a decision on cost alone would suggest otherwise. The opposite is true for detergents.

"What we find, though, is that consumers don't pick up on this difference in consistency very well," McGill says. "As a result, if quality is consistent across higher-priced goods, consumers may err and predict that a lower-priced item is lower quality than it really is."

The researchers conducted three studies to inspect how people perceive the relationship between price and quality under different conditions — when they had other information on quality in one price region, but not another, for example.

They noted that the price-quality relationship is learned in two major ways — when price and quality information for many products are simultaneously listed together, for example on websites like Yelp, and about one product at a time, over time.

"The relationship between price and quality is rarely perfect," they write. "The price-quality relationship is characterized by random error around the regression line. Often, this error is not constant across the price range."

McGill says that if consumers learn that quality is consistently high at high prices, they will assume low-price options are worse than they are.

"We find the reverse also — if they learn that quality is consistently low at low prices, they may assume quality is consistently high at high prices, when that might not be the case," she says. "In some categories, some of the more expensive items might be great but some not so great."

Consumers Spending More, Just Not on What They Want

Slightly less than half of all Americans (45%) report spending more than they did a year ago, while just 18% report spending less.

A closer look at these numbers reveals Americans' increased spending is on household essentials, such as groceries, gasoline, utilities, and healthcare, rather than on discretionary purchases.

At the other end of the spectrum, approximately one-third of Americans report spending less on discretionary items such as travel (38%), dining out (38%), leisure activities (31%), consumer electronics (31%), and clothing (30%).

More than half of Americans say they are spending roughly the same for rent or mortgage, household goods, telephone, automobile expenses other than fuel, personal care products, and the Internet.

All of this suggests that the rising cost of essential items is further inhibiting family budgets that have already been hit hard by the Great Recession and are still reeling from a sluggish economy.

Summer travel plans of Americans clearly indicate the tension between increased spending on essentials and reduced spending on discretionary items.

While considerably more Americans said they are traveling this summer (69%) than said so in 2009 during the Great Recession (52%), over one-third of travelers plan to travel less (36%) than last year. This is roughly comparable to Gallup's findings in the summers of 2010 and 2011 (33% and 35%, respectively).

Furthermore, many travelers planned to stay close to home: More than two-thirds of those who traveled this summer intended to take a trip longer than an overnight trip.

Among those, most traveled by car (81%), whereas, just less than half took at least one trip by air (47%). Less than 10% intended to travel by bus or train this summer.

Slightly more than half expected both transportation and non-transport expenses for their summer trips to cost more this year than last.

These results paint a picture of consumers straining against rising prices on daily essentials to afford summer travel, dining out, and discretionary household purchases — the kinds of purchases that normally keep an economy humming.

And while the two-thirds of Americans who planned to travel this summer is the highest level Gallup has measure since 2006, virtually one-third planned to spend just one night or less away from home, meaning it is not much of a vacation.

Those who did intend to travel expected to spend more in all travel categories — transportation, food, lodging, and entertainment — than last year, further pressuring their already-strained budgets.

Most said that they would take their own cars despite the relatively high gas prices.

If there was any doubt that the U.S. economy is still struggling to get back on its feet, the results of this poll bolster that reality.

Because consumer spending is the lifeblood of a healthy economy, these findings suggest that discretionary spending still has a ways to go before it will fuel the kind of economic growth Americans have been hoping for.

Majority of Consumers Willing to Wait -- If Shipping Is Free

Today's consumers are willing to wait longer to receive purchases made online if it means shipping is free, this according to a new survey by UPS and comScore.

According to the third annual joint survey, which polled 5,849 consumers this past February and March, four out of five respondents said free shipping is an important consideration when buying online, with 83% saying they were willing to wait an extra two days or more if it meant they did not have to pay for shipping.

More than half of consumers said they would choose a slower delivery time to get free shipping.

Retailers have to provide reasonable delivery schedules, UPS and comScore found, because consumers will not wait forever. Half of those surveyed said they have abandoned an online shopping carts because of lengthy delivery times or no date provided at check out.

More than half of respondents said they will opt for ship-to-store at some point — with 40% of those consumers making other purchases during their visit — while one in four packages shipped are directed at a location other than the home address (i.e. carrier retail stores, retail outlets, office).

An additional 82% of shoppers liked the option of being able to return the product to the store or ship it back using a free prepaid label.

With channel choice mattering less than convenience and flexibility — and with repeated improvements to shipping and fulfillment capabilities — the survey found that retailers need to differentiate themselves by delivering both compelling online and in-store experiences and exceptional service.

Bala Ganesh, director of marketing for UPS, said consumers are asking for more shipping destination options, including ship to store, to the office or to a family member. "This trend fits in with people's busy lifestyles, and their demand for convenience and flexibility," he said.

Retailers have some work to do in the customer experience area, comScore and UPS found:

Fifty-nine percent of consumers said they were satisfied with the ability to find a customer service phone number or other contact option during the search/browse phase of their shopping experience;

Fifty percent of consumers said they were satisfied with making a return and the clarity of retailers policies;

Forty-four percent were satisfied with the post-shipment flexibility to choose another delivery date, while 43% are content with the ability to reroute package; and sixty percent of shoppers were satisfied with the ability to find a retailer's return policy.

The growing impact of e-commerce was also seen in the survey findings: 40% of mobile users said they look for or redeem coupons on their devices, while 36% said they compare prices in store on their smartphones.

However, laptop/desktop remains the primary choice for both researching products (61% of respondents) and purchasing (44%), in contract to 21% and 11% for smartphones and tables respectively.

Retailer's return policies are also being checked out by consumers prior to purchase, while pursuing options for free shipping, said Susan Engleson, senior director at comScore.

"Two years ago, 17% of consumers said they did not look at a retailers' return policy before purchasing, but this year it was just 11%." Engleson said.

Engleson continued, "More 90% said they would take action to qualify for free shipping, 58% said they would add more items to their cart to qualify, and 50% said they would choose the slowest shipping time to qualify."

Engleson said the desire of consumers for a full range of delivery options at checkout, and for convenient and flexible returns, should be key areas of focus for retailers.

Some comparison of matrices from past surveys:

- Overall satisfaction with online shopping stayed the same from 2013, at 83%;
- Since 2012, retail returns volumes have grown (62% say they have returned/exchanged an item bought online in the 2014 study versus 51% in 2012); and
- Online shopping cart abandonment has grown (90% have abandoned an online shopping cart in 2014 versus 88% in 2013).

Recommendations made in the report are for retailers to improve the customer experience from a fulfillment standpoint:

- Provide easy access to the returns policy throughout the site and in post-purchase communications;
- Make customer service contacts readily available;
- Offer different shipping options to accommodate shopper needs;
- Display the expected delivery date in the shopping cart;
- Assess whether you can absorb free shipping costs as a marketing expense, and how to preserve margin while remaining competitive;
- Include a return label in the box, or at least make it easy for shoppers to print a return label from your website;
- Let shoppers know about availability on both the product page and in the shopping cart; and
- Provide notification tools (email, text) when items become available to capture sales.

More Than Half of Back-to-School Shoppers Discover Products on Social Media

Nearly 65% of last minute back-to-school shoppers planned to use social media sites such as Instagram, Pinterest or Facebook for the best deals, this according to a surgery by Crowdtap.

More than 45% of those surveyed said they considered peer reviews before making a purchase, while only 33% took expert reviews into account.

The survey also indicates that more than 60% of shoppers purchased items they found on social media.

Facebook might be the obvious leader, but Pinterest beats out all the other social networks as a source of back to school inspiration.

Shoppers are not only looking for recommendations, they are also sharing ideas as well.

Twenty-five percent of those surveyed said they would likely share digital coupons, and 21% said they would share information about deals and sales, or link to a contest.

Reviews Most Important Info
On Retailer Websites to Shoppers

Almost three-quarters of U.S. online shoppers find product reviews influential when visiting a retailer's website, making reviews the most influential content type of those identified, according to recently-released results from a UPS and comScore study.

The new data – specific to online shoppers in the U.S. – also demonstrates the influence of Q&A (48%) and product and brand videos (47%) among shoppers.

Previous research has similarly found that product videos boost purchase likelihood among their viewers.

The study also finds that consumer and peer reviews are important factors in the path to purchase, with 55% of shoppers deeming these important when searching and selecting products.

However, detailed product information (73%) is the most important factor in the search and selection process, followed by retailer reputation (66%), return policy (62%), and the presence of multiple images or the ability to zoom in (59%).

Similar factors are important when shopping via mobile applications. Indeed, product images (54%) and product reviews (53%) are considered the most important retail app features among users, with these followed by relevant search results (50%) and mobile coupons (50%).

While the study cautions that "apps... aren't a must for every retailer," four in five mobile shoppers surveyed reported having used a retailer's app rather than a browser to access a retailer at some point.

Returning to purchase influence, reviews or posts from marketplaces have influenced almost two-thirds (65%) of shoppers, with friends and family (55%) following.

Fewer (29%) claim to have been influenced by reviews or posts found on social media (29%). Respondents noted that the types of retailer posts that they are most likely to view on Facebook are promotions (47%), new product announcements (38%) and sweepstakes (38%).

Asian-Americans Have Almost 4 Times Buying Power of Millennials

There's far less research devoted to Asian Americans than to Millennials, but with an estimated buying power of $770 billion last year (as opposed to Millennials' $200 billion), Asian-Americans are a force to be reckoned with, according to data cited in a new Nielsen report.

Indeed, given their relatively long life expectancies and young median age, Asian-American households are expected to outspend all other races and ethnicities over their remaining lifetimes, per recent research.

Citing data from the **Bureau of Labor Statistics**, the Nielsen report notes that Asian-Americans' average annual expenditures, at $61,700, are 19% higher than the U.S. consumer average of $52,000. Among the various spending categories, Asian-Americans over-index in particular in spending on housing ($22,000, 26% higher than the average consumer), food ($8,000; +19%), personal insurance ($7,900; +41%), apparel ($2,150; +28%) and furniture ($420; +17%).

The Nielsen report covers the Asian-American consumer segment from a number of different angles, combining Nielsen data with third-party figures to offer a host of intriguing statistics. Below are some highlights from the report, organized by topic.

Do Teens Wield Over Their Parents' Purchase Decisions?

Children are "active decision makers in family economies," according to YouGov in releasing the results of a recent survey examining kids' influence on their parents' buying decisions.

The survey analyzes kids' influence across a range of categories, noting that young children can hold as much persuasive power as teens in those decisions..

While the study analyzes responses from parents with children aged 6-17, the following results pertain solely to those parents with children aged 12-17.

Examining categories in which an adult makes the purchases, the report finds – not surprisingly – that teens are most likely to have at least some degree of influence over purchases the adults make for them:

- Apparel for the teen to wear (96% of teens having some degree of influence);
- Personal care products for the teen (93%); and
- Footwear for the teen (93%).

Teens also wield a significant amount of influence over adults' purchases of in-home entertainment content (78%) and in-home gaming systems (74%), but less so over in-home entertainment devices (47%) and the parents' hand-held mobile products (42%).

Still, roughly 1 in 5 say that the teen picks the parent's mobile device independently (7%) or with the parent (11%).

When it comes to categories in which households have made a purchase during the prior year, parents were most likely to ascribe some degree of purchase influence to their teens in the following areas:

- Which fast-food restaurants to go to (95%);
- Types of out-of-home entertainment/sports/recreation to attend or do (93%);
- Where to shop for clothes for the teen (90%);
- Which sit-down restaurants to go to (88%); and
- Where to shop for footwear for the teen (88%).

Interestingly, half of parents said their teens influence where to shop for in-home entertainment and technology devices, and close to half said they influence which vehicle to purchase or lease (45%) and where they go on vacations without their children (44%).

Which Digital Tools Impact Online Shoppers?

Retailer sites, printable coupons, and retailer emails are the most commonly used digital tools by online shoppers, but they don't yield the greatest impact on shoppers' journeys.

That's the conclusion of a new study by Epsilon, which found the digital tools with the highest overall impact score were retailers' social media activity and price comparison sites, although they had relativity low penetration rates. Shopping applications, brands' social media activity and product reviews were also among the most highly rated by their users.

The influence of product reviews has also been noted in a separate recent study of e-commerce behavior, in which online shoppers cited them as important content on retailer websites and in retailers' shopping apps.

Some tools may have had low average impact scores but rank better in certain criteria. For example, retailer emails ranked higher in influence than in utility or overall impact. Indeed, recent survey results suggest that they are useful promotional vehicles, with emails offering free shipping and those offering discounts being the most likely to prompt shoppers to shop at a retailer.

Meanwhile, the Epsilon report notes that the average influence of the digital tools identified has grown markedly from the previous year, with influence in this case referring to the degree to which they have swayed respondents' shopping and decision-making behavior. Utility scores (improving the shopping experience) have remained generally flat, with several tools (including websites and emails from both retailers and brands) actually receding in perceived utility.

Notably, social media emerged as a top influencer of product trials, as three types of social activity were among the top 5:

- Retailer social (29% saying it influences them to try new brands and products);
- Brand social (28%);
- Printable coupons (23%);
- Daily deal sites (23%); and
- Friend social (22%).

Those results are supported by a recent study from Nielsen, which indicated that social media posts are a growing source of new product awareness.

After surveying more than 2,800 respondents on line, the report determined an impact score for each tool by averaging the percent of its users saying it has influenced them across 10 areas.

Those areas range from influencing choices (e.g. "it influences my choice of stores," "it influences my choice of brands") to impulse buying ("I make more unplanned purchases," "I spend more than initially planned") and utility (e.g. "it makes shopping easier," "it makes shopping faster").

Top Stated Reasons for Abandoning a Mobile Transaction

A majority (56%) of U.S. smartphone owning adults have abandoned a mobile transaction, according to Jumio, though this figure is down from 66% in a similar survey conducted in 2013.

Among those who have abandoned a mobile transaction, purchase uncertainty (45%) was the top reason cited, followed by slow load times (36%) and difficulty with navigation (31%).

These usability concerns appear to outweigh security concerns around payment (27%) and personal (26%) information, per the survey's results.

8 Key Trends Shaping U.S. Co-Branded Credit Card Market

Nearly 43% of U.S. adult consumers own at least one co-branded or affinity credit card, according to market research publisher Packaged Facts.

By year-end 2014, co-branded credit cards alone generated 31% of general purpose credit card purchase volume, or $809 billion out of $2.63 trillion, among Visa, MasterCard, Discover and American Express branded credit and charge cards.

Competition in the segment is fierce with a growing multitude of players chasing a finite universe of affluent prospects with more rewards and broader, deeper card features and benefits. Packaged Facts outlines eight important trends that will shape the market for co-branded and affinity cards. These include:

1. **Continued push and pull regarding transparency:** Card players are employing a broad range of rewards redemption strategies that translate to different values when using the same card. But some cards are promising eye-catching rewards tier architectures that do not translate, point for cent, as cardholders may expect. This strategy stands out when other cards provide transparency. Consumers may not begrudge this in light of the wider range of options they are provided—as long as the methods employed are not perceived as deceptive.

2. **Rewards that tie back to the partner in a unique way:** With the percentage of rewards offered clearly on the upswing, issuers and partners can choose to compete toe to toe on the rewards rate. But players need to differentiate their card programs in other ways, by offering something unique and highly aspirational to incent frequent usage. For cards attracting high-net worth users, cash back goes only so far: it means delivering on brand

expectations and enhancing the experience, offering intangible, aspirational value to the card user.

3. **New and growing co-branded entrants:** Citi is rejuvenated, Capital One and TD Bank are relatively new to the market, Wells Fargo has finally stepped in, and Alliance Data and Synchrony are shifting their emphasis to co-brand. Behind the scenes, the Visa, MasterCard and American Express networks are also jockeying for position. Need we say more?

4. **An industry chasing a finite universe of prospects:** With all of the attention paid to the affluent consumer—the mainstay of co-branded cards—one would think they are in endless supply. They aren't. More issuers, more cards, more rewards, but you can't mint the affluent on an assembly line. Consumers of all shapes and sizes continue to pace their spending, and issuers have not forgotten the pain of the recession either, resulting on only modest loan and purchase value growth.

5. **Owned-branded competition:** Major issuers continue to burnish their own-branded card programs: card players including American Express, Capital One, Bank of America, Wells Fargo, JPMorgan Chase, Citibank and U.S. Bank have each refined and tweaked their own-branded card programs very carefully, streamlining offerings and tailoring their target audiences accordingly. While the co-branded proposition is fundamentally different in an obvious way, moving from own-branded to co-branded or vice versa is likely a matter of consumer circumstance and evolving need (relationship building strategies aside), creating fluidity in the use of one card type over the other.

6. **The need to draw younger adult consumers into the card—and broader banking—mix:** Traditional financial institutions are losing the battle with Millennials, who maintain banking and card relationships at lower rates than Generation Xers did at their ages, and are flocking to online-only and emerging financial services competitors. To keep people in the fold, Chase, Citi and Bank of America have caught on to the power a unifying rewards program can have on customer retention and cross-selling. Importantly, they go beyond American Express' Membership Rewards by offering opportunities to earn more with the institution directly. Co-branded cards tied to these types of platforms may help bring Millennials back into the fold because they have what an own-branded card may lack: the power and cache of the partner brand. While brand power may be on the wane, it still has merit, especially among Millennials.

7. **Going mainstream:** Co-branded cards can move downstream to catch Middle America. Cards such as the Walmart MasterCard won't win prizes on bells and whistles, and they don't have to, as long as they give reason enough (a 1% earn rate, in this case) to incent enough usage to build loans and spend—less rewards, less expense. It will be interesting to see how mainstream hotel player Red Roof Inn navigates its rewards structure.

8. **The need for loyalty and the use of more sophisticated loyalty marketing strategies:** More than ever, the concept of loyalty is on the ropes, a victim of consumer empowerment driven by technology and online/mobile engagement. This is one BIG reason private label retail card partners have been quick to embrace increasingly sophisticated digital loyalty programs that, while still relying on cards, place the card as a spoke among many spokes in an omni-channel marketing wheel. The quest? As dimensional a portrait of the customer as technology and related card management prowess allows. Co-branded cards clearly fit into this mix and must compete on the granularity of purchase (private label cards can deliver SKU-level data to the partner) and on what can be done with the information about that purchase. For card issuers, this is a big bargaining chip at a time when merchants have the upper hand at the contract negotiating table.

Black Friday is Better Online

Consumers will spend a record $630.5 billion during the 2015 shopping season, the National Retail Federation predicts.

Nearly half of these people will either browse or buy online, spending $105 billion and using multiple devices in the process, including desktops, laptops, tablets and smartphones, according to Criteo, a performance marketing technology company, which released original data on Black Friday, Cyber Monday and "Bounceback Tuesday" shopping trends to help marketers navigate the consumers' evolving path to purchase.

Findings are based on an analysis of nearly 200 retailers and 63.7 million online transactions during the 2014 holiday season, and provide actionable insight for retail brands to effectively plan for this year's shopping rush.

Because four in 10 eCommerce sales in the U.S. include a cross-device journey, every device and platform counts for retailers as they strategically invest significant resources to engage and convert consumers through promotion and advertising.

Criteo's deep-dive into consumer browsing and buying activity uncovers two trends:

First, Black Friday is increasingly turning into an online sales event as consumers are more frequently using mobile devices to make purchases, and online shopping is extending further into the work week.

Second, for companies focused on attracting and retaining consumers during this time period, online advertising campaigns should be fully optimized across all devices.

Black Friday is Becoming Cyber Monday

While Black Friday has historically been an in-store, discount-driven event, Criteo data based on last season's transactions reveals that for many retailers online sales on Black Friday were nearly equal to those of Cyber Monday. Driving the growth of eCommerce during Black Friday is the adoption and use of mobile devices to browse and buy online.

- Mass merchants experienced online sales 275% higher on Black Friday than during non-holiday periods—nearly equivalent to Cyber Monday sales.
- Sales volumes on smartphones and tablets on Black Friday were 18% higher than on Cyber Monday.
- On Black Friday, 32% of eCommerce transactions occurred on a mobile device (tablet or smartphone), compared to 24% on Cyber Monday.

"Bounceback Tuesday" Sees Strong Online Sales

Online shopping peaks are spreading further into the week, with sales remaining steady on the Tuesday after Black Friday and Cyber Monday—defined by Criteo as "Bounceback Tuesday."

- In 2014, sales across all key retail categories were 159% above the average on Bounceback Tuesday.

- Specific retail sectors, such as sporting goods, experienced 224% above average online sales on Bounceback Tuesday, which were higher than Black Friday, despite the rise of online sales on that date.
- The toys and gadgets (+223%) and computers and technology (+190%) retail sectors also saw a sales lift on Bounceback Tuesday.

"The path to purchase for today's consumer has evolved and, as a result, people are doing a tremendous amount of online shopping across all devices on Black Friday. Sales on mobile especially have hit record numbers, according to 2014 data. Retail companies have a huge opportunity to engage consumers through personalized and relevant online advertising during the entire spending period, including Black Friday, Cyber Monday and Bounceback Tuesday," said James Smith, EVP, Americas at Criteo.

Cyber Monday Surpasses $3 Billion in Total Digital Sales To Rank as Heaviest U.S. Online Spending Day in History

For the holiday season-to-date, $27.9 billion has been spent online, marking a 6% increase versus the corresponding days last year, according to comScore.

Cyber Monday reached $2.28 billion in desktop online spending, up 12% versus a year ago, representing the heaviest online spending day in history and the first day of the 2015 season to surpass $2 billion in sales.

The weekend after Thanksgiving also reached a major milestone as it saw its first ever billion-dollar online shopping day on Sunday, while Saturday sales reached the $1 billion mark for second year in a row.

The two days combined posted particularly strong growth online, raking in $2.169 billion for an increase of 8% compared to the same weekend last year.

For the five-day period from Thanksgiving through Cyber Monday, online buying from desktop computers totaled $7.201 billion, up 10% versus last year.

Mobile Commerce Brings Total Cyber Monday Spending to More Than $3 Billion

Total digital spending on Cyber Monday, when inclusive of comScore's preliminary mobile commerce estimates, reached $3.118 billion, a 21-percent annual gain vs. $2.586 billion spent on Cyber Monday 2014.

This marks the first time in history that total digital spending surpassed the $3 billion milestone in a single day. Mobile commerce is estimated to have accounted for 27% of total digital commerce on Cyber Monday 2015, with $838 million spent via smartphones and tablets.

Amazon Ranks #1 Among Online Retailers on Cyber Monday

Some 107.8 million Americans visited online retail properties on Cyber Monday using a desktop computer, smartphone or tablet, representing an increase of 23% versus year ago. Amazon ranked as the most visited online retail property on Cyber Monday, followed by Walmart, eBay, Target and Best Buy.

"Cyber Monday maintained its reputation as the most important online spending day of year, exceeding $3 billion in total digital spending and once again becoming the heaviest online spending day of all-time," said comScore chairman emeritus Gian Fulgoni.

"Despite some talk of Cyber Monday declining in importance, the day's historical highs and continued strong growth rates confirm it is still a hugely important shopping event."

Fulgoni added, "It comes as no surprise that Amazon led all online retail properties in Cyber Monday traffic, but several multi-channel retailers such Walmart and Target also had very strong showings. Although some web sites experienced unfortunate server problems on Cyber Monday that appear to have been caused by heavy mobile traffic, it's not yet clear what the impact was for those retailers. What is clear is that the consumer economy is still healthy, and it's looking optimistic that the success of Black Friday weekend and Cyber Monday will carry on throughout the rest of the season."

Shopping at Work Accounts for More Than Half of Cyber Monday Spending

More than half of desktop e-commerce dollars spent in the U.S. on Cyber Monday originated from work computers (52.2%), while buying from home computers comprised of the remaining share (47.8%), despite more buyers opting to make purchases from this location. Consumers between 35 and 54 years old accounted for 46.5% of total dollars spent on Cyber Monday, while females (61.6%) spent significantly more than males (38.4%).

Americans Expect to Go $140 Over Budget for Holiday Gifts

Sixty-two percent of Americans who set a holiday budget go over their limit by an average of $140, marking a 20% increase from what people estimated they would overspend last year, according to a new holiday shopping survey released by Coinstar.

In order to buy gifts for everyone on their list, 66% of shoppers find they need to cut back on things they enjoy like dining out (43%) and entertainment (42%), or even take on credit card debt (27%) or purchase an item on layaway (22%).

Not only do people have to sacrifice before the holidays, but this overspending leads to post-holiday money issues, too. Americans reported they find themselves saving less money (20%), having to set a budget (19%) or dealing with debt (18%) in the first few weeks after the holidays.

"The holidays can be a stressful time of the year, particularly when it comes to money," said Andrea Woroch, a nationally recognized consumer and money saving expert. "Fortunately, there is hidden money throughout most homes in the form of coins and gift cards that can help people avoid taking on debt because of their over-spending."

Additional survey findings include:

- **Credit card use grows:** Gifters are nearly 20% more likely to use credit cards instead of cash or gift cards to pay for their holiday gifts this year (49% in 2015 vs. 41% in 2014);

- **Budgeting needs for the younger crowd:** More than twice as many people ages 18-34 admit they need to set a budget after the holidays when compared to people over the age of 35 (30% vs. 14%); and
- **Millennials are making sacrifices:** Eighty percent of people ages 18-34 admitted to needing to make trade-offs to ensure they can purchase gifts for everyone on their list, while 47% of people that age need to use credit cards to pay for their presents.

Retail Sales Expected to Rise 3.7% This Holiday Season

Retailers have their work cut out for them during the 2015 winter holiday season. In 2014, retailers experienced one of the strongest holiday seasons in recent years, according to a report by Mintel International provided by MarketResearch.com.

And this year, the continued economic growth, improving job market, and lower gas prices are all positive factors contributing to high sales in 2015.

Holiday shoppers plan on spending an average $463 on family members. This year, a common theme many merchandisers are seeing is self-shopping. With gifts for family and friends and themselves, consumers are planning to spend $805 on holiday merchandise, up from $802 in 2014.

The holiday season, November and December, is one of the most important times of the year for retailers. Many companies account for nearly 30% of their annual business during the holidays. Retail sales are expected to increase by 3.7% this year, which will hit an estimated $630.5 billion.

Smartphones

Smartphones are inescapable it seems, flip-phones are a thing of the past and many people even question how we ever lived before having everything available on our phones. An increasing share of U.S e-commerce traffic is coming from smartphones.

Roughly 58% of American adults consider themselves addicted to their phone, with that figure rising to 76% among Millennials (18-34). A little more than two-thirds of American adults (68%) now own a smartphone, representing a rapid rise from about half that proportion (35%) in mid-2011. Some 91% of U.S. adult smartphone owners have heard of a mobile payment service such as PayPal (85%), Google Wallet (51%) and Apple Pay (45%), and of those almost six in 10 currently use at least one.

One-Quarter of U.S. E-Commerce Traffic Came From Smartphones in Q3

An increasing share of U.S. e-commerce traffic is coming from smartphones, reports Monetate in its latest quarterly study. During this past quarter, smartphones comprised 24.8% of traffic for the e-commerce sites analyzed, up from 17.9% during the year-earlier period.

But the devices continue to lag in other metrics: traffic from computers (3.71%) and tablets (3.4%), for example, converts at a rate almost three times higher than smartphones (1.3%).

Similarly, add-to-cart rates and page views are almost twice as high on computers and tablets as they are on smartphones.

Separately, the study identifies three "matches made in e-commerce heaven" that should be optimized:

- Direct-to-site + desktop;
- Email + tablet; and
- Search + mobile.

How Are Millennials Using Their Phones?

Roughly 58% of American adults consider themselves addicted to their phone, and that figure rises to 76% among Millennials (18-34), finds Invoca in a recently-released study.

The report shows that amid the numerous activities being performed on phones, calls remain popular – and frequent text messaging remains the most frequent activity performed on a mobile phone by Millennials, with two-thirds using their phone to send messages more than 5 times a day.

The second-most frequent activity is making calls, which 37% of Millennials do more than 5 times a day. After that, one-third update social media with that frequency, while slightly more than one-quarter watch videos (27%), take pictures (27%) and send emails (26%) more than 5 times a day using their phone.

Interestingly, Millennials are more likely than their older counterparts (45+) to make calls with that regularity, as fewer than one-third (29%) of respondents aged 45 and older said they make calls using their mobile phone more than 5 times a day

Overall, respondents to the Invoca survey identified calling as the single most valuable function of their phone, ahead of messaging, social media, email and video.

This has some implications for businesses; in comparing mobile purchases to calls to businesses, the study notes that "sometimes a call is just easier than a click."

In fact, 59% of respondents report calling businesses at least a few times a month, and 42% call a business at least once a week. Additionally, respondents are more than twice as likely to have called a business in the past month (65%) than to have used their phone to fill out a form (24%), and Millennials are three times more likely to call a business (66%) than to use social media to contact one (22%).

The Demographics of U.S. Smartphone and Tablet Users

A little more than two-thirds of American adults (68%) now own a smartphone, representing a rapid rise from about half that proportion (35%) in mid-2011, details the Pew Internet & American Life Project in a recent study.

Tablet ownership has also been on a rapid upward trajectory, increasing from 3% of American adults in 2010 to 45% this year. So who owns these devices?

Not surprisingly, smartphone ownership is highest among youth, with 86% of 18-29-year-olds reporting ownership of a smartphone, although 30-49-year-olds (83%) are close behind. A majority (58%) of 50-64-year-olds also own a smartphone, though adoption falls to 30% among those aged 65 and up.

It's a slightly different pattern for tablet adoption, with ownership highest among the 30-49 groups (57%), followed by the 18-29 bracket (50%). While ownership is again lower among older generations, the gap isn't as large as with smartphones, as 37% of those aged 50-64 and 32% of adults aged 65 and older report owning a tablet.

Smartphone and tablet ownership also have different patterns when sorting by gender and race/ethnicity. While smartphone ownership is slightly higher among men (70%) than women (66%), the opposite is true for tablets, owned by 47% of women and 43% of men.

And while tablet ownership is considerably higher among non-Hispanic whites (47%) than Blacks (38%) and Hispanics (35%), smartphone ownership rates are generally consistent, highest among Blacks (65%) and lowest among Hispanics (64%).

Smartphone and tablet ownership patterns are more similar when looking at income and education, with penetration rising alongside educational attainment and household income.

For example, adults with at least a college degree are almost twice as likely as those without a high school degree to own a smartphone (81% vs. 41%). And while a bare majority (52%) of lower-income (<$30k) adults own a smartphone, that figure rises to 87% among those in higher-income ($75k+) households.

The gaps in ownership are wider, however, among tablet owners. For example, adults in higher-income households are more than 3 times as likely as those in lower-income households to own a tablet (62% vs. 19%). And those with at least a college degree are more than twice as likely as those without a high school degree to own the device (67% vs. 28%).

The Pew study also looks at ownership of several other devices, including computers, game consoles, e-readers, MP3 players, and gaming devices.

Unlike with mobile devices, penetration rates of these other gadgets have either stalled or gradually declined in recent years, with e-reader ownership down substantially this year (19%) from early last year (32%). Some notable demographic results from these analyses include:

- Computer ownership being far higher among non-Hispanic whites (79%) than Blacks (45%);
- A majority of adults in the 18-29 (56%) and 30-49 (55%) brackets owning a game console, with this figure down to 8% among those aged 65 and older;
- Gaming console ownership being higher among women (42%) than men (37%);
- About half (51%) of adults aged 18-49 owning an MP3 player;
- E-reader ownership being consistent at 18-19% across age groups; and
- Ownership of portable gaming devices being broadest among 18-29-year-olds (21%) and higher-income households (21%).

Smartphone-Owning Millennials Say Most Retail Browsing Occurs In-Store

With all the hype about e-commerce, it's sometimes easy to forget that it remains a fraction of total retail spending.

Now, new survey results from Adroit Digital show that the retail store is also Millennials' preferred place to browse for retail purchases, even among smartphone owners. Among the 1,000 U.S. and Canadian Millennial smartphone owners surveyed, a majority (57%) reported spending most of their time browsing for retail purchases in-store rather than on a mobile device (15%) or PC (28%).

Also of interest, Millennials were twice as likely to say they *never* (34%) browse online before buying in-store as to say they always (16%) do so.

Majority of U.S. Smartphone Owners Say They've Used A Mobile Payment Service

Some 91% of U.S. adult smartphone owners have heard of a mobile payment service such as PayPal (85%), Google Wallet (51%) and Apple Pay (45%), and of those almost six in 10 currently use at least one, according to recent survey results from YouGov.

While estimates of mobile payment services adoption vary quite markedly from one survey to the next, the YouGov research offers some insights as to how these services are being used.

Asked for which reasons they had used a mobile payment service, respondents who currently use one noted these as the top 5:

- To make a purchase online (50% of users; 27% of smartphone owners overall);
- To pay or send money to a business/store for a product or service (39% of users; 21% of smartphone owners);
- To send money to a friend or family member (37% of users; 20% of smartphone owners);
- To transfer money between their own accounts (33% of users; 18% of smartphone owners); and
- To receive money from a friend or family member (28% of users; 15% of smartphone owners).

There were some notable disparities when sorting the results by demographic group. For example, among mobile payment service users, men were more likely than women to send money to a friend or family member (41% vs. 34%), while women were more apt to make a purchase online (55% vs. 46%).

And while 35-54-year-olds were less likely than 18-34-year-olds to report being mobile payment users, those who are were more apt to say they had used one to make a purchase in a physical store (23% vs. 15%).

Overall, slightly fewer than 1 in 10 (9%) of adult smartphone owners said they have used a mobile payment service to make an in-store purchase, with this more common among men (12%) than women (6%) and among Hispanics (13%) than White (8%) or Black (9%) respondents.

Of the few making an in-store purchase using a mobile payment service, the most common types of purchases were clothing (46%), on-the-go food such as snacks and coffee (45%), electronics such as tablets and smartphones (44%) and personal care items (37%).

Finally, among those respondents who are aware of mobile payment services but don't currently use one, the main reasons given were: having no need for them (59%) and not trusting the internet with their money (35%).

Out-of-Home Media Touted for Ability
To Reach Consumers Before Mobile Activities

Out-of-home (OOH) media outpace other traditional media in reaching smartphone users in the hour before they engage in specific mobile activities such as mobile shopping, mobile search, and mobile social networking, according to the Outdoor Advertising Association of America (OAAA) in a recently released study conducted by RealityMine.

The study was based on a sample of 1,837 smartphone users (aged 18-64) whose location, mode of transport, media activity behavior, purchase behavior and emotional context were collected via a smartphone e-Diary at each half-hour throughout the day during a week-long period.

The results indicate that:

- OOH media reached panelists in the hour prior to 43% of mobile shopping activity, ahead of TV (27%), AM/FM radio (12%) and print newspapers (3%);
- OOH media similarly reached participants in the hour before 32% of mobile search activity, outpacing TV (26%), AM/FM radio (9%); and print newspapers (2%);
- OOH media reached panelists in the hour prior to 28% of mobile social media activity, matched by TV (27%) in this instance, but ahead of AM/FM radio (8%) and newspapers (1%); and
- OOH media reached participants in the hour before 34% of brand-related social media activity, again on par with TV (34%) and ahead of AM/FM radio (15%) and print newspapers (7%).

In each of these cases, OOH media exposure was greater for transit/bulletins/street furniture than for place-based media.

(Also, brand-related social media activity includes location-based services or interacting with brands, products, services, celebrities, personalities, fan pages, non-profits, charities or cause-driven organizations).

OOH advertising has previously been touted for its ability to spur mobile behaviors. A couple of years ago, a CBS Outdoor study claimed that a significant percentage of urban Europeans responded to OOH advertising through various mobile activities, such as downloading an application (13%), scanning a QR/barcode (11%), redeeming a voucher with a mobile device (8%), and using a mobile phone to make a purchase (7%).

According to the OAAA study, OOH isn't effective in just reaching consumers prior to mobile activities. It also outpaces other traditional media in reaching smartphone users in the hour prior to QSR visits and mall visits, and in the same half-hour as considering purchases in the automotive, fashion and apparel, and fast food categories.

In other words, these media (in most cases transit/bulletins/street furniture rather than place-based) could potentially influence consumers' purchase decisions in these and presumably other categories.

Indeed, the study found that overall, OOH media reached consumers in the same half-hour as 68% of purchase activity.

Separately, the OAAA reports that OOH advertising revenues were up by 4.7% year-over-year in Q1, the 20th consecutive quarter of growth. The fastest-growing advertising categories were government, politics and organizations (11.5%), financial (10.5%) and media and advertising (9.4%).

Social Media/Social Networking

Social media seems to be everywhere, but somewhat surprisingly is not number one. Social media/networking is the preferred customer service channel for just 2% of customers, far behind channels such as phone (43%) and email (22%).

However, mobile, digital, and social brands continue to exhibit loyalty supremacy, with new brands and categories marking up for that a third of 2014's Top-100 leaders list. Local deals and offers on Facebook have a strong pull among 18-29 year-olds who own at least a smartphone or tablet and a desktop computer, who have an interest in making purchases from local/small businesses. Teens prefer Instagram for their social networking, gravitating more away from Facebook. There are four primary motivations for going online: interpersonal connections, self-expression, exploration, and convenience.

Top Brands Ranked by Customer Loyalty

Mobile, digital, and social brands continue to exhibit loyalty supremacy, with new brands and categories making up more than a third of this year's Top-100 leaders list, according to Brand Keys Loyalty Leader 2014 report.

Topping this year's list are Apple, Amazon, What's app, Google, YouTube, and Kindle.

Thirty six of the top 100 Loyalty Leaders are new brands or categories.

Most new arrivals facilitate communication and social outreach: tablets, smartphones, and social networks, with What's App (instant messaging), Netflix, and Amazon (video streaming), Instagram, and PayPal (online payments) now representing that trend.

Other, new, non-digital/social categories include Fast-Casual Restaurants (Chipotle, Panera, Chick-fil-A), Insurance (USAA), Credit Cards (Discover, American Express), and Beer (Sam Adams).

Dunkin' Donuts was the only non-digital/social brand in the top-10, up 7 spots from last year, but not astonishing when you realize their customers have rated them #1 in the out-of-home coffee category for years.

The 2014 Brand Keys Loyalty Leaders top-10 rank as follows:

1. Amazon: tablets
2. Apple: tablets
3. Apple: smartphone
4. YouTube: social networking
5. What's App: instant messaging
6. Amazon: online retail
7. Google: search engines
8. Kindle: e-readers
9. Samsung: smartphones
10. Dunkin' Donuts: coffee (out-of-home)

Some 45% of the top-100 brands account for consumer outreach and engagement via cellular and social networks, and the phones, smartphones, computers, and tablets needed to meet ever-increasing expectations related to outreach and personal connectivity the consumer uses as a yardstick to measure brands.

Last year beauty and personal care brands accounted for approximately a fifth of the top-100 but this year represent only 13%.

Traditional retail brands were down 50%. The ineptitude for many retailers to provide meaningful differentiation — beyond low-lower-lowest pricing strategies — has seriously eroded loyalty levels in the retail category.

That, and a shift to buying online and via mobile devices.

Retail brands that remain among this year's Loyalty Leaders include J. Crew (#50), The Gap (#80), Macy's (#88), Victoria's Secret (#75) and T.J. Maxx (#92).

Six automotive brands made the top-100, including: Hyundai (#23), Ford (#26), Toyota (#48), Jeep (#70), Nissan (#94), and KIA (#99).

Nissan appears on the list for the first time while Ford and Toyota moved up the list +12 spots each, Jeep moved up +11.

The brands that showed the greatest loyalty gains this year were:

- Netflix (+79)
- Estee Lauder (+31)
- MAC Cosmetics (+28)
- HTC smartphones (+26)
- Cover Girl (+25)

With a few exceptions, it turns out that the biggest Loyalty Leader losers were primarily categories, with certain categories just disappearing.

Those categories included Breakfast Cereal, which should not come as a shock to anyone.

Perennial Loyalty Leaders absent from this years list include Pepsi and Coke, ABC News, NBC News, CBS News, the Today Show, Bing, and Yahoo.

When it comes to the search category, only Google (#7) appears.

Not surprisingly General Motors did not make this year's list.

McDonald's, which had appeared since the List's 1996 inception, dropped off the top-100 list too.

In a study conducted earlier this year by Brand Keys, Millennials, a key audience for fast food chains, reports a 20% decrease in visits to them, with 42% reporting increased visits to fast-casual restaurants, a category whose brands *have* shown up for the first time on this years list.

Other brands *not* appearing on the loyalty Leaders List this year included Ben & Jerry's, Canon (point-and-shoot cameras), H&M, Haagen-Daz, Skechers, Skype, Southwest Airlines, Walgreens, and Walmart.

Brands with the greatest loyalty and engagement erosion:

- Max Factor (-20)
- Clinique (-16)
- Grey Goose (-13)
- Revlon (-13)
- Apple Computers (-11)
- Costco (-11)
- Sam's Club (-11)

While it is true that some of the shifts are due to the creation and adoption of new categories and brands that better meet — even exceed — customer expectations, brands that understand that real emotional connections can serve as a surrogate for added-value.

The brand which have made loyalty and emotional engagement one of their real strategic priorities and KPIs will always show up at the top of a consumer's list.

Teens Choice of Social Network: Instagram

Teens continue to gravitate away from Facebook in favor of Instagram, according to Piper Jaffray's latest semi-annual survey of American teens.

Roughly three-quarters of respondents reported using the visual platform, up from 69% in the previous survey.

By comparison, just 45% said they use Facebook, a significant drop from 72%, the decline was enough to move it behind Twitter in the popularity stakes.

The micro-blogging site is now the second-most used among teenagers, but does not seem to be making strides: the 59% endorsement rate in this latest survey marks a slight drop from 63% in the preceding report.

Meanwhile, Pinterest and Tumblr have continued to be relatively flat, used by slightly more than 1 in 5 teens, while Google+ usage plunged from 29% to 12%.

Instagram's rise to the top of social media has been quite rapid: in Piper Jaffray's Spring 2014 survey, 30% of teens called it their "most important" social network, overtaking Twitter (the fall 2013 favorite) and putting even more distance between itself and Facebook (the Spring 2013 favorite).

The latest study notes that 38% of teens believe Instagram is a positive marketing channel through which to reach them, compared with 34% saying the same about Twitter and 21% about Facebook, with only 4% of teens using Snapchat.

Social Media Is Not Number One

Social media is the preferred customer service channel for just 2% of customers, far behind other channels such as phone (43%) and email (22%), this according to a Parature survey of roughly 1,000 United States adults.

Yet, respondents are not shy about using social media to interact with brands: 35% claim to have asked a customer service question on social media, while 35% have complained about a brand and 52% have praised a brand. Some 51% among those that got a response said it gave them a somewhat or much more favorable view of the brand.

The survey does not detail whether the response was for a question, praise, or complaint. Research from Bazaarvoice has shown that brands can benefit from responding to negative reviews. Even so, a recent survey found that 1 in 5 brands rarely, if ever, respond to complaints on social media.

It is interesting to note, however, that survey respondents are more likely to take to social to praise rather than complain about a brand, as previous research has found that consumers are more likely to share bad than good service experiences.

Nevertheless, recent research from NewVoiceMedia suggests that half of US consumers will tell friends and colleagues not to use a business following an inadequate customer service experience – while 7 in 10 will recommend a company following a positive experience.

Overall, 59% of the Parature survey respondents who interacted with a brand on social media (be it praising, complaining, or asking a question of it) said they received a response from the brand. By comparison, Socialbakers data indicates that US Brands responded to just 38% of Facebook users' wall posts in June, down from February's high of 59%.

When looking for a rapid response, however, social media is not the preferred choice. When asked which channel they would use if they needed a fast or immediate response, a dominant 57% of respondents cited the phone, followed by live chat (24%). Just 1% of respondents said they would use social media.

Sponsorship

If you're using sponsored content, paid posts, partner stories to promote your products, you might want to think again. Roughly 54% of Internet users aged 18-65 say they largely do not trust sponsored content, with most of the remainder only trusting such content if they trust the publication it runs on (19%) or they already trust the brand (23%).

Trust in Sponsored Content Runs Low

If you're using sponsored content, paid posts, partner stories to promote your products, you might want to think again.

Roughly 54% of internet users aged 18-65 say they largely do not trust sponsored content, with most of the remainder only trusting such content if they trust the publication it runs on (19%) or they already trust the brand (23%), according to survey results from Contently.

The study also found that two-thirds of those surveyed have at some point felt deceived upon realizing that an article they read or a video they watched was sponsored by a brand.

The results are interesting in light of a Polar analysis of data within its native advertising platform suggesting that the more closely aligned a native unit is with the publisher's content (on a style basis), the better it will perform.

In February, Chartbeat CEO Tony Haile, revealed that only 24% of readers were scrolling down on native ad content on publisher sites, compared to the 71% of readers who scroll on "normal content."

It was a damning indictment of the quality of sponsored content at large.

A separate survey conducted by Hexagram and Spada found that 8 in 10 publishers and 2 in 3 brands that have used native advertising reported having received no backlash at all to their use of the campaigns.

That is despite almost 6 in 10 respondents to the Contently survey who believe a news site loses credibility if it runs articles sponsored by a brand.

Two-thirds of respondents to the Contently survey said they would not be as likely to click on an article sponsored by a brand as they would to click on editorial content.

A key finding in the Contently study is that while most publishers assume that readers know what it means when a post is labeled "Sponsored Content," the majority of readers cannot agree on one clear answer.

While a bulk of respondents (48%) believe that "Sponsored Content" means that an advertiser paid for the article to be created and had influence on the article's content, more than half (52%) thought it means something different.

But that's not where the confusion ends. Some of the most striking revelations include:

- Two-thirds of readers have felt deceived upon realizing than an article or video was sponsored by a brand;
- 54% of readers do not trust sponsored content;
- 59% of readers believe a news site loses credibility if it runs articles sponsored by a brand;
- As education level increases, so does mistrust of sponsored content; and

- Respondents rated branded content as more trustworthy than Fox News, and nearly equally as trustworthy as MSNBC, indicating that content has a mistrust problem overall.

Even if readers do not understand what branded content means, do they prefer it to the often scorned banner ad? The answer may surprise you if you work in digital media.

More than half (57%) of readers said that they would prefer that their favorite blogs and news sites run banner ads instead of sponsored articles.

In a ranking of perceived quality, respondents ranked articles in print newspapers and print magazines as having the highest quality, followed in descending order by:

- articles on a news website;
- advertorials in a printed magazine;
- sponsored articles on a news website;
- articles on a brand's website; and
- blog posts by mommy bloggers.

None of this means that sponsored content is "dead in the water," it just means that it is time to get it right.

Sports

Baseball might be America's past time but 50% of Americans are professional football fans. In fact, professional baseball (32%) is actually third on American sports fans must-watch list behind college football (35%) and before professional basketball (30%).

Watching sports is no longer limited to attending a game or watching on TV, in 2014 more than 70 million consumers watched sports on either their smart phones or computer. It's pretty common knowledge that a lot of people watch the Super Bowl solely for the commercials, and in 2015 BMW and Mercedes-Benz saw the biggest increase in car shopper interest on edmunds.com, while the most popular ad was Budweiser's "Lost Dog,"

Football Frenzy: Half of Americans Are Professional Football Fans

After six months football that counts is back, as the NFL regular season kicked off yesterday. Half (50%) of Americans are professional football fans, making the sport a clear fan-favorite among U.S. adults, this according to new research from Mintel.

Joining professional football at the top of sports fans' must-watch list are college football (35%), professional baseball (32%) and professional basketball (30%).

According to Mintel research, roughly two thirds of U.S. adults are sports fans (67%), individuals who watch at least half of their favorite team's games or events in at least one sport.

By Mintel's definition, 56% of women and 80% of men qualify as sports fans. Though men (63%) are much more likely than women (38%) to watch football, it is the most popular sport among fans regardless of gender.

In fact, 38% of men report that they almost never miss their favorite football team's game. A similar trend is seen among college football fans, with 45% of men and 26% of women reporting that they are fans.

In conjunction, baseball and basketball rank third and fourth most popular among men and women, with men (43%) being twice as likely as women (22%) to be fans of professional baseball and professional basketball (40% vs. 21% of women).

Additionally, male sports fans are more likely to play fantasy sports (23%) than women (13%), with men (45%) showing greater interest in game and player statistics than women (31%).

"Following sports is a widely popular tradition in the U.S. due to a rich history at both the collegiate and professional levels, as well as the notion that athletics embody the American ideals of hard work, perseverance and striving for greatness. Our research shows that sports like college and professional football have strong fan bases among male and female sports fans and are as much of an American pastime as baseball," said Lauren Bonetto, Lifestyles and Leisure Analyst at Mintel. "Furthermore, the popularity of fantasy sports illustrates the level of dedication Americans have to sports overall and could lead to increased engagement as those in fantasy leagues may watch additional games to gain a competitive edge."

Importance of the tailgate spread   The majority of sports fans agree that eating and drinking is a big part of watching sports (60%).

Nearly all sports fans consume beverages while watching sports at home with at least half reaching for water, soda or beer.

Among sports fans age 21 and older, 63% report consuming alcoholic beverages while watching sports, with 50% of these fans drinking beer. In comparison, 54% of fans report drinking soda and 64% drink water while watching sports.

Though many fans drink alcohol while watching sports, it appears few are "drinking to get drunk;" sports fans tend to opt for beer (50%) and wine (31%) over mixed drinks with hard alcohol (28%). In particular, male sports fans are significantly more likely than female fans to consume beer while watching sports (56% vs. 42%).

Overall, 83% of fans snack while watching sports. Mintel research shows that 82% of U.S. adults buy salty snacks for themselves, and sports fans are no exception: 68% of fans eat salty snacks while watching sports. Outside of snacks, chili, a staple of some football tailgate spreads, is eaten by nearly one third of sports fans (29%) during games.

Millennials use game time to socialize   While two thirds of fans prefer to watch games from the comfort of their own home rather than in person (69%), roughly half of American sports fans view sports as a tool for socializing. A full 46% agree that following sports is more about being social than anything else, including 59% of Millennials.

Millennials are also most likely to agree with similar motivations for watching sports. Three quarters (74%) of sports fans agree that following sports is a good way to bond with family and friends, increasing to 78% of Millennials.

Further, 52% of sports fans overall and 67% of Millennials agree that following sports makes them feel more connected to their community. Millennial sports fans are the most likely generation to watch sports with others, including 45% who report watching with friends, compared to 34% of fans overall.

Compared to Millennials, children show less interest in watching sports. In 2014, a third of kids age 6-11 watched sports on TV at least occasionally (33%). This is down from 39% in 2013, and is a sharp decline from 2008, when nearly half of children age 6-11 reported watching sports (45%).

"Millennials tend to agree that following sports is about being social. Our data indicates Millennials prefer to watch sporting events as part of a larger group and gravitate towards social media in order to stay connected and engaged both online and offline," concluded Bonetto.

The Year in Sports: Digital Steps Up to Plate

With the rise of technology, media content is no longer synonymous with TV. Consumers can connect with media across a variety of devices, anytime, anywhere — at work, during a daily commute, or during outdoor activities — with just a few screen taps.

According to Nielsen's 2014 Year in Sports Report, more than 70 million people consumed sports on either their smart phones or computer in the third quarter of 2014.

Of that group, the top 20% — 10 million on phones, 15 million online — consumed 85% of the total sports minutes viewed in that quarter.

Fans insatiable appetite for sports spans all forms of media, including radio. Sports radio attracts 23 million weekly listeners, who tune in for an average of four hours a week.

A cumulative 72.3 million Americans consumed a staggering 7.1 billion minutes of sports content on their smartphones in October 2014 with 79 million online users consuming over 8.7 billion minutes of content.

From October 2012 to 2014, the average user increased their monthly smartphone time spent by 35%.

Super Bowl Advertisers Mercedes-Benz and BMW See Biggest Increases in Car Shopper Interest on Edmunds.com

Mercedes-Benz and BMW saw the most compelling spikes in traffic on edmunds.com after their ads ran during Super Bowl XLIX, according to a real-time analysis by the car shopping website.

By the end of the game, the Mercedes-Benz AMG GT had the biggest cumulative spike in traffic, with a 2189% jump over previous Sunday averages on edmunds.com. The BMW i3 captured the second most buzz on edmunds.com; its cumulative traffic climbed 583%.

"Even though these two advertised vehicles are likely to be sold in small volume to niche audiences, the BMW and Mercedes brands will enjoy the overall buzz they have generated, especially as both continue their efforts to grow their overall reach into new car shopper segments," said edmunds.com Sr. Analyst Jessica Caldwell. "Both brands will be quite happy that the millions of dollars they invested had the desired effect."

edmunds.com also tracked the immediate traffic lifts enjoyed by Super Bowl advertisers during and after their commercials ran:

- Chevrolet sponsored the pre-game show and showed four Colorado ads; site traffic to Colorado pages increased 25% during the pregame and 1104% during the first quarter of the game;
- During the third quarter of the game, Dodge Challenger ads lifted its traffic on Edmunds 232%;
- Fiat 500x increased 3981% in the moments following its second quarter ads; interest remained high in the third quarter, delivering a 986% life for the vehicle;
- Jeep Renegade was advertised in the third quarter of the game and traffic to its pages immediately increased 1031%; during fourth quarter the increase was 5720%;
- Kia Sorrento traffic increased 213% immediately following its third quarter ad;
- Lexus NX's second quarter ad generated an increase of 341%. The brand did even better immediately after its RC 350 ad ran in the third quarter, increasing vehicle's page traffic on Edmunds 5702%. The RC continued to enjoy success in the fourth quarter with a 690% lift in traffic to its pages on edmunds.com;
- MINI sponsored an early part of the pre-game show and showed five ads; site traffic to MINI Cooper increased 48% during that period;
- Nissan brand consideration increased 90% immediately following its second quarter ad; and
- In the moments following its halftime ad, Toyota Camry site traffic increased 364%

Super Bowl Ad Rankings Go to the Dogs

Anheuser-Busch's 'Lost Dog' spot was ranked the top commercial in the 27th annual USA TODAY Ad Meter, the most widely recognized barometer and industry-leading tool used to measure public opinion surrounding Super Bowl advertising.

AB won for the third straight year, taking home its 13th Ad Meter title in three years.

The top five ads, as voted upon by this year's Ad Meter panel, including final ratings are:

1. Anheuser-Busch — Lost Dog (8.10)
2. Always — Like a Girl (7.10)
3. Fiat — Blue Pill (6.87)
4. Microsoft — Braylon (6.74)
5. Doritos — Middle Seat (6.71)

Some services are more popular in some markets than others: San Francisco (48%) edges Washington DC (47%) in Netflix penetration, while Washington, DC (24%) takes the lead over Seattle (23%) in Amazon Instant prime penetration, with San Francisco further back (18).

Seattle, meanwhile, has the largest share (9%) of homes with access to Hulu Plus.

The Super Bowl Ad Meter was created by USA TODAY in 1989 to gauge consumers' attitudes about television's most expensive commercials.

Football Still Doing Touchdown Dance Around Baseball

Back in 1985, there was only a one-point difference between the percentage of American adults who followed at least one sport and considered pro football (24%) or baseball (23%) to be their favorite.

Today, "America's pastime" remains in the past, as pro football is still America's Favorite Sport — now by a 16-point margin over baseball.

Pro football is the top pick among 32% of sports fans, while baseball only garners "favorite" status among half as many Americans (16%), according to a new study from The Harris Poll.

However, baseball aficionados can feel good that their sport of choice has managed a 2 percentage point increase from last year's 14%, while football saw a three- point decrease from 2013's 35% — meaning the gap between the two narrowed by five points year-over-year.

As if only to confirm the sport's widespread appeal, men's college football comes in as America's third favorite sport, with 10% of adults supporting its claim, though, like its professional counterpart, this sport has also seen a narrow decrease from last year's 11%.

The next two top sports have maintained their same fan percentages, with auto racing at 7% and men's pro basketball, part of a three-way tie at 6%. Tied with basketball at 6% and up from only 2% last year, the most notable increase across the board, men's soccer has made the list of America's top five favorite sports.

The final member of the 6% three-way tie for America's fifth favorite sport is ice hockey, most beloved by one percent more of the population compared with last year (5%).

Though the total number of sports fans considering pro football to be their favorite is 32%, some demographics are more attached to the game than others are. Generation X (43%),

- Easterners (37%), and moderates (35%) are the demographics most likely to consider pro football to be their favorite sport.
- Meanwhile, the lowest numbers can be found among Millennials (25%), adults who have competed post- graduate degrees (25%), and liberals (26%).
- As for those who believe RBIs and home runs are number 1, the largest percentages can also be found among Easterners (23%), Liberals (22%) and Baby Boomers (20%). Meanwhile, those who consider baseball their favorite sport are less abundant among Midwesterners (12%), and adults with children in their households (10%).

Streaming Devices

Regular television is now a thing of the past, a growing portion of Americans own a TV with built-in streaming functionality: some 19% of U.S. households have a smart TV as of September 2015, up from 15% in November 2014.

Almost 1 in 5 Americans aged 18-54 use a digital streaming media player monthly to watch TV and movies, that's more than double in proportion in 2013 (9%). Video ad completion rates were lower on devices with smaller screens as smartphone (46%) and tablet (54%) viewers completed ads at roughly half the rate of those watching on gaming consoles (95%) and over-the-top (OTT) boxes (99%). Consumers are viewing more ads on OTT streaming devices such as Apple TV and Chromecast, which have moved ahead of tablets and desktops in digital video monetization.

Digital Streaming Media Player Use Continues to Grow

Almost 1 in 5 Americans aged 18-54 use a digital streaming media player monthly to watch TV and movies, more than double the proportion from 2013 (9%), reports GfK in newly-released data.

Smart TVs (television sets with integrated Internet) are also growing quickly, with 19% of 13-54-year-olds using them at least monthly to watch TV and movies.

As GfK notes, "the TV set will continue to be the hub for video entertainment for the foreseeable future," with the change instead being in the mix of content sources.

Smart TVs Now in Almost 1 in 5 Households

Streaming media players are gaining in popularity, but a growing portion of Americans own a TV with built-in streaming functionality: some 19% of U.S. households have a smart TV as of September, reports Nielsen in a new study, up from 15% in November 2014.

Washington, DC (26%) ranks as the market with the broadest smart TV penetration and the largest absolute year-over-year gain (11% points).

Smart TV ownership is also high in Houston (24%) and New York (24%) among others, per the report.

When It Comes to Video, Bigger Screens Are Better

Video ad completion rates were lower on devices with smaller screens last year, says Vindico, as smartphone (46%) and tablet (54%) viewers completed ads at roughly half the rate of those watching on gaming consoles (95%) and OTT boxes (99%).

The overall video ad completion rate stood at 78%, but just 37% of video impressions were both viewable and viewed to completion. (Completion rate figures exclude skippable ad impressions from Google/YouTube.)

Separately, the average click-through rate for video ads was 0.62%, with that figure highest for tablets (3.62%) and smartphones (2.36%) and lowest for OTT boxes (0.01%) and game consoles (0.11%).

OTT Streaming Devices Overtake Tablets In Digital Video Ad Views

Consumers are viewing more ads on over-the-top (OTT) streaming devices such as Apple TV and Chromecast, which have moved ahead of tablets and desktops in digital video monetization, according to FreeWheel in its Q4 2014 Video Monetization Report.

During the quarter, OTT devices accounted for 8% of ad views for professional, rights-managed video content, up from just 2% during the year-earlier period and moving ahead of tablets (7% share) in the process.

Not too surprisingly, viewing on OTT devices tends to mirror TV viewing habits, with 91% of video ad views on the devices coming during long-form and live content.

By comparison, 54% of ad views on tablets came during long-form and live content, as did just 30% of views on desktops and laptops and 25% on smartphones.

FreeWheel explains the discrepancy by noting that "computers and smartphones are used to 'snack' on content throughout the workday while tablets and OTT devices tend to live in the home and are 'binge viewing' portals."

As a result of their heavy emphasis on long-form content, OTT devices accounted for a hefty 37% share of live viewing by device in Q4, second only to desktops and laptops (50%).

Live content itself has grown as a content monetization force, accounting for 23.2% of ad views for programmers (see methodology below for a description of "programmers") during Q4 2014, up from 9.9% share a year earlier.

In other trends identified in the report:
• Both video ad views (+30%) and video views (+27%)

- On a year-over-year basis, ad views during long-form and live content grew by 43% in Q4, more than twice the growth rate of ad views during short- and mid-form content (+19%);
- Sports content accounted for the vast majority (83%) of ad views during live and simulcast viewing;
- Video ad views of Broadcast shows' current seasons grew by 67% year-over-year, and for programmers, 94% share of ad views during Q4 came for current season shows rather than archival content;

  • Even so, digital viewers are watching on their own schedules, as 64% of programmers' ad views came at least 8 days after air date;

  • Viewers saw 3.9 ads per mid-roll break, dipping slightly from Q3 (4) after several quarters of increases; and

  • Authenticated viewing continued its fast growth as Q4 marked the first quarter in which a majority (56%) of long-form and live monetization derived from authenticated viewing (defined as viewing that occurs after viewers enter their MVPD subscription credentials). That 56% figure is more than 4 times the share from Q4 2013 (13%).

Digital Streaming Media Player Use Continues to Grow

Almost 1 in 5 Americans aged 18-54 use a digital streaming media player monthly to watch TV and movies, more than double the proportion from 2013 (9%), reports GfK in newly-released data.

Smart TVs (television sets with integrated Internet) are also growing quickly, with 19% of 13-54-year-olds using them at least monthly to watch TV and movies.

As GfK notes, "the TV set will continue to be the hub for video entertainment for the foreseeable future," with the change instead being in the mix of content sources.

Smart TVs Now in Almost 1 in 5 Households

Streaming media players are gaining in popularity, but a growing portion of Americans own a TV with built-in streaming functionality: some 19% of U.S. households have a smart TV as of September, reports Nielsen in a new study, up from 15% in November 2014.

Washington, DC (26%) ranks as the market with the broadest smart TV penetration and the largest absolute year-over-year gain (11% points).

Smart TV ownership is also high in Houston (24%) and New York (24%) among others, per the report.

When It Comes to Video, Bigger Screens Are Better

Video ad completion rates were lower on devices with smaller screens last year, says Vindico, as smartphone (46%) and tablet (54%) viewers completed ads at roughly half the rate of those watching on gaming consoles (95%) and OTT boxes (99%).

The overall video ad completion rate stood at 78%, but just 37% of video impressions were both viewable and viewed to completion. (Completion rate figures exclude skippable ad impressions from Google/YouTube.)

Separately, the average click-through rate for video ads was 0.62%, with that figure highest for tablets (3.62%) and smartphones (2.36%) and lowest for OTT boxes (0.01%) and game consoles (0.11%).

Technology

Snapchat may be more popular with youth but the social media app has infiltrated about half of 18-24-year-old smartphone users, closing in on Instagram.

Almost half (45%) of shoppers do not trust retailers to keep their credit and debit card information safe from potential hackers. U.S. adults will spent more than 5-and-a-half hours per day with digital media in 2015, up by almost a half-hour year-over-year. Virtually all (95%) of commercial emails generate some forwarding behavior. Nearly three-quarters of adults in the U.S. believe that technology has become too distracting, with Millennials (18-35) slightly above-average in their agreement.

Who's Using SnapChat?

It is well established that Snapchat is more popular with youth, but new data from comScore and CivicScience offer some updated figures detailing Snapchat's popularity. According to comScore's numbers, Snapchat infiltration is now at about half of 18- to 24-year-old smartphone users, up from less than one-third a year earlier and closing in on Instagram (54.6%). And while Snapchat's popularity does tail off among older smartphone users, it has still been growing quickly.

Per comScore, 1 in 5 smartphone users aged 25-34 used Snapchat in June, with that being more than triple the percentage (6.3%) from a year earlier. Among smartphone owners 35 and older, Snapchat's penetration stood at 7.6% in June, more than double the year earlier rate of 3%.

Not surprisingly, CivicScience's poll shows a similarly young demographic. Among the 14% of survey respondents who claimed to use Snapchat, 71% were under 25-years-old, with a majority 43% between the ages of 18 and 24. Interestingly, the results of the survey indicated that Snapchat fans lean heavily female with just 31% being men.

The CivicScience study also looked at behavioral traits of Snapchat users, many of which are consistent with traits commonly attributed to youth.

Compared to the general population, Snapchat fans are 86% more likely to say their friends and other contacts on social media influence the products they buy, fans are 89% more likely to often post comments on Facebook or Twitter while watching a show or movie, ad fans are 43% more likely to say they are "addicted" to their digital devices.

Security Breaches Affect Shopping Behavior

Almost half (45%) of shoppers do not trust retailers to keep their credit and debit card information safe from potential hackers, according to a report from Interactions, which noted that up to 44% of respondents have had their personal information stolen as a result of a security breach.

A new report from Retail Perceptions offers insight into how the loyalty to brands of consumers changed following highly publicized data breaches. Up to 12% of shoppers said they stopped shopping with retailers that experienced a breach, with another 36% indicating they shopped at the retailer less frequently.

With debit and credit cards being the top targets for hackers, shoppers may be inclined into making purchases via other means, namely cash. The majority (79%) of respondents said they were more likely to use cash as opposed to credit cards to purchase products in-store.

Buyers have varied opinions regarding their comfort levels shopping with retailers after they experience a security breach.

Roughly one-fifth (19%) of those surveyed feel comfortable going back to the same retailer to shop immediately, while another 19% said they would prefer to hold off for three to six months. Conversely, some people do not care as long as the breach is corrected quickly (22%).

Shoppers provided four key stipulations retailers would have to adhere to in order to regain their trust after a breach:

- provide free credit monitoring capabilities;
- offer additional incentives or discounts;
- provide clear and honest explanations to shoppers regarding the breach; and
- increase security measures and communicate the changes that have been made.

With What Major Media Do U.S. Adults Spend Most Time?

U.S. adults will spend more than 5-and-a-half hours per day with digital media this year, up by almost a half-hour year-over-year, per eMarketer's latest estimates.

The majority (2:51) of that time will be spent with the mobile internet, which will have seen a compound annual growth rate of 37.2% between 2011 and 2015.

TV will occupy the second-largest chunk of adults' daily media time, at 4-and-a-quarter hours this year, down less than 20 minutes from 2011.

By year's end, print newspapers will have seen the largest decline in daily time, although newspaper ads continue to have a sizable influence on consumers' purchases.

How Often Are Emails Forwarded?

Virtually all (95%) of commercial emails generate some forwarding behavior, according to a Litmus analysis of more than 400,000 commercial sends with at least 500 opens between January 2013 and March 2015.

The median email (by forward-to-open rate) generated 1 forward for every 370 opens, or a 0.27% forward-to-open rate, per the analysis.

However, there is exponential growth in this rate when looking at the top percentiles, with the top 1% being 17.6 times more likely to be forwarded than the median, generating 1 forward for every 21 opens.

Interestingly, the analysis found that the forward-to-open rate was higher for emails with small audiences (those with 500 to 50,000 opens) than for those with larger audiences, which the study author attributes to smaller audiences tending to "coalesce around narrow interests, specialty products, niche services, and local attractions."

Examining the top percentile of emails against the 50th percentile, the study finds that the most-forwarded emails were more likely to center around topics such as event registrations/RSVPs, transactions, and new product or service/store openings, and far less likely to be centered on promotions, deals and discounts. News and helpful content was the second-most common topic for both the top percentile and 50th percentile.

Americans' Views of Impact of Technology on Everyday Life

Nearly three-quarters of adults in the U.S. believe that technology has become too distracting, with Millennials (18-35) slightly above-average in their agreement, according to a recent Harris Poll.

A strong majority also agree that technology is corrupting interpersonal communications (69%) and having a negative impact on literacy (59%) with these figures highest among Baby Boomers.

However, there are positive associations with technology use, as 71% (73% of Millennials) believe it has improved the quality of their life and 51% (67% among Millennials) feel that is enhances their social life.

Indeed, more respondents believe that technology is having a positive than negative effect on various aspects of their lives, including their ability to learn new skills, their relationships with friends, their ability to live life the way they want to, and their happiness.

Traditional Media

Traditional media is no longer the most trusted source of news and information around the world.

 Among online U.S. adults, Baby Boomers (46-65) spend almost twice as much time on a daily basis with TV, radio and print as do Millennials (16-34).

 A slight majority (53%) of U.S. consumers agree that, compared to 5 years ago, there is too much content out there, and 45% wish they could frequently unplug from all content and devices. While most feel that content has become easier to create and more visual, levels of skepticism regarding the authenticity of content are running high.

 U.S. magazines' total print and digital audience rose 7.6% to 1.68 billion in July 2015 from 1.57 billion in July 2014, yet it should be noted that magazines now includes not only the familiar print versions, but mobile.

Consumers are more likely to trust brand content found in a print newspaper and on TV than in a variety of social platforms including Instagram, Twitter or blogs.

Globally, revenues from newspaper circulation exceeded advertising revenues in 2014 for the first time this century.

U.S. adults will spend more than 5-and-a-half hours per day with digital media this year, up by almost a half-hour year-over-year.

Traditional Media Consumption Estimates, by Generation

Among online U.S. adults, Baby Boomers (46-65) spend almost twice as much time on a daily basis with TV, radio and print as do Millennials (16-3) per newly-released data from a TNS study.

In fact, while Baby Boomers report spending more than double the time with TV (3.4 hours per day) as with TV and video online (1.3 hours), Millennial estimate spending more time with digital than offline TV (2.7 vs. 1.9 hours per day).

For comparison, Nielsen figures suggest that while youth watch substantially less traditional TV than their older counterparts, traditional TV viewing among Millennials is in excess of 2 hours per day, surpassing 3 hours per day for the 25-34 demographic.

Authenticity and Design: How Consumers Feel About Online Content

A slight majority (53%) of U.S. consumers agree that, compared to 5 years ago, there is too much content out there, and 45% wish they could frequently "unplug" from all content and devices. While most feel that content has become easier to create and more visual, levels of skepticism regarding the authenticity of content are running high, according to a recent study from Adobe.

Indeed, a majority of adults report being likely to question the authenticity of a variety of forms of content, including:

- Whether a news article is biased (61%);
- Whether a photo in an ad has been altered (60%);
- Whether the author has been paid or otherwise incentivized to provide a positive review (60%); and
- Whether a photo or image posted by a company has been altered (58%).

Similarly, a majority are likely to question the authenticity of photos and videos posted by people they don't know, among other forms of content.

Indeed, the only content forms that a minority will question are photos and videos posted by peers. As such, content shared by friends and family members (72%) and content shared by a work colleague or peer (59%) – independent of who created the content – are the most trusted, according to the study.

Few other content sources earn trust from a majority of respondents. Only a slight majority trust content from a traditional broadcast media network (55%), from a company whose products they buy (54%), or from a traditionally printed newspaper or magazine such as the New York Times (54%).

Yet, trust in content from traditional media still beats other sources, per the study. For example, few trust content from a professional blogger (36%), an entertainment news outlet such as Buzzfeed (34%), from an entertainment celebrity (31%) or a YouTube celebrity (31%).

These are interesting findings in light of other research that has found a higher degree of trust in branded content that appears on TV and in print than on social channels, with Facebook being the notable exception.

A key theme to emerge from Adobe's study is the greater degree of trust in information from those considered more likely to be peers. For example:

- 68% consider breaking news to be more trustworthy when coming from an eyewitness than from a news anchor;
- 84% consider a product endorsement to be more trustworthy from an ordinary user than a celebrity; and
- 73% would trust a music recommendation from a close friend over one from a music service based on past preferences.

The study notes that Millennials are more likely than Gen Xers and Baby Boomers to question the authenticity of online content, using skepticism around photo and video alterations as examples.

At the same time, maybe Millennials only have themselves to blame. After all, separate results from the report indicate that 35% of Millennials deem entertaining content more important to them than accurate content. By comparison, only 20% of Gen Xers and 10% of Baby Boomers feel the same way.

Further, Millennials emerge as the generation least likely to confirm the accuracy of content before sharing, with almost 4 in 10 not checking to see if the information they are about to post is accurate. And only a minority (43%) think about the appropriateness of a photo they are about to post.

Beyond content authenticity, the Adobe research also examines interactions with content, with some interesting findings:

- Millennials use more devices and consume more sources of content than adults on average;
- While laptops and desktops are the digital devices most commonly used by Gen Xers and Baby Boomers, Millennials use their smartphones most frequently;
- Online search engines are the most common sources of content for Millennials and Gen Xers on a daily basis, while cable and satellite TV lead among Baby Boomers;
- Given 15 minutes to consume content, 66% of respondents would watch a video report on breaking news rather than read a report on breaking news, and 59% would skim articles on trends rather than read a long article on one issue;
- Design matters to consumers, as two-thirds (73% among Millennials) would rather read something beautifully designed than something simple and plain if they had only 15 minutes with which to do so;
- When viewing content across their personal and professional lives, roughly two-thirds or more value content that holds their attention, displays well on the device they're using, and has overall good design; and

More than one-third of respondents will stop engaging with content altogether if images won't load (39%), it takes too long to load (39%), the content is too long (38%) or the content is unattractive in its layout or imagery (38%).

Why You Should Keep Advertising in Magazines: Audience Grows 7.6%

Don't fail to keep promoting your brands in magazines.

That's the clear message from the latest Magazine Media 360° Brand Audience Report from the **MPA – The Association of Magazine Media**, which covers both print and online readership.

U.S. magazines' total print and digital audience rose 7.6% to 1.68 billion in July from 1.57 billion in July 2014, the report said. But note that "magazines" now includes not only the familiar print versions, but mobile.

And that's where most of the growth came from. The total mobile Web audience jumped 58.3% to 445.5 million from 281.4 million, and the size of the audience accessing magazine content via desktops or laptops edged up 3.2% to 256.9 million.

Digital growth more than offset a smaller decrease in magazines' total print audience. But some *print* categories were doing well.

For example, some food and epicurean titles enjoying big increases. *Allrecipes* — Meredith Corp.'s new food title based on the Web site of the same name — saw the audience for its combined print and digital editions soar 38.9% to 7.5 million, with most of this in print. EatingWell was up 9.9% to 5.74 million, *Vegetarian Times* jumped 35.7% to 2.45 million, and *Every Day with Rachael Ray* edged up 1.9% to 5.21 million.

Smaller increases were seen at *Food Network Magazine,* up 0.5% to 12.4 million, and *Bon Appetit/Epicurious,* up 0.4% to 6.64 million.

A number of automotive enthusiast titles also saw their combined print and digital editions grow, with *Car Craft* up 3.4% to 1.93 million, *Motor Trend* also up 3.4% to 7.34 million, *Popular Mechanics* up 3.3% to 7.6 million, and *Street Rodder* up 4.3% to 2.11 million.

Last but not least, some highbrow journals experienced growth in this category, with *New York Magazine* up soaring 34.5% to 2.38 million, *The New Yorker* up 7.2% to 4.49 million, and *Vanity Fair* up 2% to 6.93 million.

Consumer Trust Brand Content in Newspapers, On TV More Than Social Platforms Including Twitter, Instagram, Blogs

Consumers are more likely to trust brand content found in a print newspaper and on TV than in a variety of social platforms including Instagram, Twitter or blogs, according to results from an Acquity Group survey. Even so, social does have its place, as Facebook beats all other channels in brand content trust, per the study.

That's largely the result of younger respondents, with the 18-22 (29%) and 23-30 (32%) age brackets about twice as likely as Baby Boomers (52-68; 16%) to give Facebook the top rank for brand content trust. Print, not surprisingly, gets the vote among older consumers.

Traditional media's continued influences comes to the fore when looking at drivers of new product or service trials. In fact, 57% of respondents reported having tried a new product or service as a result of a campaign or ad on TV, far ahead of print magazines or newspapers (38%) and social media (34%). TV was also a top paid medium in a recent Nielsen study examining drivers of new product awareness.

Again, though, there are generational divides at play. While TV was the top medium influencing new product and service trials for each age group in the Acquity Group survey, it was rivaled by social media among 18-30-year-olds, for whom print is a lesser influence.

Unsurprisingly, print is a greater influence than social media for older Americans (particularly those older than 50), as is direct mail.

The study finds that respondents are considerably more likely to view on social media a link sent directly to them by a friend or family member than a post by a favorite brand. (Recommendations from family and friends continue to hold sway...)

As for the types of content that consumers are most likely to share with their network? The pervasive "funny video" is top of the heap, echoing earlier research, although it's closely followed by a video that spreads awareness for a cause.

By comparison, respondents report being far less likely to share a video that evokes negative emotions or a link to a product they're excited to have just purchased.

The report notes that brand matters in social amplification: 63% of respondents said that the brand or organization producing the content is a factor they take into account when deciding to share content such as a blog post, video or link with their social network.

Global Newspaper Revenues: Circulation Overtakes Advertising

Globally, revenues from newspaper circulation exceeded advertising revenues last year for the first time this century, according to the World Association of Newspapers and News Publishers (WAN-IFRA) in its latest annual World Press Trends survey.

Of the estimated US $179 billion in circulation and advertising revenue generated last year, $92 billion derived from print and digital circulation compared with $87 billion for advertising.

The Newspaper Association of America (NAA) has previously detailed a shifting revenue mix for newspapers in the US, though advertising had remained the dominant source of revenues at the time.

The data shows that print circulation revenues grew by 6.4% in 2014 and has increased by 16.4% over 5 years. However, print advertising spending declined by 5.2% year-over-year and by 17.5% over the 5-year period.

The report indicates a wide disparity in newspapers' fortunes when sorting by region:

North America

Print circulation was down by 1.3% year-over-year, and by 8.8% over 5 years.
Print ad revenues were down by 7.5% year-over-year, and by 28.2% over 5 years.

Europe

Print circulation decreased by 4.5% year-over-year, and by 21.3% over 5 years.
Print ad revenues declined by 5% year-over-year, and by 23.1% over 5 years.

Asia-Pacific Region

Print circulation was up by 9.8% year-over-year in Asia, and by 32.7% over 5 years, largely on the back of large increases in India.
Print circulation declined by 5.3% year-over-year in Australia and Oceania, and by 22.3% over 5 years.
Print ad revenues were down 6.5% year-over-year in Asia and the Pacific, and declined by 7.3% over 5 years.

Latin America

Print circulation increased by 0.6% year-over-year, and by ~3% over 5 years.
Print ad revenues grew by 4.9% year-over-year, and by 27.7% over 5 years.

Middle East and Africa

Print circulation rose by 1.2% year-over-year, and by 3.7% over 5 years.
Print ad revenues grew by 2.2% year-over-year, but declined by 22.1% over 5 years.

Other Findings:

- Globally, some 93% of newspaper revenues are derived from print;
- While newspapers' digital ad revenues aren't expected to overtake print ad revenues, they grew by 8.5% in 2015 and by nearly 60% over 5 years;
- Paid digital circulation increased by 56% year-over-year and by more than 1,420% over the past 5 years, says WAN-IFRA citing PricewaterhouseCoopers data, though this growth has been from a small base; and
- Roughly 2.7 billion people globally read print newspapers, and more than 770 million read them on desktop digital platforms.

U.S. Adults Daily Major Media Consumption, 2011-2015

U.S. adults will spend more than 5-and-a-half hours per day with digital media this year, up by almost a half-hour year-over-year, per e-Marketer's latest estimates.

The majority (2:51) of that time will be spent with the mobile internet, which will have seen a compound annual growth rate of 37.2% between 2011 and 2015.

TV will occupy the second-largest chunk of adults' daily media time, at four-and-a-quarter hours this year, down less than 20 minutes from 2011.

By year's end, print newspapers will have seen the largest decline in daily time, although newspaper ads continue to have a sizable influence on consumers' purchases.

Traditional Media No Longer Most Trusted For News and Information

Traditional media is no longer the most trusted source of news and information around the world, according to the latest annual Edelman Trust Barometer.

The study surveyed 6,000 "informed publics" aged 25-64 across 27 markets, finding that online search engines are now the most trusted source of general news.

Search also widened its lead over newspapers and TV as the first source for general information and the source used by most to confirm and validate news,

("Informed publics" are college- educated respondents in the top 25% of household income per age group in each country. They report significant media consumption and engagement in business news and public policy.)

Informed publics were asked to rate their level of trust in various media sources when looking of general news and information.

On a 9-point scale (where nine represents the greatest amount of trust), 64% rated their trust in search engines a top-4 box score, with traditional media slightly behind at 62%.

Only a minority (albeit an increasing one) trust social media (48%) and owned media (47%) for general news and information.

Overall, trust in the media as an institution declined a couple points year- over-year to 51%.

Indeed, in only 12 of the 27 countries measured did respondents average a greater level of trust in the media than in the prior year.

Moreover, 16 of the 27 countries (almost 60%) failed to record a majority of respondents trusting the media.

One of those countries was the US, with just 43% rating their trust in the media a top-4 box, although that was a point higher than in last year's study.

The annual study contains a host of intriguing data points, some of which include:

- Friends and family (72%) and academic experts (70%) are the most trusted sources of information consumed by informed publics on social networking sites, content sharing sites, and online- only information sources;

- Informed publics are almost twice as likely to trust content created by companies they use (60%) as content from brands they don't use (32%);
- Informed are most likely to trust technology (78%) and consumer electronics (75%) companies to "do what is right," though trust in each industry declined by 2 points. The least trusted industries continue to be financial services (54%), bank (53%) and the media (51%);
- When it comes to information about a company's engagement, integrity, just 22% of informed publics from developed countries trust global companies that are headquartered in developing countries. By contrast, 77% of respondents in developing countries trust multinationals that are headquartered in developed countries;
- Informed publics in developed countries are far more likely to trust family-owned businesses (72%) than big business (45%). But in developing countries, big business (75%) is more trusted than family-owned businesses (69%);
- Academic or industry experts (70%) are the most credible spokespersons among informed publics, while CEOs (43%) and government official or regulators (38%) are considered credible by the fewest;
- When it comes to information about a company's engagement, integrity, and operations, employees are more trusted than CEOs. Academics are most trusted with information about a company's products;
- Some 51% of informed publics believe that the pace of development and change in business and industry today is too fast, versus 19% who feel it is just right and 28% who find it to be too slow;
- Almost seven in 10 informed public trust electronic and mobile payments, though fewer (55%) trust cloud computing. Trust in electronic and mobile payments, electronic and personal health trackers, and cloud computing is much higher in developing than developed countries;
- Trust in industry sectors does not necessarily translate to trust in their ability to responsibly develop and release industry-specific innovations. Trust in innovation can be increased by making test results available publicly for review and by partnering with an academic institution; and
- Eight in 10 informed publics have chosen to buy products and services from a company they trust during the past year, and 68% have recommended them to a friend or colleague.

Television

Pay-TV subscribers were down in Q3 of 2014, with the 13 largest providers losing about 150,000 video scribers.

Some 51% of TV viewers reported that they multitask everytime or almost every time they watch TV, up from just over one-third (36%) in 2014.

Online millennials (18-34-year-olds) report spending two-thirds of their time watching original series on traditional TV, compared to 84% for online adults aged 35-54 and 90% aged 55 and up.

Alcohol brands shown on popular youth television programs are three times more likely to be consumed by underage drinkers compared to other alcohol brands, providing new and compelling evidence of a strong association between alcohol advertising and youth drinking behavior.

2015 RESEARCH ALERT YEARBOOK

Pay-TV Subscribers Down in Q3

The 13 largest pay-TV providers in the U.S. — representing about 95% of the market — lost about 150,000 net video subscribers in 3Q 2014, according to a new study from the Leichtman Research Group, Inc.

This is compared to a loss of about 25,000 video subscribers in 3Q 2013, and more net losses than in any previous third quarter.

The leading pay-TV providers make up 95.3 million subscribers — with the top nine cable companies having around 49.5 million video subscribers, satellite TV companies having more than 34.2 million subscribers, and the top telephone companies having 11.6 million subscribers.

Other key discoveries for the quarter include:

The top 9 cable companies lost about 440,000 video subscribers in 3Q 2014 — compared to a loss of about 600,000 in 3Q 2013;

Time Warner Cable lost 182,000 subscribers in 3Q 2014 — compared to a loss of 304,000 in 3Q 2013;

Satellite TV providers lost 40,000 subscribers in 3Q 2014 — compared to a gain of 174,000 in 3Q 2013;

DirecTV lost 28,000 subscribers in 3Q 2014 — compared to a gain of 139,000 subscribers in 3Q 2013;

The top telephone providers added 330,000 video subscribers in 3Q 2014 — compared to 400,000 net additions in 3Q 2013;

Over the past year, major pay-TV providers lost about 105,000 subscribers — compared to a loss of about 45,000 over the prior year.

TV Multitasking Continues to Grow

Some 51% of TV viewers multitask every time or almost every time they watch TV, up from just over one-third (36%) last year, according to a new report from TiVo in its second annual study of multitasking and social TV.

Still, viewers are keeping the TV screen the center of their attention: an estimated 47% of their TV time is spent with their primary focus on the TV show even while multitasking, up from 39% in 2013.

Interestingly, the estimated amount of TV time spent multitasking with the focus on something else has stayed flat at 26%.

Instead, there has been a decline in the estimated amount of TV time spent only watching TV (without multitasking), from 35% to 27%.

In other words, while more time is being spent multitasking, all of that time is being spent with the TV as the primary focus.

While that may be the case, TV is not extending its reach to viewers' multitasking activities.

Only 5% of respondents — who were required to watch at least 7 hours of TV per week on any device — reported engaging in TV-related multitasking every time or almost every time they watch TV.

That compares with 50% who never or almost never engage in TV-related activities.

Instead, the most common activities include browsing the internet (74%), reading or sending email (73%) and text messaging (71%).

"Even given the proliferation of multitasking, viewers remain primarily focused on the television shows they are watching," said TiVo Chief Research Officer Jonathan Steuer. "To paraphrase the Bard, the program's the thing!"

Online engagement with favorite programs has become mundane: 61% of respondents report searching the Internet for information about the programs they watch and 47% have "liked" a show's official Facebook page.

However, these activities do not usually occur while watching the program.

The TiVo results widely support conclusions from a Deloitte report released earlier this year, in which a greater bulk of respondents reported frequently multitasking while watching TV, with web browsing, emailing and texting the top activities.

However, they run contrary to a report last year from the Multimedia Research Group which had seen TV multitasking trending towards related activities.

Multitasking raises questions about TV advertising effectiveness, particularly as 56% of the TiVo survey respondents say they multitask every time or almost every time during commercial breaks.

Though to be fair, the most popular reported activities during a commercial break are going to the bathroom (85%), getting a drink or snack (78%) and talking to people in the house (50%) — not considered "multitasking".

Additional key findings:

- 94% of respondents reported that they have multitasked while watching TV;
- Smartphones (78%) and laptops (72%) emerge as the top devices used while watching TV;
- Almost 6 in 10 respondents report using another device every time or almost every time they watch TV;
- During commercial breaks, 56% of respondents report multitasking every time or almost every time;

- More than 6 in 10 have noticed Twitter hashtags during TV shows, but this group was more apt to dislike (53%) than appreciate (12%) seeing them;
- Only about 1 in 5 say they've ever posted on social media about the shows they watch; and
- Of those who do post to social media about their TV faves, the majority (71%) selected Facebook as the site they most commonly post about TV, Twitter came in a distant second with 24%.

Time Spent Watching Original TV Series, by Platform

Online millennials (i.e. 18-34 year-olds) report spending two-thirds of their time watching original series on traditional TV, compared to 84% for online adults aged 35-54 and 90% for those aged 55 and up, according to a new report from comScore.

Desktops and laptops are the next-most preferred platform for each group, accounting for an estimated 19% of time spent watching original TV series among Millennials.

Overall, more than 8 in 10 Millennials and more than 9 in 10 adults aged 35 and older have watched original TV series on traditional TV during the past month, while close to half of Millennials have watched on desktops and laptops (44%) and tablets (49%).

Underage Youth More Likely to Drink Alcohol Brands Shown on TV

Alcohol brands shown on popular youth television programs are three times more likely to be consumed by underage drinkers compared to other alcohol brands, providing new and compelling evidence of a strong association between alcohol advertising and youth drinking behavior.

A new study from the Center on Alcohol Marketing and Youth (CAMY) at the John Hopkins Bloomberg School of Public Health and Boston University came to this conclusion after examining whether exposure to brand-specific alcohol advertising on 20 popular youth television shows was associated with brand-specific consumption among underage drinkers.

The find was published in *Alcoholism: Clinical and Experimental Research* and comes on the heels of a study from the same researchers earlier in July which discovered underage drinkers are heavily exposed to magazine ads for the alcohol brands they consume.

"Taken together, these studies strengthen the case for a relationship between brand-specific alcohol advertising among underage youth and brand specific consumption," said lead author Craig Ross, PhD, MBA, president of Virtual Media Resources in Natick, Massachusetts.

Among youth, alcohol is the number one drug and responsible for 4,300 deaths per year.

Uncategorized

Local deals and offers on Facebook have a strong pull with youth, according to a survey fielded among 18-29 year-olds who own at least a smartphone or tablet and a desktop computer, who have an interest in making purchases from local/small businesses.

There are 4 primary motives for going online, yet the extent to which those factors motivate consumers can differ quite widely across various countries, with few connected consumers in the U.S., for example, motivated by the potential to express their opinions and be heard.

Social media is the preferred customer channel for just 2% of customers, far behind other channels such as phone (43%) and email (22%). More than one in seven U.S. adults ages 18-39 (15%) do not currently hold a valid driver's license, and, among these 22% intend never to obtain one.

Almost one in four U.S. Latinas (24%) are contributing more to their household's total income now than they were in 2014. Almost half of U.S. shoppers (46%) believe in-store prices are higher than prices at the same retailer online, three in 10 (31%) think online prices are higher, while 23% believe prices are about the same online and in-store.

Americans are more likely to read nutritional information on food packages than on restaurant menus, while almost two-thirds (68%) pay a great deal or a fair amount of attention to nutritional labels on food packages, and only 43% pay as much attention to nutritional information given on menus.

One in three Americans (33%) have searched for online coupons on mobile devices, and more than one in four (26%) have purchased items in physical stores using mobile coupons.

One in Seven Adults Under Age 40 Aren't Licensed to Drive

More than one in seven U.S. adults ages 18-39 (15%) do not currently hold a valid driver's license, and, among these, 22% intend never to obtain one, according to the Transportation Research Institute at the University of Michigan. When asked to name the main reason they don't currently have a license, these adults are most likely to cite being too busy or not having enough time to go through the process of obtaining one, followed by the high costs of vehicle ownership and maintenance.

Adults under 30 are more likely than those 30-39 to say they don't have enough time to get a license or that they're able to depend on other people for transportation. Nondrivers ages 20-39 are four times more likely than those under age 20 to cite a preference for public transportation as the primary reason they don't have a driver's license. Women are more likely than men to cite fear or dislike of driving or never having learned to drive as their primary reason for not having a license, while men are more likely than women to cite being able to conduct business online as their primary reason.

Men are also more likely than women to say they never plan to get a driver's license-27% vs. 19%. Non drivers age 30 and older are more likely than those under 30 to plan never to get a license.

Among adults 18-39 who currently don't hold a driver's license, 16% have had a license at some point in the past. Two-thirds of non drivers who are married or partnered (66%) say their spouses or partners have a valid driver's license. Almost half of the study participants (46%) are unmarried/unpartnered, however.

Latinas Are Increasing Their Earnings and Making Family Purchase Decisions

Almost one in four U.S. Latinas (24%) are contributing more to their household's total income now than they were a year ago, according to Nielsen. They plan to spend any extra money they earn in the next five years primarily on paying off debt (73%), building up general savings (63%), and saving for retirement (38%). Latinas are much more likely than non-Hispanic white women to earmark extra money for purchasing a new home (250% more likely) or furthering their education (163% more likely). They are also 21% more likely than non-Hispanic white women to have purchased a first home in the past year.

Nearly nine in 10 Latinas (86%) say the primary shopper in their household is a woman. Areas in which Latinas say women are the primary decision-makers in their homes include food and beverages, clothing, and pharmaceuticals. Decisions about social activities, family finances and insurance, and personal and home electronics are most likely to be shared.

Latinas are highly connected and are especially active users of mobile Internet. More than three-quarters of online Latinas (77%) own smartphones, compared to 55% of non-Hispanic white online women. They're twice as likely as non-Hispanic white women to use mobile devices for streaming audio or watching video, 76% more likely to use mobile banking, and 56% more likely to shop via mobile.

Most Latinas rely on online information to help them make decisions about purchases, daily life choices, and significant events. Latinas search online most frequently for recipes and cooking information, beauty tips, and information related to their personal health and wellness.

More than six in 10 Latinas (62%) wish there were more online lifestyle information written "for Latinas like me," and 56% wish there were more online lifestyle information written in Spanish. The majority of online Latinas (55%) surf the Web at least partly in Spanish, including 31% who surf equally often in Spanish and English. More than three-quarters of Latina (77%) social media users say the majority of their friends on social networks are Hispanic.

Almost Half of Shoppers Think Retailers' Prices Are Higher In-Store Than Online

Almost half of U.S. shoppers (46%) believe in-store prices are higher than prices at the same retailer online, according to a survey of online consumers by Accenture Interactive. Three in 10 (31%) think online prices are higher, while 23% believe prices are about the same in-store and online.

Eight in 10 consumers (80%) consider it important for prices to be the same in-store and online (rating of 4 to 5 on a five-point scale, where 5 = very important). Nine in 10 (92%) consider it important for product descriptions in-store to match those online, and 87% consider it important for product availability to be the same in-store and online.

In reality, fewer than half (46%) say product availability is the same in-store and online most or all of the time (4 to 5 on a five-point scale). One in six (16%) say product availability is rarely the same in-store and online. Just over half (53%) say online and in-store prices are the same most or all of the time, while 84% say product descriptions are mostly or always the same.

When in-store prices differ from online prices, 46% of shoppers purchase via mobile devices, while 42% purchase in-store and 12% choose not to purchase at all. When product availability differs, 62% purchase via mobile devices, while 28% purchase in-store and 9% don't purchase at all.

Three-quarters of shoppers (75%) use a smartphone or tablet to compare prices when shopping in-store. Among these showroomers, 46% typically make their final purchases online, while 20% make them in the store, and 34% make them in a different retail store from the one in which they were comparing prices. Almost three-quarters of showroomers (74%) say they compare prices via mobile in-store every time they shop, while the remaining 26% only do so when shopping for items priced over $250.

Although 82% of U.S. consumers say they're concerned about websites tracking their online behavior, 61% prioritize receiving relevant offers over ensuring that their online habits aren't being tracked. Almost two-thirds (65%) would be receptive to receiving a text message alert while shopping in-store with an offer that matches their current shopping needs and/or history.

Consumers Read Nutritional Information
on Packages but Not Menus

Americans are more likely to read nutritional information on food packages than on restaurant menus, according to Gallup. Almost two-thirds (68%) pay a great deal or a fair amount of attention to nutritional labels on food packages, while only 43% pay as much attention to nutritional information given on menus.

One in Three Americans Seek Out Mobile Coupons

One in three Americans (33%) have searched for online coupons on mobile devices, according to RetailMeNot. More than one in four (26%) have purchased items in physical stores using mobile coupons, and among these, 90% have done so in the past month.

Shoppers are especially receptive to mobile offers that coincide with retail shopping trips. More than half (51%) say they're more likely to enter a store and make a purchase if they receive a coupon for that store while they're nearby. More than six in 10 (63%) say receiving a mobile coupon while shopping in-store makes them more likely to buy something there. Adults under 35 and parents are more active users of mobile shopping and mobile coupons than are adults 35 and older and people without children.

Six in 10 U.S. Men Wear Fragrance

More than six in 10 men ages 18-64 (63%) wear fragrance at least occasionally, according to The NPD Group. Four in 10 male fragrance wearers (40%) have just one chosen scent at home. More than seven in 10 men who wear fragrance (72%) started doing so when they were age 17 or younger. One in four male fragrance wearers (25%) say they never purchase it for themselves but receive fragrance items as gifts.

Men's top consideration when choosing a fragrance is whether their romantic partner likes it.

Dads More Receptive Than Moms to Mobile Marketing

Among parents who own smartphones, dads are more receptive than moms to mobile marketing efforts, according to Placecast. Almost six in 10 dads (58%) have taken action in response to a promotion or coupon they received on their phones, compared with 46% of moms and 31% of smartphone owners without children at home. Almost seven in 10 dads (69%) who aren't currently receiving opt-in mobile promotions are at least somewhat interested in receiving them, compared to 60% of moms and 42% of nonparents who'd be interested.

The majority of dads (53%) who receive mobile promotions or are interested in receiving them say they'd recommend retailers offering such promotions to others, compared with 48% of moms and 35% of nonparents who'd recommend them. Parents are more likely than nonparents to consider location-based mobile offers useful-81% of dads and 79% of moms find local offers useful, compared with 55% of nonparents.

Among smartphone owners, dads are more likely than moms or nonparents to own tablets-55% of dads have tablets, compared with 39% of moms and 30% of people without children at home.

Workforce/Employment

Forty percent of American workers who received paid vacation as a job benefit did not use all of their available paid vacation days. In addition, half of them did not unplug while on vacation, with one in four reporting they worked every day of their vacations.

Sixty percent of Americans are happy with the opportunity for a person in the U.S. to get ahead by working hard, up from 54% in 2014 which was comparable to satisfaction levels measured in the prior three years.

40% Don't Take All Their Vacation Time, 50% Don't "Unplug"

Forty percent of American workers who received paid vacation as a job benefit did not use all of their available paid vacation days. In addition, half (50%) did not unplug while on vacation, with one in four reporting they worked every day of their vacations, according to new research from Alamo Rent A Car.

When asked why they didn't use all their vacation days, 47% reported they were too busy at work.

In fact, 19% reported five days or more of paid vacation went unused in 2014.

Interestingly, Americans who used all of their paid vacation were more likely to unplug while on their trips (54% vs. 37%).

The study also found that parents are more likely to get paid vacation than non-parents (59% vs. 47%). However, parents tend to take shorter vacations than non-parents, with 37% reporting their family vacation lasted five days or less (vs. 26% of non-parents).

"Our research indicates work increasingly remains top of mind for many people, even when they're vacationing with their families," said Rob Connors, assistant vice president of brand marketing for Alamo Rent A Car. "But, while Americans may be working while traveling, they are still reaping benefits from time away from the office, with 71% of people feeling more positive after their vacations and 40% reporting they are more productive when they return to work."

However, the research also revealed that younger American workers are finding it increasingly difficult to leave work behind, with 35% of millennials reporting they work every day while on vacation and come back from vacation less productive (21%). Millennials also said getting all their work done is a big stressor before leaving for vacation (29%).

Other family travel preferences and trends identified through the research include:

Vacation frequency, length and timing

- Thirty-eight percent of Americans prefer taking two vacations per year and are six times more likely (31%) to choose summer vacations over any other season, especially parents (41%);
- Thirty-six percent of families report six to seven days is the average length of a vacation with their immediate family members.

Destinations:

- Thirty-one percent of Americans prefer beach vacations, or somewhere sunny and warm, beating out theme parks (10%), cruises (8%) and ski trips (1%);
- More than half of families taking recurring vacations like to mix it up, choosing different locations most times or each time they travel;

- When asked how far families are willing to travel, 46% said there's no limit – they'll travel anywhere in the world.

Technology Use:

- Fifty-three percent of Americans use screen time on vacation to keep everyone entertained during the flight or drive;
- Dads are more likely than moms to approve the use of electronic devices for their children on vacation (98% vs. 93%);
- Six percent of parents do not let their children use any electronic devices on vacation.

Car Games:

- Despite a high percentage of families using screen time, almost two-thirds of parents report they still play traditional car games with their family while driving to a vacation destination;
- I-Spy is the favorite traditional car game for 45% of parents on family vacations. The License Plate Game is second (28%), and the Alphabet Game is third (24%);
- Single parents are more likely to play car games with kids on vacation than married parents (73% vs. 59%).

Stressors:

- Americans are most concerned about over-spending on family vacations. Forty-six percent of Americans report feeling apprehensive and nervous about spending too much money on a family vacation;
- A big stressor before leaving for vacation is packing (26%). Women are twice as likely as men to report packing as the biggest stressor before vacation (30% vs. 16%).

Regional Differences:

- Midwesterners are most likely to get paid vacation (62%). They are most likely to prefer a beach vacation, or someplace warm and sunny (43%);
- Westerners are most likely to play traditional car games with children (67%). In addition, Westerners prefer outdoor vacations (13%);
- Southerners prefer weekend trips more than all other regions combined (6 % vs. 3.6 % of Americans from all other regions). They also are the most likely to prefer a cruise vacation (11%);
- Northeasterners are the most likely to prefer to take vacations to theme or water parks (14%). This region is also the most likely to take a vacation during the summer (42%).

60% of Americans Satisfied With Ability to Get Ahead

Sixty percent of Americans are happy with the opportunity for a person in the U.S. to get ahead by working hard, according to Gallup's Mood of the Nation survey.

This is up from the 54% last year, which was comparable to satisfaction levels measured in the prior three years. However, from 2001 through 2008, Americans' satisfaction with the ability to get ahead by working hard was higher, ranging from 77% to 66%.

Americans' satisfaction with the chances to get ahead are clearly linked to their views of the economy; when the recession hit and economic confidence dropped, so did Americans' satisfaction with the chance to get ahead. With economic confidence moving back up again, so are views on mobility.

The ability to get ahead by hard work is just one component within the broad spectrum of concerns about economic inequality. Another component is satisfaction with the way income and wealth are appropriated.

Americans' satisfaction is much lower on this level, with 31% satisfied and 67% dissatisfied, then on the ability to get ahead.

Americans can be placed into four categories based on their responses to these two questions:

- A little less than a third (31%) of Americans are not satisfied with both the opportunity to move up and the current system of income and wealth distribution;
- Another quarter (24%) of Americans are satisfied with both economic mobility and economic equality;
- Most of the rest (35%) are satisfied with the opportunity for mobility in the country, but not the amount of equality; and
- A small group (7%) are dissatisfied with mobility, but OK with the distribution of income and wealth.

Youth

Local deals and offers on Facebook have a strong pull with youth who have an interest in making purchases from local/small businesses.

Teen employment figures improved in 2014 and as a result, spending rebounded. Yet, teen perception of the economic climate worsened with roughly 73% seeing the economy as staying the same or getting worse, up from just 57% in 2013.

Snapchat might be more popular among youth than adults, but teens prefer Instagram over every other form of social media.

Alcohol brands shown on popular television programs are three times more likely to be consumed by underage drinkers compared to other brands.

Slightly more than six in 10 youth aged 13-24 would try a product or brand suggested by a YouTube star (YouTuber), while fewer than half would try a product or brand suggested by a movie star.

A vast majority of Millennial teens (16-19) say that a recommendation from a friend or family member would influence them to try a new mobile application, making it a bigger influence than social media recommendations (35%) or an online video (34%).

Teens (aged 13-19) in the United States spend roughly 9 hours per day with media, including more than 6-and-a-half hours with screen media. Listening to music and watching TV emerge as the more frequent media activities among this demographic, though TV takes a backseat to videogames among favored activities.

As far a social media platforms are concerned, teens think YouTube (80%), Snapchat (79%) and Instagram (78%) are cool.

Who's Using SnapChat?

It is well established that Snapchat is more popular with youth, but new data from comScore and CivicScience offer some updated figures detailing Snapchat's popularity. According to comScore's numbers, Snapchat infiltration is now at about half of 18- to 24-year-old smartphone users, up from less than one-third a year earlier and closing in on Instagram (54.6%). And while Snapchat's popularity does tail off among older smartphone users, it has still been growing quickly.

Per comScore, 1 in 5 smartphone users aged 25-34 used Snapchat in June, with that being more than triple the percentage (6.3%) from a year earlier. Among smartphone owners 35 and older, Snapchat's penetration stood at 7.6% in June, more than double the year earlier rate of 3%.

Not surprisingly, CivicScience's poll shows a similarly young demographic. Among the 14% of survey respondents who claimed to use Snapchat, 71% were under 25-years-old, with a majority 43% between the ages of 18 and 24. Interestingly, the results of the survey indicated that Snapchat fans lean heavily female with just 31% being men.

The CivicScience study also looked at behavioral traits of Snapchat users, many of which ore consistent with traits commonly attributed to youth.

Compared to the general population, Snapchat fans are 86% more likely to say their friends and other contacts on social media influence the products they buy, fans are 89% more likely to often post comments on Facebook or Twitter while watching a show or movie, ad fans are 43% more likely to say they are "addicted" to their digital devices.

Facebook Offers Draw Youth to Local Businesses

Local deals and offers on Facebook have a strong pull with youth says G/O Digital in a new survey fielded among 18-29 year-olds who own at least a smartphone or tablet and a desktop computer, who have an interest in making purchases from local/small businesses.

Of the various Facebook marketing tactics identified, respondents were most likely to attribute influence to Facebook offers that can be redeemed at a local store.

When presented with seven Facebook marketing tactics and asked which would be more likely to impact them to make an in-store purchase from a local or small business, a majority 40% of respondents cited Facebook offers which can be redeemed at a local store, distantly trailed by promoted posts (12%); photos/videos that encourage choice of favorite products, styles and colors (11%); and loyalty app promotions (10%), among others.

Similarly, the largest share of respondents cited Facebook offers when asked which marketing tactic would most influence them to visit the website, mobile site or app of a local/small business.

Overall, 84% of those surveyed said that local deals and offers on Facebook have some impact on their decision to make a purchase in-store.

Aside from offers, the study demonstrates that customer reviews and ratings are an influential element when it comes to respondents' decision to interact with local businesses on Facebook.

Asked which of five factors they care more about when engaging with a local or small business online, 41% of those surveyed cited customer reviews/ratings, far outweighing others such as "featured products/services relevant to your needs" (19%) and "number of page 'Likes'" (15%).

Furthermore, eight in ten said they would be more likely to purchase products or services in-store from a local/small business if there were more positive customer reviews/ratings on the brand/s website, mobile site or Facebook page.

A recent study from BrightLocal similarly demonstrated the power of customer reviews for local business, discovering that 88% of those who responded claimed to regularly (39%) or occasionally (49%) read online reviews to determine the quality of a local business.

G/O Digital's study focused on Facebook marketing merits special attention, given that 62% of respondents indicated that it is the most useful social channel to research products and services before visiting a local/small business, far ahead of Pinterest (12%), Twitter (11%), Instagram (9%) and others (6%).

Taking Stock With Teens – Fall 2014

Piper Jaffray has completed its 28th semi-annual Taking Stock With Teens market research project, which indicates increased spending across categories despite decreased optimism about the economy.

Key findings from the survey in fashion, beauty and personal care, digital media, food, gaming and entertainment include the following:

Spending rebounds as teen employment figures improved modestly and parent contribution returned to historical levels in the 70% range. Yet, teen perception of the economic climate worsened with roughly 73% seeing the economy as saying the same or getting worse, up from just 57% a year ago.

Male spending increased in the spring while females turned this fall and contributed to gains year over year and sequentially in total spending. This is the first period of improved spending, specifically on fashion-related goods, in nearly two years.

Fashion spending improves with a mid/high single digit increase in apparel spending. Beauty spending increased, mainly on color cosmetics, while spending declined in accessories.

Shopping frequency stabilizes after several years of declines but remains below historical averages, suggesting capacity rationalization is needed as teens continue to shop "on demand." While teens still prefer to shop in-store for their fashion needs, they are increasingly shopping online and via mobile, preferring sites associated with stores versus pure play e-commerce sites.

Teen closets are diverse. A key fashion trend among teens is the spirit of choice – demand for action sports, fast fashion, refined classics and fashion athletic brands stabilized or increased.

Demand for legacy brands stabilizes – AE, A&F, Hollister and Aero – but is still significantly below peak mindshare and current capacity.

This generation of teens are creating their own "stories" through purchases, experiences and activities in order to cultivate their personal brands, primarily in domains like social media and friend networks.

Friends and the Internet dominate teen influences and combine in social media environments. Instagram and Twitter are the two most used social media sites, implying teens are increasingly visual and sound bite communicators.

The percentage of teens asking for a GoPro as a gift more than doubled sequentially and more than quadrupled year-over-year.

Apple remains the top consumer electronics brand for teens. 67% own iPhones, up 6% from spring 2014. 73% of teens expect their next phone to be an iPhone.

A key food trend amongst teens is the increasing consumption of organic food, especially among upper-income teens.

Mobile gaming interest declines to 80%, but 22% of those that play spend money on virtual goods or extra levels, up 4% from spring 2014.

Teens Choice of Social Network: Instagram

Teens continue to gravitate away from Facebook in favor of Instagram, according to Piper Jaffray's latest semi-annual survey of American teens.

Roughly three-quarters of respondents reported using the visual platform, up from 69% in the previous survey.

By comparison, just 45% said they use Facebook, a significant drop from 72%, the decline was enough to move it behind Twitter in the popularity stakes.

The micro-blogging site is now the second-most used among teenagers, but does not seem to be making strides: the 59% endorsement rat in this attest survey marks a slight drop from 63% in the preceding report.

Meanwhile, Pinterest and Tumblr have continued to be relatively flat, used by slightly more than 1 in 5 teens, while Google+ usage plunged from 29% to 12%.

Instagram's rise to the top of social media has been quite rapid: in Piper Jaffray's Spring 2014 survey, 30% of teens called it their "most important" social network, overtaking Twitter (the fall 2013 favorite) and putting even more distance between itself and Facebook (the Spring 2013 favorite).

The latest study notes that 38% of teens believe Instagram is a positive marketing channel through which to reach them, compared with 34% saying the same about Twitter and 21% about Facebook, with only 4% of teens using Snapchat.

Underage Youth More Likely to Drink Alcohol Brands Shown on TV

Alcohol brands shown on popular youth television programs are three times more likely to be consumed by underage drinkers compared to other alcohol brands, providing new and compelling evidence of a strong association between alcohol advertising and youth drinking behavior.

A new study from the Center on Alcohol Marketing and Youth (CAMY) at the John Hopkins Bloomberg School of Public Health and Boston University came to this conclusion after examining whether exposure to brand-specific alcohol advertising on 20 popular youth television shows was associated with brand-specific consumption among underage drinkers.

The find was published in *Alcoholism: Clinical and Experimental Research* and comes on the heels of a study from the same researchers earlier in July which discovered underage drinkers are heavily exposed to magazine ads for the alcohol brands they consume.

"Taken together, these studies strengthen the case for a relationship between brand-specific alcohol advertising among underage youth and brand specific consumption," said lead author Craig Ross, PhD, MBA, president of Virtual Media Resources in Natick, Massachusetts.

Among youth, alcohol is the number one drug and responsible for 4,300 deaths per year.

Youth Say YouTube Stars More Influential Than Big-Screen Ones

Slightly more than six in 10 youth aged 13-24 would try a product or brand suggested by a YouTube star ("YouTuber"), according to results from a DEFY Media survey, while fewer than half would try a product or brand suggested by a TV or movie star.

There appears to be an age trend when it comes to following stars on social media, though: 13-year-olds are far more likely to follow a YouTube (59%) than TV/movie (32%) star, while the gap is closer for 14-17-year-olds (53% and 44%, respectively).

Among 18-24-year-olds, slightly fewer follow YouTube (51%) than TV/movie (54%) stars.

The results bring to mind a separate survey released last year by Variety, in which US teenagers (13-18) named YouTube stars their most influential figures, ahead of film, TV and music celebrities.

Hispanics to Comprise One-Third of Under-18s in 2060

Hispanics will account for 33.5% of the under-18 population in 2060, growing from 24.4% last year to rival the non-Hispanic white population (35.6% share) in number, according to the latest projections from the U.S. Census Bureau.

Indeed, minorities' share of the under-18 population will rise from 48% last year to 64.4% in 2060, per the study.

Meanwhile, as of last year, Hispanics comprised 17.4% of the total population, a figure that will rise to 28.6% by 2060.

Asian-Americans are another fast-growing group, and are expected to increase from 5.2% share of the total population last year to 9.1% share in 2060.

Teens & Social: What's the Latest?

Instagram remains the most important social network to teens, widening its lead over Facebook and Instagram, according to the latest semi-annual teen survey from Piper Jaffray.

The results indicate that:

- Instagram is the "most important" social network to the largest proportion (32%) of teens surveyed, up a couple of points from a year earlier;
- Twitter continues to be the second-most important social network, cited by 24%; and
- Facebook (14%) is narrowly ahead of Snapchat (13%) for the third spot.

It is interesting to see Snapchat – identified for the first time in the survey – rivaling Facebook in the survey results. Its inclusion appears to have diluted the share of respondents citing Facebook or Twitter as their most important, although it had no such effect on the results for Instagram, further cementing that platform's popularity with this sample demographic.

The previous survey from Piper Jaffray (released in October 2014) had reported just 4% of teens using Snapchat, a surprising result given that network's growing popularity with youth.

In that survey, Instagram was the most popular social network, used by 76% of teens, ahead of Twitter (59%) and Facebook (45%).

In other words, it's probably safe to assume that Facebook-owned properties (whether Facebook or Instagram) are among the most popular with teens, with Snapchat very much in the conversation.

Twitter's position seems a little more difficult to ascertain, although it's clearly in the top four. It will be interesting to see the next edition of Piper Jaffray's survey now that they are including Snapchat as an option.

Radio Listeners: AM/FM Still Strong;
Digital Platforms Key for Youths' Music Discovery

AM/FM radio continues to be the preferred medium among core radio listeners, with 81% of weekly radio station listening taking place on an AM/FM radio in a vehicle (51%) or at home, work, or school (30%), according to the latest annual TechSurvey from Jacobs Media.

Consistent with recent research, AM/FM radio continues to benefit from the in-car environment, with roughly half of respondents saying that most or all of their radio listening takes place in the car.

Overall, survey respondents were almost twice as likely to say they had increased (18%) than decreased (10%) their AM/FM radio listening (on any device) over the previous year.

Interestingly, the share of listening attributed to digital platforms didn't rise from last year, although the survey authors note that this year's sample skews older than last year.

Interestingly, though, recent research from Edison Research and Triton Digital found that while online radio's reach continues to grow, consumption this year is flat.

Meanwhile, as in previous years, the Jacobs Media survey finds that emotional connections are a primary driver of radio listening. Among the main reasons given for listening to AM/FM radio, 55% said they enjoy working with the radio on, 45% said it keeps them company, and 40% said they listen to get in a better mood.

The top reason, though, continue to be a desire to hear favorite songs/artists, cited by two-thirds of respondents.

Fewer respondents (34%) reported that a main reason for listening is to discover new music.

Even so, among those interested in new music and new artists, AM/FM radio is not only the most widely used discovery source (56%), but also the primary source for the most respondents (40%).

Still, there are wide generational gaps in music and artist discovery, with Gen Z respondents about half as likely as the survey average to cite AM/FM radio (on any device) as their primary source for finding out about new music and new artists (23% vs. 40%).

Instead, Gen Z respondents are more likely to turn to Facebook (11% vs. 5%), iHeart Radio (9% vs. 2%) and Spotify (5% vs. 2%). (The report's authors caution that the Gen Z sample size is small.)

Pandora, meanwhile, is particularly more influential than average among Gen Y respondents (12% vs. 5%) for music discovery.

The platform continues to lead all radio applications among respondents who own mobile devices, two-thirds of whom download radio-centric apps.

Games, Music Preferred App Categories Among Older Teens

A vast majority of "Millennial teens" (16-19) say that a recommendation from a friend or family member would influence them to try a new mobile application, making this a bigger influencer than social media recommendations (35%) or an online video (34%), finds Refuel Agency in a recent survey.

In its study, Refuel examines a wide variety of digital behavior among older teens, including the types of apps that they're most likely to download and use. Games (70%) and music (59%) led in those popularity rankings, followed by social networking (49%), video/photography (35%) and book (29%) apps.

Narrowing the analysis to messaging apps, the survey reveals that half of respondents often use Facebook Messenger, slightly ahead of the 47% often using Instagram and Snapchat.

Indeed, Facebook remains a highly popular platform for teens, as other research has found.

In the Refuel Agency study, teens were asked which sites or apps they spend most of their time on (multiple responses allowed): Facebook (51%) was second only to YouTube (64%), and was slightly ahead of both Instagram (45%) and Snapchat (42%).

Still, YouTube's popularity endures, as three-quarters of older teens say they use it on a regular basis. Other streaming platforms often used by teens include Netflix (55%), Pandora (39%), Spotify (24%) and Google Play (24%).

In other survey findings:

- Apple tops Samsung and Google as the top brand that Millennial teens say they cannot live without;
- Teens estimate spending almost twice as much time daily using their cellphones and smartphones than watching TV (6.3 hours vs. 3.5 hours);
- Cellphones and smartphones (55%) outrank computers/laptops (18%) and other devices including the TV (7%) as teens' most important device;
- Musicians/bands (43%), TV shows (43%) and movies (42%) are the categories that older teens are most likely to follow or like on social media; and
- More than one-third (37%) of teens say they have a lot or some influence on their parents' electronics purchases.

Instagram Remains Most Important Social Network For Teens; Snapchat Gains Steam

Instagram continues to be at the top of the heap when it comes to teens' most important social networks, details Piper Jaffray in its latest semi-annual "Taking Stock With Teens" report. While Instagram remains popular with teens, Twitter's influence appears to be declining, and it is now challenged by Snapchat.

According to the results from Piper Jaffray's survey, one-third of teens name Instagram their most important social network, up slightly from the prior edition. Twitter – which was briefly teens' favorite network in late 2013 – was cited by 20% of teens, down from 24% in the previous survey.

As such, Twitter is now rivaled by a rapidly-growing Snapchat, which was cited by 19% of respondents as their most important network, up from 13%.

Snapchat's rise means that it has now overtaken Facebook, which is now the most important network to 15% of teens, stable from the previous survey, but considerably down from its leading position in late 2012 and early 2013.

This may serve to re-ignite the conversation about Facebook's appeal to teens, which has ebbed somewhat from the fever-pitch it reached a couple of years ago. Of course, Facebook-owned Instagram is still tops among teens, and Facebook itself isn't exactly doing too badly.

Also, it's important to remember that the Piper Jaffray survey asks teens about their most important network, which doesn't necessarily equate with their most-used network. Indeed, research from the Pew Internet & American Life Project indicates that Facebook is still the most commonly used — and the most frequently used — social network by American teens.

In other interesting results from the Piper Jaffray teen survey:

- Amazon Prime penetration is rising across all household incomes, and tends to increase alongside household income levels;
- Apple iPhone ownership and interest has moderately increased from the last survey;
- Netflix now reportedly accounts for the largest share of time (38%) watching media content, followed by cable TV at 29% share and YouTube at 21% share;
- The percentage of teens who don't believe they need cable has increased from this time last year, and there has similarly been a decrease in the percentage of time that TV shows are watched on TV by teens; and
- AM/FM occupies the greatest share of time spent listening to audio in the car (37%), but when it comes to time spent listening to music overall, MP3s dominate (37%), followed by streaming other than Pandora (21%) and Pandora (17%).

Teens Most Common — and Preferred — Media Activities?

- Teens (aged 13-18) in the United States spend roughly 9 hours per day with media, including more than 6-and-a-half hours with screen media, reports Common Sense Media in a new study. Listening to music and watching TV emerge as the most frequent media activities among this demographic, though TV takes a backseat to video games among favored activities.
- The study is based on a nationally representative survey of more than 2,600 tweens (8-12) and teens (13-18), with teens representing slightly more than half of the respondents. Among these teens, almost two-thirds (66%) report listening to music every day, with a majority (58%) also watching TV on a daily basis.
- Somewhat surprisingly, fewer than half (45%) say that they use social media every day, with online video viewing (34%) and mobile game playing (27%) further behind.
- Likewise, listening to music tops the charts when it comes to enjoyable media activities, with close to three-quarters (73%) of teens saying they enjoy this activity "a lot." TV trails in the second spot, bringing a lot of enjoyment to 45% of teens, rivaled by watching online videos (also 45%). Somewhat surprisingly again, social media is further down the list, with only 36% of teens saying they enjoy using social media "a lot."
- In fact, social media is passed on the enjoyment stakes by playing video games. While only 15% of teens reported playing console video games every day, 42% say they enjoy doing so "a lot." And when teens were asked to identify their single favorite media activity, playing video games (15% share) fell second only to listening to music (30%).
- Social media ranked more highly on this measure, with 10% of teens saying it's their favorite media activity, on par with reading (also 10%) and slightly ahead of watching TV (9%).

2015 RESEARCH ALERT YEARBOOK

- There are some notable gender-based differences in teens' favorite media activities, however. For example, 27% of boys surveyed said that playing video games is their favorite activity, compared to just 2% of girls. That made video games the preferred activity overall among boys, ahead of listening to music, the favorite for 22% (as opposed to 37% of girls).
- Girls were also far more likely than boys to cite reading and social media as their favorite activities (14% vs. 5% in each case).
- Although watching TV is ahead of online video viewing among teens in both daily viewership and preference, digital platforms do play a significant role in teens' TV and video viewing.
- Breaking down all of TV and video viewing time among teens, the study notes that live TV captures half of that time, with time-shifted TV capturing another 8%. But 36% of video time is apportioned to online videos (22%) and TV on digital platforms (14%), with smartphones being the device most commonly used to watch video digitally.

In total, the report indicates that the media activities that occupy the most daily time per day for teens are:

- Watching TV/DVDS/videos (2:38);
- Listening to music (1:54);
- Playing video, computer or mobile games (1:21); and
- Using social media (1:11).

These were the only media activities to average at least one hour of use per day among teens. By comparison, teens average slightly more than a half-hour per day browsing websites (36 minutes) and slightly less than half reading (28 minutes).

Which Social Media Platforms Do Teen Users Rate as "Cool"?

YouTube (80%), Snapchat (79%) and Instagram (78%) are considered "cool" by the largest share of US online teens (12-17) who are monthly users of the platforms, according to a report from Forrester Research. While Facebook (65%) isn't considered to be "cool" by as many of its users, it does have the largest share of "hyperusage" of any platform.

In other words, compared to users of other platforms, teens using Facebook are the most likely to say that they're on the site "all the time."

Facebook is also considered important for keeping in touch with friends by 66% of its teen users, behind only Instagram (70%) and Snapchat (74%).

In a separate question which asked the full sample of more than 1,200 respondents (13-19) to cite the sites or apps they spend the most time on, both Facebook (58% vs. 38%) and Snapchat (42% vs. 33%) were indicated more often by the older than younger set.

By contrast, younger teens were more likely than their older counterparts to say they spend most of their time on YouTube (73% vs. 60%) and Instagram (46% vs. 43%).

These findings are interesting in light of other research on teens' social preferences.

The popularity of Instagram, for example, is supported by studies conducted by Piper Jaffray, the most recent of which revealed that Instagram is teens' "most important" social network, ahead of Twitter and a fast-rising Snapchat. (YouTube was not an option in that survey.)

It seems that young teens likely stick to those leading social platforms, as relatively few (39%) said that social networking apps are among the types they are most likely to download and use. Instead, games (72%) and music (57%) apps are the types of apps that younger teens are most likely to download.

As for music apps, a majority (58%) of the young teens surveyed reported sometimes or always using apps with music identification capabilities such as Shazam and SoundHound, while only 19% said they never use such apps.

Meanwhile, when it comes to the activities these young teens most commonly perform on their phones during the school day, texting (52%) and playing mobile games (52%) top the list, followed by social media (44%), taking and looking at pictures (42%) and browsing the web (38%).

In other findings from the Refuel Agency report:

- While younger and older teens estimate spending the same amount of time each day with various devices, younger teens spend more time with tablets and video game consoles and less time with computers, mobile phones and TV;
- Still, younger teens are more likely than older teens to cite tablets, TVs and MP3 players as their most important device;
- Both younger and older teens cite privacy and security as their top 2 features in a browser;
- Online videos would influence the most younger teens to try a new app, while older teens are most influenced by social media recommendations; and
- As with older teens, younger teens name Apple, Samsung and Google (in that order) as the brands that they cannot live without.

U.S. Teens Used Less Ecstasy, Heroin, Synthetic Marijuana, Alcohol, and Cigarettes in 2015

The use of licit and illicit drugs by American teens show that some important improvements are taking place, this according to the results from the latest national survey in the Monitoring the Future series.

The use of alcohol and cigarettes reached their lowest points since 1975 when the study began. Use of some especially dangerous illicit drugs — such as MDMA (ecstasy, Molly), heroin, amphetamines and synthetic marijuana — also showed a drop in use this year. However, use of Marijuana remained the same.

The study tracks the trends in substance use by polling over 40,000 8th, 10th, and 12th-graders each year in about 400 public and private secondary schools across the contiguous 48 states.

Alcohol

Use of alcohol by U.S. teens continued it's long-term decline. Those in grades 8, 10, and 12 displayed a further decline in the proportion of students reporting any alcohol use in the year preceding the survey.

"The recent peak rate in annual prevalence of alcohol use was in 1997, at 61% for the three grades combined. Since then, there has been a fairly steady downward march in alcohol use among adolescents," said Professor Lloyd Johnston, the study's principal investigator. "The rate has fallen by about a third, to 40%. More importantly, the percentage who report binge drinking has fallen by half, from 22% to 11%."

Some 12th-graders drink even more heavily than five or more drinks in a row, reporting 10 or more, or 15 or more, drinks in a row on at least one occasion in the prior two weeks—dangerously high levels of consumption that the investigators have labeled "extreme binge drinking."

Peer disapproval of binge drinking had been rising since 2000 among teens, though it did not rise further in 2015. Declines in availability may be another contributing factor to the declines in teen drinking.

"In recent years, there has been a fair decline in all three grades in the proportion saying that alcohol is easy for them to get, with the steepest decline among the youngest teens," Johnston said. "This suggests that state, community and parental efforts have been successful in reducing underage access to alcohol."

Illicit Drugs

Multiple illicit drugs dropped in use this year.

There were declines in use of MDMA (ecstasy, Molly), heroin, synthetic marijuana ("K2," "Spice") and amphetamines.

Investigators say there were no statistically significant increases for any of the more than 50 classes and subclasses of drugs that MTF tracks among 8th, 10th and 12th-grade students.

The use of MDMA, known as ecstasy and more recently Molly, has been tumbling in use since around 2010. Inclusion of Molly in the question about perceived risk to the user produced a considerable jump in the proportions of 8th and 10th-graders saying MDMA use is dangerous to the user.

Reported availability of ecstasy (MDMA), specifically, has been declining since the peak year of use in 2001, but there was little further decline in 2015.

Heroin, which is one of the most dangerous illicit drugs, is of particular importance. The amount of secondary school students using heroin has been declining steadily in the past few years, and it continued to fall a little in somewhere grades in 2015.

Among 8th-graders, the proportion reporting any heroin use in the prior 12 months fell significantly from 0.5% to 0.3%; and their annual prevalence is down by two-thirds since 2008, when it was 0.9%.

In both 10th and 12th grades, annual prevalence fell in 2015 by one-tenth of 1% to 0.5% (not a statistically significant change, but the decline for the three grades combined was significant). Both of these upper grades did have an annual prevalence above 1.0% at the beginning of the 2000s, so their rates of heroin use have now fallen by more than half.

This year's improvements were almost entirely in taking heroin using a needle, which is the most dangerous form of use. There was little change in the taking of heroin without a needle.

Synthetic marijuana has been sold over the counter in multiple states — notably in gas stations, convenience stores and head shops. It is often imported from overseas and can be very potent and unpredictable both in its chemical content and in its effects, resulting in a number of emergency room admissions.

Use fell by a statistically significant amount in 2015 for the three grades combined. The proportions saying they used any synthetic marijuana in the past 12 months now stand at 3%, 4% and 5% in grades 8, 10 and 12, respectively—down substantially from the 4%, 9% and 11% observed in those same grades in 2012.

"While there has been some increase in the proportion of students seeing use of this drug as dangerous, it hardly seems enough to account for the considerable declines in use, which leads us to conclude that efforts to reduce availability have been successful to some degree," Johnston said.

"Efforts at the federal and state levels to close down the sale of these substances appear to be having an effect," Johnston said.

The use of amphetamines also showed some decline in 2015.

While the fall in annual prevalence for the three grades combined from 6.6% to 6.2% did not reach statistical significance, the decline in past 30-day prevalence from 3.2% to 2.7% did, suggesting that the decline is fairly recent. Reported availability of amphetamines has been in decline in all three grades for some years.

Among the many other drugs covered in the study, none showed significant increases or decreases in use this year. A number already have shown appreciable declines in use in the past, such as "bath salts," LSD, other hallucinogens, salvia, crack, methamphetamine and inhalants.

The most widely used of all the illicit drugs, marijuana, showed no significant changes in annual prevalence this year in any of the three grades, separately or combined.

While the use of pot rose for several years, the annual prevalence of marijuana has essentially leveled out since around 2010.

This year, 12% of 8th-graders, 25% of 10th-graders and 35% of 12th-graders reported using marijuana at least once in the past year.

However, their daily or near-daily marijuana use (defined as smoking marijuana on 20 or more occasions in the past 30 days) is of more importance. These rates stand at 1.1%, 3% and 6% in 8th, 10th and 12th grades, respectively.

In other words, one in every 16 or 17 high school seniors is smoking marijuana daily or near daily. While these rates have changed rather little since 2010, they are from three-to-six times higher than they were at their low point in 1991.

Teens using cigarettes also reached an all-time low in 2015.

YouTube

Mothers are avid viewers of YouTube videos, being slightly more likely than the overall internet browsing population to visit YouTube on a monthly basis.

Slightly more than six in 10 youth aged 13-24 would try a product or brand suggested by a YouTube star (YouTuber), while fewer than half would try a product or brand suggested by a movie star.

Top-Indexing YouTube Video Categories Among Mothers

Mothers are avid viewers of YouTube videos, being slightly more likely than the overall internet browsing population to visit YouTube on a monthly basis, according to data from Compete.

While music (26%) videos capture the greatest share of mothers' viewing, this demographic under-indexes the average viewer when it comes to watching music videos.

Instead, the top-indexing categories for mothers are family (+63%), how-to (+37%) and animals (+34%), per the report.

Want Influence Perform on YouTube, Teens Say

Slightly more than six in 10 youth aged 13-24 would try a product or brand suggested by a YouTube star ("YouTuber"), according to results from a DEFY Media survey, while fewer than half would try a product or brand suggested by a TV or movie star.

There appears to be an age trend when it comes to following stars on social media, though: 13-year-olds are far more likely to follow a YouTube (59%) than TV/movie (32%) star, while the gap is closer for 14-17-year-olds (53% and 44%, respectively).

Among 18-24-year-olds, slightly fewer follow YouTube (51%) than TV/movie (54%) stars.

The results bring to mind a separate survey released last year by Variety, in which US teenagers (13-18) named YouTube stars their most influential figures, ahead of film, TV and music celebrities.

www.ingramcontent.com/pod-product-compliance
Lightning Source LLC
Chambersburg PA
CBHW061358210326
41598CB00035B/6027